THE ADOLESCENT

THE ADOLESCENT
Case Studies
for
Analysis

NANCY C. RALSTON

G. PATIENCE THOMAS
University of Cincinnati

Chandler Publishing Company
An Intext Publisher
New York and London

Library of Congress Cataloging in Publication Data
Ralston, Nancy C
   The adolescent: case studies for analysis.
   1. Adolescent psychology—Cases, clinical reports,
statistics. 2. Adolescent psychiatry—Cases, clinical
reports, statistics. I. Thomas, G. Patience, joint
author. II. Title. [DNLM: 1. Adolescent
psychology—Case studies. WS462 R164a 1974]
BF724.R34   616.8'9'09   73–17320
ISBN 0–8102–0473–8

Chandler Publishing Co.
257 Park Avenue South
New York, New York 10010

78-6196

Text design by Design 110

To our parents

GAIL C. and ROBERT E. HUFFMAN
MARTHA R. and OVERTON E. THOMAS

Contents

Preface

The scientific study of human behavior has developed numerous methods of investigation, and there are conflicting views as to their validity and effectiveness. One method, however, the case study, is a generally accepted and widely used means of collecting and analyzing behavioral data. We employ it here to gain information about some typical behavior patterns in adolescence and to develop insight into causes and meanings.

Chapter 1 introduces the method and its historical background, pitfalls to be avoided, primary uses, and philosophical assumptions. A representative case study outline is provided and discussed. Chapter 2 describes the developmental psychologist's approach to the study of adolescence and briefly explores a few of the developmental tasks that young people have in today's society. The remaining chapters are devoted to actual case studies of adolescents encountering normal developmental crises or such disturbances as drug abuse and suicidal tendencies, which may require professional attention. Each chapter begins with a discussion of the specific developmental area under consideration. These discussions focus on pertinent psychological concepts and are designed to establish a frame of reference within which the subject of the study may be better understood.

The individuals studied are representative of the population in terms of sex, race, religion, and socioeconomic background. At the end of each section of every case study there are questions designed to stimulate a more than superficial acquaintance with the factual material of the case study and to encourage careful, analytical scrutiny of the data and descriptive information each study provides.

While the cases themselves suggest many reasons for certain types of behavior, the questions require the reader to identify possible relationships and help to guide thinking into areas which otherwise might not have been explored. Care should be taken to differentiate fact from interpretation and justifiable from unjustifiable conclusions.

We developed these materials initially for use in graduate and undergraduate courses in Adolescent Psychology. Almost without exception, students report that studying a case helps to integrate their reading and observation, aids them in understanding theory and applying it to real situations, and makes the material in the course come alive. Encouraged by the response to our first book, *The Child: Case Studies for Analysis,* we have gone further here to offer larger amounts of psychological theory in addition to the cases.

1

The Case Study

THE NATURE AND CHARACTER OF THE CASE STUDY

The case study is a highly concentrated, specific approach to the process of understanding human growth and development, involving an in-depth study of a single individual. Other approaches employ large numbers of subjects and may eventually result in the production of norms, principles, and generalizations that one can understand and appreciate more fully when they are applied to an individual with whom one is familiar. The case-study method, by comparison, permits the application of general knowledge within a very personal frame of reference, and in turn helps develop an understanding that has broad applications to all individuals. Using the case-study method, we move from specific to broad applications, in contrast to other methods which operate in the opposite direction.

Because of its built-in characteristic of specificity, the case study is, of necessity, very comprehensive. It is a collection of all of the pertinent information about an individual, involving the use of any tools or techniques which may contribute to each phase of the study. After all of this relevant information has been collected, it must be organized and recorded in a meaningful way so that the subject—the *individual* about whom the study is written—emerges as a very real person, accurately described. This individual's own perspective toward himself and his life should be apparent. From this total description, inferences can then be drawn and predictions can be made about the future course of this person's growth and development.

The scope of the case study is virtually limitless, as long as the detailed information contributes to an understanding of the unique organization of the particular personality involved. One phase of the study is usually the case history, which involves pertinent facts about the individual and his environment. Information about his family, birth, development, health, education, personal and social adjustment, work, and many other facets of his life are included in the case history, so that it becomes a record of his physical, mental, and emotional development up to the time of the study. The case study may be expanded with anecdotes, conference or interview reports, samples of work, test scores, diagnostic reports, sociometric records, or reports from specialists. The case study goes beyond the case history because all the facts are organized until some patterns of behavior emerge which can be used for predictive purposes, and if desired, for diagnosis and assistance.

The case study is probably the most comprehensive of all the methods used to study an individual, and scientific procedures should be followed to ensure as much objectivity as possible. This method of investigation should be used with full knowledge of its advantages and disadvantages, both of which are numerous.

The most severe limitation is that of time, for the process of collecting relevant information is a long and tedious one. Since many of the controls present in the experimental method are absent, data may be based on biased impressions or imperfect memory of events. No matter how practiced we become in our observational and recording techniques, we are still victimized by the vagaries of our human memories, which do not always serve us well. As a result, we impose serious limitations upon the scientific accuracy of the case study. Details will be misinterpreted, exaggerated, glossed over, or even forgotten. When interpreting information, it is easy to infer too much, to oversimplify, and to make generalizations or judgments on the basis of little evidence. Cause and effect are difficult to determine from a single case. However, since no two individuals are alike, focusing attention on a single person and attempting to understand him thoroughly is a challenging task. It might be helpful to think of the person who conducts the case study as a photographer, in that he is attempting to create a snapshot totally free of any distortion; a picture as accurate and unflattering, if necessary, as an X-ray photo of an individual. His method depends upon words rather than film, and the developing process must be a very scientific one so that the final picture will not be either underexposed or overexposed.

The reader of a case study cannot be sure, however, that it presents a picture of camera-like objectivity. It is very easy for an author to be influenced by his own evaluations of the individuals and situations that he observes, to make judgments consistent with his own set of values rather than those of the people in the study, to formulate opinions consistent with his own stereotypes, and to permit his own previous experiences to color his presentation of the material. For example, each of us has certain preconceived notions about the way parents should behave toward their children. In reporting the same bit of interaction between mother and child, one observer may state that "Mrs. Brown gave Tommy a threatening look, walked over to the boy, and shoved him down the corridor ahead of her," while another would say, "Mrs. Brown looked sympathetically at Tommy, walked over to him, and gently nudged him down the corridor in front of her." Each report has been colored by the feelings of the observer toward Mrs. Brown, toward Tommy, and about the manner in which a mother should treat her son, and each creates a very different impression in the mind of the reader. However, some description and interpretation is vital to the case study in order to fully convey the atmosphere in which the subject lives. "Sally walked into the room, sat down at a desk, and looked around her" is an underexposed picture which tells us virtually nothing. However, "Sally dragged dejectedly into the dark, dreary room, glanced disconsolately about her depressing surroundings, slouched down into a well-used, long-suffering desk, and proceeded to glare defiantly at everyone" is an example of overexposure which involves too much attention to detail.

Another kind of distortion which may creep into a case study involves over- or underemphasis on some particular kind of behavior on the part of the subject. In dealing with adolescents, the inexperienced observer is sometimes prone to read too much into the perfectly normal rebellious behavior and rejection of parental standards and values which most teenagers exhibit. On the other hand, some observers tend to dismiss as a "harmless prank" antisocial behavior which is indicative of serious maladjustment, and to ignore or gloss over instances of such behavior in their reporting. A great deal of the validity of the final case study depends upon the skill of the observer.

It is obvious that the case-study method is by no means perfect. There are numerous limitations, and some of them are quite serious. However, even these should be viewed in an objective light. While the method may not be recognized as an acceptable means of validating hypotheses, this is not to say that it cannot generate hypotheses about a specific individual or about behavior in general.

THE HISTORY OF THE CASE STUDY

The origin of the case-study method would be difficult, if not impossible, to trace. Its initial employment is usually attributed to the field of medicine, where it is still used today. A patient's medical history is his case history from a medical perspective. Studying it helps the physician make his diagnoses and prescribe treatment or other measures to promote the health of the individual.

In the psychological realm, one of the best-known advocates of the case-study method was Sigmund Freud. By analyzing the data included in case studies of his numerous patients, Freud developed entirely new and highly controversial psychological theories based upon a process which he called psychoanalysis. As a natural outgrowth of this type of application, the case study evolved into a very important clinical tool, and is used today by many types of professionals who are responsible for making human behavior more comprehensible. Psychologists, social workers, educators, and others in similar lines of work use it to help them formulate hypotheses, make predictions, identify causative factors, and plan preventive and therapeutic measures, in a variety of circumstances.

Historically, the case-study method has been used primarily in an effort to understand problem behavior such as delinquency, school failure, or emotional maladjustment. Psychologists and counselors have employed it to help others learn to solve their own problems and better understand their own behavior. This use implies a diagnostic and remedial function. Only recently in its history has the case-study method been recognized as a useful and worthwhile tool to describe normality as well as abnormality. Since there is an expressed need among individuals who study human behavior for more research concerning typical rather than atypical development, the case-study method has barely achieved a good start in making valuable contributions to our knowledge of the human being and why he behaves as he does.

That an individual uses and is familiar with the case-study method does not imply that he is either a trained clinician or that he is qualified to give advice to parents or teachers on the basis of his investigations. The case study, with this caution, is useful as a learning tool to facilitate continued growth toward an understanding of human behavior.

THE FORM AND INTERPRETATION OF THE CASE STUDY

There is no single universally accepted form for the case study. The purpose of the study will, in great measure, determine what material must be included. A social worker, a psychologist, and a probation officer, for example, might all have different approaches and therefore their respective outlines would reflect different emphases. Regardless of the purpose for which the case study is intended, an outline is essential to ensure that the material is organized in an orderly way and follows a logical sequence of presentation. Major topics and subsequent subtopics of related material help the reader to draw reasonable conclusions about the effects of both hereditary and environmental factors as they influence the development of the individual.

The following outline is offered for study because it is representative of some which are currently in use by various individuals and agencies studying adolescent behavior. Though it is very comprehensive, it should be viewed as flexible and adaptable to each individual case. The types of information which might be included are described in detail, followed by some general questions which the reader should be able to answer after each section of the outline has been read.

The Outline for the Case Study

I. IDENTIFICATION OF SUBJECT AND SOURCES OF INFORMATION

What is the adolescent's name, address, race, sex, and age? Does he work or go to school? What are the sources of information: parents, teachers, school records, and other sources?

II. THE FAMILY HISTORY

A. Health and Physical Characteristics

Each member of the family should be described in terms of health and physical traits. Are they of large or small stature? Are they relatively active or have any serious diseases or injuries occurred? Is anyone physically handicapped in any way?

B. Educational Status

What level of education has been attained by each of the parents, by siblings, and by other close relatives? What seems to be the interest in and attitudes toward educational achievement?

C. Economic Status

This information should provide an accurate picture of the family's socioeconomic level. The father's occupation, the mother's work experience, if any, and the occupations of other close relatives, if these are pertinent, should all be described. Have the family members been responsibly employed? That is, have they worked consistently or sporadically? Have they ever been dependent upon welfare funds? Are they well-liked and respected by their fellow workers? Specifically, how is their economic level best described— wealthy, moderate, poor, or destitute? What are their living conditions— superior, average, or deprived? What visible evidence is there to substantiate the above descriptions: cars, home ownership, type of neighborhood, home furnishings, condition of the home and yard, and the like?

D. Social Status and Adjustment

Who are the members of the immediate family? How is the family life best described—harmonious, chaotic, quarrelsome, restrictive, or by some other word? Are there specific, obvious problems with relationships in the family, such as an indulgent grandparent or a favored child? What is the status of the family within the neighborhood? Are they highly respected, prominent, isolated, or ostracized? Does the family membership include any specific social problems—delinquents, criminals, dope addicts, alcoholics, or the like? Is there any membership in community or church organizations? What is the social life of the family—full, limited, wholesome, or nonexistent? Are there many friends and what are they like?

E. Interests and Recreation

What are the most obvious interests of each family member? Are they athletic, intellectual, musical, social, or of some other type? Do they like to travel? What hobbies are apparent? What do they read? What evidence of various interests can be seen in the home or is reflected in conversations?

F. Ideology

What are the dominant ideals and attitudes of the family? Is there actually a philosophy which they express or which possibly can be inferred from their attitudes and behavior? Is this family characterized as liberal or conservative, public-spirited or isolationist, optimistic or cynical, religious or indifferent?

Interpretive Questions

After each section of the case studies in the following chapters is a group of interpretive questions. The nature of these questions is indicated in this chapter in generalized form; the specific questions in the actual case studies necessarily vary.

1. Which of the factors described above seems to be most significant in terms of determining the development of the adolescent? What factors might be due to (a) heredity, (b) environment?
2. Which factors are most likely to exert the greatest influence in the future, in your opinion, and why?
3. Might any of these previous influences be subject to change in some positive way that would be to the adolescent's advantage?
4. What evidence, if any, do you find of a pattern of influences that consistently appears in succeeding generations?

III. THE CASE HISTORY

In this section the topics are similar to those covered by the family history, but closer attention is paid to chronological events in the adolescent's development. Our motive is to present an accurate longitudinal study of all of the factors operating in an adolescent's life.

A. Health and Physical Characteristics

What is the general picture of development—normal or otherwise? Was birth normal? What was the age of walking, talking, toileting, and other developmental accomplishments? What has been the history regarding diet, digestion, sleep, and exercise? What diseases or injuries have been incurred? What is the general level of emotional stability and physical vigor? How is the adolescent's physical build best described?

B. Educational History

What was the individual's age at his initial school experience, and what has been his school progress? Is there any evidence of academic successes or difficulties? Does he have any special interests or aptitudes? Is he a willing or uncooperative student? How does he get along with other pupils and with teachers? What kinds of evaluations regarding his school performance are available? What are his future educational plans, if any?

C. Emotional Development and Adjustment

Is this individual basically dependent or independent, cooperative or noncooperative, confident or insecure? What are his attitudes toward his parents, siblings, and peers? How well developed is his emotional control? Does he exhibit tantrums, aggressiveness, hostility, or antisocial behavior? Does he have phobias, anxieties, or other irrational fears? Can he generally be described as well-balanced, apathetic, moody, withdrawn, hostile, or by some other term?

D. Psychosexual Development and Adjustment

How well has this individual achieved a male or female role identity? What evidence is available concerning physical sexual development and acceptance of the physical self? Are heterosexual interests present? How does the individual feel about and relate to members of the opposite sex? Can development in this area be classified as normal or abnormal?

E. Social Development and Adjustment

What kinds of social experiences does the individual have? What kind of "social self" does he exhibit? What is his part in family life, and in the neighborhood or community? Does he seem introvertive or extrovertive, aggressive or withdrawn? Does he have friends of both sexes or only one? Are they about the same age, older, or younger? In general, what are the characteristics of his friends, and how well does he get along with them? Does he belong to any organizations, and if so, is he a leader or a follower? Has he ever exhibited any antisocial behavior or experienced other social difficulties?

F. Interests and Recreation

What does the individual do with his spare time? Does he have any hobbies, collections, special talents, or favorite activities? How much and what does he read? Does he prefer activities which can be done alone, or those which involve other people? What were his play patterns and interests as a child? How much time is spent in recreation, and what are his attitudes toward these activities? Are these worthwhile, or done just to "kill time?"

G. Ideology

Describe the self-concept of the individual, his thinking about himself, and about his world as he sees it. The individual may not have formulated his own thinking, and if not, this should be noted. However, inferences can be made as to his underlying attitudes, ideals, and ambitions.

Interpretive Questions

1. How would you characterize the adolescent's overall adjustment at present?
2. What handicaps, if any, has he overcome in the past, or will he have to overcome in the future?
3. What aspects of the adolescent's development may have been the result of the role of each parent? What future effects do you forsee in these areas?
4. How have school experiences influenced the adolescent's personality development?
5. What are the effects of his social status and peer associations, including his position in the family and relationships with siblings?
6. What critical factors in the adolescent's life may have contributed to the kinds of social and emotional behavior which he currently exhibits?
7. What kind of adjustment has he made to his emerging adult sexuality? How important a part of his total personality has this area of development become?
8. How well has the adolescent mastered the developmental tasks of childhood? Evaluate his success thus far with the tasks of adolescence and describe any probable future difficulties.

IV. CURRENT STATUS; DIAGNOSIS AND PROGNOSIS; RECOMMENDATIONS

This section will include the more salient or critical features of the case in its present state. Any crisis regarding health, education, adjustment, behavior, self-concept, or related areas should be explored. The situation is subject to diagnosis if a problem exists. A forecast or prognosis regarding the adolescent's future is in order. An appropriate recommendation of means to effect a more wholesome developmental process or more desirable future experiences for the adolescent would be pertinent.

Interpretive Questions

1. Evaluate the author's summary and conclusions in the above areas.
2. What additional suggestions and evaluations would you like to add?
3. How well do you feel you know this individual after reading his case study?
4. What new information and insight into adolescent behavior have you gained from this study?
5. How typical of adolescents in general is this individual?

SUMMARY

Having now seen the contents of a representative outline of the type utilized by professionals who use the case-study method, the reader is in a better position to appreciate the comprehensive nature of this method of studying human behavior. A conscientious attempt is made to omit no bit of data, no item of information that might possibly contribute to the total picture we are trying to construct. Frequently materials obtained by means other than those described in this outline are integrated into the final case study. An effort is made to include documentary evidence of various kinds—psychological, personality, and aptitude test results; clinical laboratory reports; and even quotations of experimental findings in some cases. Thus it requires a complex process of selecting, weighing, interpreting, and comparing evidence of various types to reach a final "orchestrated" result.

Understanding
Adolescent
Behavior

"Individualization" is the key concept in describing the adolescents reported in this book and it is obtained by means of an intensive investigation of all of the factors affecting an individual's life, not just those details which may be entertaining or particularly descriptive. These case studies will include various types of data: school and medical records, personal documents, family histories, interviews, and other contributions from various individuals and institutions in addition to those of the person being studied. These data should encourage the reader to form a mental picture and ultimately lead to a greater understanding of the individual under consideration. As a bonus, in analyzing the motivations of others, and in learning about their modes of behavior, the reader becomes better prepared to understand himself.

ADOLESCENCE, A CULTURAL PHENOMENON

There is some disagreement among social scientists as to whether adolescence is a universal experience, because it is not found in all existing cultures. The primary reason for the disagreement seems to lie in the confusion evoked by the term "adolescence" itself. Some people wish to use this term primarily to allude to the physical changes which take place in the young person's body during the so-called adolescent period. Others, taking a more holistic view, use "adolescence" to describe everything that takes place in an individual's life during a transitional period separating childhood from adulthood. This latter approach is the more acceptable one. Granted, physical changes, dramatic ones, do take place. This is a developmental stage referred to as "puberty." These bodily changes, dominated primarily by the development of sexual characteristics, are, of course, universal and are as old as the history of mankind. Adolescence, however, when referred to in the broadest sense, is a relatively new social phenomenon.

Detailed studies of cultures other than our own reveal that the adolescent period, as we know it, simply did not or still does not exist in other parts of the world. Extensive research conducted by the eminent social anthropologist Margaret Mead,[1] for instance, throws considerable light upon this topic. Dr. Mead's work reveals that the transition from childhood to adulthood is sometimes accomplished in more primitive societies by means of a ceremonial ritual. Prior to the ceremony, the individual is a child but he or she emerges as a fully confirmed adult. This transitional experience is of extremely brief duration when compared with that of a young person in our society, who spends years undergoing this metamorphosis.

Most of the world's western nations do see evidence of some form of adolescence, but nowhere else do we find the exaggerated form which is typical of the United States. These facts contribute to the accuracy of describing adolescence as a social or cultural phenomenon rather than a physical one. In addition, even in our own country, adolescence has made a fairly recent appearance. Only a few generations ago there was very little, if any, time in a young person's life-span for the transitional period which denotes adolescence today. Boys and girls of the past were expected to finish limited schooling, assert their own economic independence, select a mate, and raise a family, all as a matter of course and as quickly as possible. Today, the picture has changed dramatically.

Modern-day American society prolongs adolescence for many individuals until they are well into their twenties. Some young people, particularly those who have not become totally independent of their parents, thus find themselves dichotomized. On the one hand, they wish to be treated as children and receive all the benefits of this status, while in different circumstances, they expect to be regarded as adults. This confusing existence can and does cause certain dilemmas for everyone: the adolescent, parents, teachers, employers, peers, and society in general.

[1] Margaret Mead, *Coming of Age in Samoa* (New York: William Morrow and Co., 1928).

YOUTH-ORIENTED SOCIETY

The emphasis which is placed upon youth in our society knows no parallel. No one cause for this has, as yet, been proven. One can speculate about any number of contributing factors. First of all, this is a young country. Compared to other societies, we are relative beginners when it comes to contributing to the cultural phenomena of mankind. Second, the pages of our country's history are replete with the contributions and accomplishments of youthful individuals; the settlers, explorers, the folk heroes of the nation's infancy. America, referred to by immigrants as "the new world," was seen as the site of rejuvenation, the beginning of a new life, and the realization of the democratic ideal where they, and especially their children, would find untold opportunities for education, employment, and the good life. These newcomers watched with admiration as their children acquired new habits, a new language, and an awesome amount of new information from their educational experiences. Emphasis soon was placed upon the wisdom of these young people. Every sacrifice was made in their behalf. Society was becoming more and more youth-oriented with each generation, an outgrowth of the child-centered home.

The evolution of this emphasis is quite apparent today. Much of the nation's business is aimed toward the youthful segment of society. Advertisements are directed to young people, to attract their attention and their dollars. Older individuals are urged to maintain "youthful" appearance, appetites, interests, tastes, and aspirations. Maturity, per se, is no longer very appealing. Middle age is a state to be abhorred, and the prospect of becoming a senior citizen is religiously ignored. Sports heroes, pop idols, movies, and other media glamorize the youthful state. So many so-called adults are proselytized and adopt youthful styles of dress and means of expression that authentic young people are forced to greater and greater extremes in order to maintain their identity, to separate themselves from adult, "square" society or the "establishment," and to preserve the sanctity of their subculture.

ARTIFICIAL ADOLESCENCE

The existence of the adolescent period in our culture is due primarily to the length of the educational process. This emphasis upon the extensive education of every child still does not exist in any other country in the world. Expanding public education to include four years of high school has postponed the assumption of adult roles for every young person in America today. The parental dream of providing a college education for every child has artificially prolonged adolescence for an even longer period, and created what Kenneth Keniston has termed the stage of youth, "a previously unrecognized stage of development that intervenes between the end of adolescence proper and the beginning of adulthood."[2]

The artificiality of the adolescent experience has caused eruptions to occur in the ranks of those most intimately involved. Pressures have been exerted in a variety of ways, and important changes have already taken place. For example, demands for a lowered voting age have been met. Other demands, made in the form of protest movements deploring war, racial discrimination, welfare inequities, and an absence of sound ecological practices are being pressed. Yet another target for expressed disenchantment has begun to emerge, as young people are zeroing in on the limitations and outright failures of our educational system. One of the most visible bits of evidence of this movement is the emerging rejection of the myth that "everyone needs a college education."

So we see that quite a bit of seasoning and numerous ingredients make significant contributions to the recipe which results in the virtual potpourri called adolescence in America today.

STORM AND STRESS

One of the first documented theories of adolescence was proposed by G. Stanley Hall in 1904.[3] As a result of his experiences with young people and their expressed problems, Hall described the adolescent period as being one of storm and stress. Many modern authorities are still inclined to agree with this description. Sadly enough, the storm and stress of today may be of greater intensity than ever before. Certainly society is much more complex and life is, therefore, much more complicated than it was in 1904. If we can agree that adolescence is a social or cultural phenomenon, then we also must assume that cultural influences upon the young person are of paramount importance. These influences contribute significantly to the storm and stress experienced by each young person in his own time.

The emphasis which Hall placed upon the negative aspects of adolescence might lead one to believe that adulthood, by comparison, is seen by proponents of the storm and stress theory to be a period of euphoria, completely devoid of trials and tribulations. This, of course, is not the case. Adulthood has its own stresses. The increased responsibilities and ever-impinging demands of society, family, and employment inevitably take their toll. However, several important factors create differing capabilities for meet-

[2]Kenneth Keniston, "Moral Development, Youthful Activism, and Modern Society," *Youth and Society* v 1, no. 1 (September, 1969): 111.

[3]G. Stanley Hall, *Adolescence: Its Psychology and Its Relation to Physiology, Anthropology, Sociology, Sex, Crime, Religion and Education* (New York: Appleton, Century, Crofts, 1904).

ing the exigencies of their respective lives in the adult and the adolescent. The adult, supposedly more mature in experience as well as in age, should be better equipped to handle the challenges his life presents than is the younger individual. The adult has had many more opportunities to profit from past mistakes. His learning opportunities have been more extensive and his judgment should be more mature. The adolescent, by contrast, may still operate frequently on a trial and error basis, learning with each mistake, but obviously still making them.

The adult has another important advantage. Having tested, and in most cases, proven himself, he has considerable self-confidence. He can trust himself. The adolescent, in many respects quite mature, especially in the physical sense, cannot trust himself. Still operating primarily on an emotional rather than a rational basis, the young person has no inhibitor mechanism to keep his emotions under control. Few adults throw temper tantrums. When they do, they have the wisdom to do so behind closed doors. The mature person, perhaps no less sensitive than the adolescent, has the benefit of a governor or inhibitor mechanism, in the psychological sense, which mediates, postpones, or even dissipates his emotional reactions. Thus the adult, who is more mature, appears to be more mature in his behavior than his younger counterpart. This is a distinction which is well to keep in mind whenever one assesses or compares the storm and stresses of adolescence and adulthood, or finds himself judging adolescent behavior.

One other disadvantage or handicap typical of adolescence involves the compounding of problems during this stage in life. Probably at no other time does an individual face so many problems all at once while so ill-prepared to contend with them. Perhaps problems of a more serious nature do occur in adulthood; however, not only is the adult better prepared to handle them, but seldom will he have such a multitude to deal with at the same time.

The adolescent's first concerns will probably involve physical factors. His or her body is changing rapidly and dramatically. Fortunately, in most cases the changes are for the better, but still the adolescent is very self-conscious. If a poll were taken of any given adolescent population concerning personal feelings regarding physical change, the results probably would be negative. The adolescent boy or girl usually is growing and changing "too slowly" or "too rapidly." Seldom do young people see themselves as "just right." Because of increased and sometimes bewildering sexuality, accompanied by an anticipated interest in the opposite sex, appearance becomes of paramount concern.

The desire to be socially accepted, to be with the "in group," and to be attractive and sought after by peers of both sexes becomes another problem area. The adolescent seeks self-esteem through his or her status in a social setting.

Recognition is also sought from older, respected, and admired individuals. To achieve status through a relationship, real or imagined, with an idol, a hero, or a favorite teacher, rewards the adolescent by tending to inflate that flaccid ego.

His status in the eyes of others is something for which he must contend within his own family as well as with peers and associates. There is a surge toward independence during the adolescent period which is more often seen as a "revolt" by long-suffering parents. The adolescent is indeed "revolting," and often in more ways than one. Parents should be assured that this drive for independence, which often turns their son or daughter into a sullen, noncommunicative despot, is a natural and quite predictable phase essential to growing up. A young person must be able to separate himself psychologically from those who have most significantly affected his life in order to prepare himself for the adulthood which lies ahead. Some psychologists will go so far as to suggest that we need to be much more concerned about the adolescent who remains totally docile and obedient during this stage in life.

DEVELOPMENTAL TASKS

Perhaps the amount of storm and stress in an individual's life is dependent upon his or her ability to perform certain tasks. The concept of developmental tasks has existed for almost 30 years, but received its greatest impetus from the work of Robert J. Havighurst in the early 1950s. As defined by Havighurst, a developmental task is one "which arises at or about a certain period in the life of the individual, successful achievement of which leads to his happiness and to success with later tasks, while failure leads to unhappiness in the individual, disapproval by society and difficulty with later tasks."[4]

Developmental tasks arise from maturation, the cultural pressures of society, the aspirations and values of the individual, or a combination of these factors acting together, and are grouped according to the appropriate age-span during which they should be mastered. The developmental tasks of adolescence, ages 12 to 18, have been defined as follows[5]:

1.   Coming to terms with their own bodies
2.   Learning new relationships to their age-mates
3.   Achieving independence from parents
4.   Achieving adult social and economic status
5.   Acquiring self-confidence and a system of values

[4]Robert J. Havighurst, *Human Development and Education* (New York: Longmans, Green and Company, 1953),p.2.
[5]S. M. Corey and V. Herrick, "The Developmental Tasks of Children and Young People," in *Readings in the Psychology of Human Growth and Development,* ed. W. Baller (New York: Holt, Rinehart and Winston, 1962).

Since adolescence in our society is often artificially prolonged considerably beyond the age of 18, it is pertinent to give some consideration to the developmental tasks of early adulthood:

1. Selecting a mate
2. Learning to live with a marriage partner
3. Starting a family
4. Rearing children
5. Managing a home
6. Getting started in an occupation
7. Taking civic responsibility
8. Finding a congenial social group

It should be apparent that considerable overlapping is possible, if not probable, in these two lists of tasks. It is also possible that for some individuals in particular circumstances this list is by no means all-inclusive. More recent investigation suggests that tasks involving academic success and/or attaining economic stability are appropriate to the young adult category, due to prolongation of adolescent status.[6]

IDENTITY CRISES

In addition to the preceding prerequisites encountered on the road to maturity, the young person frequently experiences a struggle caused by an "identity crisis." Erik Erikson has proposed that for each developmental level there is a series of ego qualities which must emerge if personality growth is to proceed smoothly.[7] For the period of adolescence, he has called these qualities "identity versus role confusion," based upon the assumption that adolescents are concerned with what they appear to be to others as compared with what they really are. The dangers inherent in this developmental stage are role confusion regarding either sexual or occupational identity. One young man has expressed this challenge as he saw it in the following statement: "I don't even know what kind of life I want to live, let alone how to make a living."

This type of identity crisis is not experienced solely by the adolescent. A similar crisis may occur at middle age. This postadolescent dilemma may be attributed again to the exaggerated emphasis placed upon youth in our society.

The frustration of middle age can cause a confused state not unlike that of the adolescent who is searching for an appropriate *modus operandi* or life

[6]Nancy C. Ralston and G. Patience Thomas, "A New Perspective on the Developmental Tasks of Adolescence and Early Adulthood," *Improving College and University Teaching*, in press.

[7]Erik Erikson, *Identity: Youth and Crisis* (New York: W. W. Norton, 1968).

style. The more mature person often becomes disenchanted with his or her status quo. He may find himself, at middle age, still searching for "the real meaning of life" and becoming painfully more aware, with every passing year, of man's ephemeral mortality. In this state of mind, the individual often panics, attempts to reassess the current situation, and sets out to make some adjustments in his personal life, involving family arrangements, social relationships, and conditions of employment. The "seven-year itch" and the "middle-aged drop out" are examples of the symptoms of an identity crisis.

The adolescent, on the other hand, bogged down in his role confusion, may experiment with drugs, hoping this will provide some magic insight. He or she may investigate different life-styles, pledge himself body and soul to the counterculture, or run away from home and join a commune of "soul mates" who are painfully eager to share role confusion and other frustrations. Many of these youngsters have seen the effects of the identity crises of their own parents and thus have become all the more determined to reject their inherited life-style for one, whatever it may be, that appears to be less threatening, less debilitating, and less futile.

The "flower children" of recent years emerged as progeny of the "beat generation" and espoused a philosophy based upon "love." There is security in numbers and the adolescent is no exception when he or she takes steps, sometimes drastic ones, to ally himself with others of common dreams and beliefs. Attitudes and values diametrically opposed to those which were imposed in the home are often appealing and, in some cases, gratifying. Closely-knit groups of young people, and especially the established communes, are a negative form of the kibbutz. They involve a subculture and, in effect, a youth society with rules and regulations of its own.

Ironically, the young person conforms to avoid casting himself in the role of a conformist. It is fashionable or "in" to be down on conformity, so the adolescent goes out of his way to be different and to distinguish himself from "squares." Dramatic, if not absurd, clothing and hair styles are adopted. These are the most obvious ways an adolescent can reveal disdain for, and rejection of, unacceptable standards and adult-imposed tastes and attitudes. In this attempt to affect nonconformity, the adolescent merely conforms to the mode of dress and behavior of his peers, thus gaining their acceptance and respect. He becomes, in essence, a nonconforming conformist or a conforming nonconformist.

Clothing manufacturers quite naturally exploit the young person's "far out" tastes. Clothing is designed to appeal to the youthful spender. Second hand clothing stores do a rushing business in selling recycled styles: faded denims, obsolete military uniforms, and moth-eaten fur coats, all of which are quickly copied and turned out at a frightening rate in new wash-and-wear form by the designers and manufacturers who know the potential of this ever-unsated market.

Adults who desperately desire to maintain a youthful aura adopt these youth-oriented creations for their own. This process creates a vicious circle of competition. Young people, rigidly conforming to nonconformity, see their image adopted by adults and seek new mantles of revolution, and so it goes.

CUSTOM-BUILT TURMOIL

The severity of any one adolescent's turmoil will depend upon the individual himself and his family background. To suggest that every young person experiences severe storm and stress would be misleading. Some young people manage to endure this period of travail with a minimum of discomfort. In such a case, we assume that the young person received considerable support from parents, teachers, and peers as well. The adolescent, for instance, who receives wholesome and comprehensive sex education is far more likely to accept with equanimity the physical changes he or she undergoes during puberty than the boy or girl who is left on his own, and whose education comes from the street or locker room and often from misinformed sources.

The adolescent who is treated with respect and regarded as an individual of worth and dignity by parents, teachers, and employers, stands a much better chance of successfully surviving the pains of growing independence than the young person who is consistently "put down" or arbitrarily relegated to a child's role. The young man or woman who is encouraged by teachers to try out ideas, to experiment, and to initiate educational experiences will benefit more from learning opportunities and find his schooling far more relevant than the student who is victimized by a structured, inflexible, lock-step type of instructional program. The adolescent who learns to control his emotions and to operate on a rational rather than an affective basis will enjoy social acceptance by peers and adults. He or she must want to be tolerant in facing the limitations of others as well as their own. It is a two-way proposition.

A smooth route to adulthood, without any stumbling blocks along the way, is perhaps too much to hope for. However, the young person who accepts the challenges proposed by developmental tasks in a wholesome manner, and who benefits from responsible leadership and encouragement, has every chance of making the most appropriate decisions regarding his or her role identification, educational and vocational plans, adjustment to emerging and continuing sexuality, and mate selection.

Sometimes, for some people, these challenges seem insurmountable. It is possible that certain individuals actually prolong adolescence for themselves because of a need to postpone the responsibilities of adulthood. Others apparently never emerge fully from the adolescent period, regardless of their chronological age, and remain partially or fully dependent upon others all their lives.

Numerous solutions or panaceas have been proposed in an attempt to relieve the adolescent of some of the pressures which cause the proverbial storm and stress. One suggestion is that our present society might become less youth-oriented and more mature in its own right, thus diminishing the attention given to adolescence and making it only one of a series of developmental stages which continue throughout life. Many educators propose that less emphasis be placed upon the need for prolonged schooling, so that there would be less frustration in the area of education. They feel that if more prestige and pride were afforded occupations which do not require college degrees, and young people were encouraged to seek realistic and practical vocational preparation, the problems of bored, unmotivated students who eventually drop out of school would be greatly reduced. Some legislators believe that additional adult privileges and responsibilities should be awarded to young people at an earlier age so they would feel that they truly have a place in this society and a voice in its affairs. Noted psychologists have asserted that too much democracy, in the home and in the school, has led to chaos and a lack of well-defined values and models from which adolescents can gain a sense of direction. They claim that what is needed is the reestablishment of adult control and authority, along with more rigorous attention to the responsibilities of parenthood. One suggestion frequently advanced by adolescents themselves is that our society would benefit from the establishment of a new value system. Until any, or all, of these proposals prove valuable and become realities, the adolescent will be helped if everyone with whom he associates makes every effort to understand the stresses with which this young person is attempting to cope.

The rest of this book is devoted to an analysis of some of the major and most prevalent problems facing adolescents today, along with descriptions of how adolescents deal with these problems.

3

Identity Crisis

The search for identity, or the process through which a self-concept emerges, begins very early in life. The infant makes the initial explorations which provide the information necessary to permit such a concept to develop. The baby examines his environment, the people and things it contains, his own body in relation to all of this, and eventually begins to establish the fact that he is, indeed, a separate, unique individual.

The child, as he matures and his experiences expand, continues to amass information which further apprises him of his individual status. He is continually responding to new clues which provide additional information in terms of how he is regarded by the significant people in his life: family, peers, teachers, etc.

The individual's self-concept is in a constant state of evaluation and revision, depending upon the type of data which is incorporated into the young person's consciousness. At no time in life is this self-concept more severely challenged than during adolescence, thus causing the "identity crisis" previously mentioned in Chapter 2. Without the security afforded by knowing "who he is," the adolescent is left floundering in the sea of confusion, bounded on one side by childhood and by adulthood on the other. To accomplish, with any degree of success, the developmental tasks of this period lacking some sense of identity is an impossible task.

Any number of factors affect the ease or difficulty with which the identity crisis is faced. The presence or absence of appropriate role-models during the youngster's childhood and preadolescence will help to determine whether or not appropriate sex roles are adopted and thereby contribute to a strong or weak self-concept. The individual learns not only how to relate to others during his data-gathering experiences, but how to regard himself as well. Parents are probably one of the heaviest contributors to the child's concept of self and the models they provide are crucial to a positive type of identification with, and acceptance of, sex roles.

A conflict-free sex role adjustment, however, does not represent the entire resolution of the identity crisis. Since the peer group has begun to exert such influence upon the adolescent, and his experiences and continued education have brought him into contact with ideas, attitudes, and values which may be quite different from those with which he has been nurtured in the home, conflicting forces often threaten the young person's fragile convictions. Confused by competing influences and the magnetism of peer pressures, the adolescent feels terribly insecure as a result of his vacillations. He finds he cannot trust himself in the sense that, while acknowledging the existence of parental standards or tastes and wanting to respect them, he finds himself leaning in the opposite direction, toward the appeal of peer approval. Conflicts of this sort were no problem during childhood because, for the most part, they did not exist. Now, however, the adolescent, in a period of self-distrust, does not feel comfortable in making the decisions necessary to decide which way to turn. Self-distrust causes the indecision which leads to insecurity, a typical component of the identity crisis. Various negative emotions contribute to this uncomfortable state of affairs: guilt, resentment, self-disgust, loneliness, helplessness, and any number of other ego-deflating forces.

The adolescent cannot avoid making choices. He is becoming more and more responsible for his own behavior and choices are inevitable. He must begin to handle problems himself, whether they are of sexual, social, economical, educational, vocational, or political origin. His own values must begin to emerge. He must learn to trust himself and to enjoy some consistency. In short, he must learn to control his own thoughts and subsequent behavior. Because of the complexity of society and the plethora of cultural pressures, the necessity for choice is sometimes overwhelming.

The popularity of "causes" in the adolescent population is a reflection of the challenges of the identity crisis. When a young person accepts a "cause" as his own, it is as though he is saying to himself, "Look at me, here is a choice I have definitely made! Here is a part of my behavior that is consistent, that is predictable. In this facet of my life, I can trust myself, my feelings, and my values. At least in this situation, I know who I am!"

As a pattern of behavioral consistencies begins to emerge, the ego becomes strengthened and the crisis begins to dissipate. The postadolescent hopefully becomes comfortable with his adult identity and becomes self-actualized. One can only speculate as to whether the self-concept ever becomes static and the crisis is ever completely resolved. We know that the characteristics of an identity crisis frequently reappear at middle age and sometimes again at retirement or at the onset of old age. This is fairly easy to explain in terms of a flexible, dynamic self-concept which must grow as the individual grows and change as the person changes throughout the stages of his life. This type of crisis, however, would seem to have its greatest impact upon the immature, unsuspecting, but fortunately resilient young people who meet these challenges with varying degrees of success.

A Case Study of Stanton Bailey

Stanton Bailey has faced a crisis in his young life and has made an important decision. He has left what few ties he has in this world. This is typical of his usual pattern of seeking escape. Hopefully Stanton can pull himself out of the rut that has so defeated him. Realistically, there is the possibility that he will remain trapped by everything that has operated against him, some of which was self-imposed.

I. IDENTIFICATION OF SUBJECT AND SOURCES OF INFORMATION

Name: Stanton Bailey
Address: 347 Summit Avenue
Race: Caucasian
Sex: Male
Age: 16
School or Occupation: McAllister Senior High School, grade 11
Sources of Information:
  1. Personal observation
  2. Interviews with subject
  3. Interviews with parents
  4. Interviews with siblings
  5. Interviews with peers
  6. Interviews with teachers
  7. Interviews with school counselor
  8. Interview with physician
  9. Interview with employer

II. THE FAMILY HISTORY

A. Health and Physical Characteristics

The members of the Bailey family are all of relatively small stature. The father, Kenneth Bailey, is 5 ft. 4 in. tall and weighs approximately 120 lb. Beulah Bailey, the mother, is 5 ft 2 in. and normally weighs around 105. Mrs. Bailey is very nervous and at times this results in a weight loss. Periodically she will remain in bed for about a week to "rest up" and expects the other members of the family to provide her meals. She usually loses weight during these intervals since no one else in the family is very accomplished in the kitchen.

There are three boys: Merton, age 23; Earl, age 25; and Stanton (Stan), age 16. Merton, who married at age 20, no longer lives at home. Melanie, age 12, is the "baby" of the family, and as such, receives preferential treatment from everyone.

No member of the family has ever suffered from a serious disease nor been physically handicapped except Stan, who during infancy suffered from a condition which eventually was corrected and will be discussed later.

B. Educational Status

Stan's parents both graduated from high school. Neither was able to attend college because of financial reasons. Both seem to resent their lack of opportunity. They are determined that each of their sons will attend college and are disappointed that at this time Merton has been forced to give up his schooling and go to work full time. Earl is hoping to complete an associate's degree in electronics. He has gone to evening school sporadically, financing most of his own education. The parents have helped out whenever possible. They have placed a great deal of hope in their youngest son, Stan, as they feel he is the most capable of the three boys and they want every possible educational opportunity for him. Stan is pressured by his parents to "do well," . . . "amount to something," and make them "proud of him." Stan has never truly exerted himself to the point of exploiting his full academic potential. His lackadaisical attitude is a source of friction in the home. Because, according to all school reports, Stan is capable of achieving a commendable academic record, his father, particularly, pushes him in the direction of winning a college scholarship so he "won't have to pay through the teeth" to provide Stan with the education he wanted so badly for himself.

No one is very concerned about Melanie's education. No plans have been made nor hopes expressed about college in her case. Mr. Bailey has definite feelings about a "woman's place," and since his wife has done all right without a college degree, he sees no need for his daughter to extend her education beyond high school. Melanie does not seem to care, one way or another, although later on she may have conflicting opinions of her own. During her entire school experience, she has earned exceptional grades. Her report cards are given a cursory glance by her father, but Mrs. Bailey usually utters some brief acknowledgment of this good work.

Stan's grade reports normally set off a session of verbal abuse that leaves the boy sullen and resentful. Sometimes days will pass before he will speak to either parent. During these spells he is seldom at home. He stays out late at night, eats his meals out, and isolates himself from his family as much as possible. This behavior makes his mother very nervous and she usually takes to her bed.

C. Economic Status

The father is a draftsman. He has worked steadily during all of his adult life, although he has had some difficulty with interpersonal relations, as he has trouble accepting the authority of others. Several times he has come close to losing his job. However, the quality of his work and his dependability have always saved him. His income is moderate. He has never been promoted, probably because of the reason already mentioned.

The mother has never worked as she married immediately upon graduation from high school. The eldest son, Earl, was born within the first year of marriage, so Beulah Bailey found herself both a housewife and mother at an early age.

Earl makes a modest contribution to the family budget and will continue to do so as long as he remains with the family. Stan works periodically for a local grocer. He and several of his close friends take turns driving the delivery truck and carrying boxes and bags of staples to people who order from the store. Stan admits that he "eats most of what he earns," while the rest goes for "cigarettes and other stuff." Mr. Bailey has tried unsuccessfully to get Stan to contribute at least a token amount to the family in order to "teach the kid some responsibility." Whenever Stan is approached with this suggestion, he gets out of it by saying he is "broke" and maybe will "kick some in next time." As far as Stan is concerned, "next time" never comes.

The Bailey home is a very modest six-room dwelling which is still not paid for. Mrs. Bailey always talks about moving to "a pretty little apartment that's easy to take care of," but her husband believes in home-ownership and wants to stay where they are.

The Baileys own one economy-type car which is four years old and a source of irritation because of its constant need for repairs. Earl has a second hand motorcycle which he purchased on an installment plan. Stan wants a motor bike of some description, but there is no hope in the immediate future. He has been known to "take off" on his brother's bike when he can get away with it. Earl has beaten him three times for this, and Stan seems to have learned the lesson, "thou shalt not covet thy brother's bike."

D. Social Status and Adjustment

This family has no noticable status within the community and is not well-known within the neighborhood. This isolationism is due, in great measure, to the personality of the father. It would seem that either friendships are unimportant to Kenneth Bailey, or that he is totally incapable of establishing such a relationship. As a result, there simply are no family friends. Relationships with neighbors are, at best, tenuous.

The Baileys have never associated with anyone outside the family. Mr. Bailey belongs to a union, but attends very few meetings and never takes part in the social activities. Mrs. Bailey attended several Parent-Teacher Association meetings when the eldest son first started school, but her husband discouraged further participation. The parents communicate with the school only when they are summoned for conferences, and then Mrs. Bailey goes alone. In every case, the conferences have been called as a result of the school's concern about Stan.

Occasionally, Mrs. Bailey will be visited by Merton's wife, Estelle. The visits are always planned for a time when Mr. Bailey is working. Merton has long since severed his family ties. He was more or less forced to do this because of his father's attitude and behavior toward him. Merton has never been forgiven for marrying and subsequently dropping out of school. Stan used to visit his brother and sister-in-law, but soon tired of the long bus rides. It is not known whether Earl associates with the couple or not. Earl is seldom in the home except to sleep, and no one keeps track of his activities.

Stan and Melanie fend for themselves. Their comings and goings are, for the most part, ignored. When notice is taken, in Stan's case at least, it results in negative reactions. Stan has learned to defend himself in the only way he knows, primarily by staying away.

E. Interests and Recreation

Mr. Bailey's interests involve watching sports programs on television, reading *Popular Mechanics,* and other "do-it-yourself" or "fix-it" publications. He spends an inordinate amount of time dismantling and rebuilding his car. The space behind the garage is a graveyard for exhausted and discarded broken parts. The neighbors bordering on the Bailey property have made repeated complaints about this eyesore. Mr. Bailey remains unmoved by these protests.

Mrs. Bailey, when she feels well, knits compulsively. She has made a total of 27 full-sized afghans, most of which are in the home, draped over various pieces of furniture in every room. They represent beautiful handwork. Unfortunately there is no one with whom Mrs. Bailey can share her accomplishments. She did give one to Merton and Estelle for a belated wedding present, but neither member of the couple shows an interest in acquiring another afghan. Melanie once suggested to her mother that she try to sell some of her work. Mrs. Bailey only shrugged and said, "Oh, I wouldn't know how to do that," and the matter ended there.

F. Ideology

If there is a family philosophy, it must revolve around a mutual concern about "life with Father." Everyone, including Mrs. Bailey, tries to stay out of his way. The children, with the exception of Melanie, who may be ignored by Mr. Bailey, but never brutalized, are alienated by his unending antagonism. The family, each in his own way, plods ahead in their respective ruts, avoiding confrontations whenever possible. If there is any joy in any of their lives, it is found outside of the home.

Interpretive Questions

1. Describe Stan's home life as it is seen from his perspective. Under what psychological pressures is he attempting to operate?
2. By what means, in addition to "staying away," do you think Stan defends himself against his father's negativism?
3. Describe Mrs. Bailey in her role as a mother. What effect does she seem to have upon her youngest son?
4. What sort of father-figure does Kenneth Bailey present? How will he, and how has he, already influenced Stan's acceptance of a sex-role?
5. The older boys have responded to the atmosphere within the home in different ways. Why, when their environment was common, have they reacted differently?
6. If Stan should follow a pattern already established by an older brother, which one is he more likely to emulate? How might he avoid following either set of footsteps? Predict what different path he might pursue.
7. How do you think Melanie feels about her father? Given the sex-role which her mother presents, how might Melanie feel about marriage when she grows up?
8. Why does Melanie continue to excel in school when she receives no motivation to do so from her parents? Do you think she will continue to achieve, or become discouraged and give up? If she does continue to achieve, what sorts of family conflict might arise?
9. How does Mrs. Bailey cope with the tensions within the home? Are her methods constructive or destructive? Are any methods of improving the situation open to her?
10. Describe the Baileys as seen through the eyes of a neighbor. How might these attitudes contribute to their social isolation? How do you think Estelle feels about her husband's family?

III. THE CASE HISTORY

A. Health and Physical Characteristics

Stan, according to medical reports, was carried full-term and birth was normal. Shortly after birth, the infant exhibited digestive difficulties. The problem was soon diagnosed as a constricture of the small intestine (pyloric stenosis). Surgery at the age of two weeks solved the problem.

There is no record of any difficulties or abnormalities concerning walking, talking, eating, toilet-training, or any other developmental area.

Stan, according to his mother, has always been a "funny eater." He uses no seasoning, not even salt and pepper, no butter on bread, and restricts his diet to very few foods. Among his favorites are "plain" hamburgers, mashed potatoes without butter or gravy, cottage cheese, hard-boiled eggs, and pudding custards. These are the things his mother fixes for him, when she is cooking, and it is assumed he eats this way when he buys his own meals. When asked what he chooses when he eats out, he admits only to "dairy whips and stuff like that." Obviously Stan does not have a balanced diet. He is short, as are his parents, has very poor posture, a blemished complexion, and unattractive and uncared-for teeth. His mother once attributed his peculiar eating habits to the digestive trouble in infancy, but this cannot be substantiated medically.

At the age of 16, Stan is an inveterate smoker. He started stealing his father's cigarettes at the age of 10. Once, caught in the act, he was physically and verbally punished to the point of hysterics on his part. He no longer steals cigarettes from his father, but from his brothers instead, with extreme caution and prudence so that his thefts are never noticed. He remains unfazed by antismoking "propaganda" disseminated in health classes. He is suspected of drug abuse by school officials; however, this has never been proven. Four suspensions for smoking have occurred. In one of the instances, marijuana was suspected.

B. Educational History

Stan entered school at the age of six. He had no nursery school or kindergarten experience because his mother felt he was too young and too little (mostly the latter), to attend school. All of the boys entered school at the first-grade level. Melanie went to kindergarten.

Stan adjusted well to his initial educational experiences. Somewhat shy, because he had had no previous experience with children outside of his own family, he soon learned the rudiments of sharing, getting in line, taking turns, and other social fundamentals of primary education. He attacked his school activities with a reasonable degree of zest and seemed to enjoy the total experience. During the first few years of the elementary grades, Stan continued to respond to the demands of an educational setting, participating in

Expanation of Marks

S   Satisfactory   N   Needs to improve

LANGUAGE ARTS

	PERIOD	
	1	2
Takes part in group discussion	S	—
Expresses ideas well	S	—
Is interested in stories and books	S	—

MUSIC AND PHYSICAL ACTIVITIES

	PERIOD	
Takes part in music activities		N
Takes part in rhythmic and play activities	S	—

ART ACTIVITIES

Shows interest in materials	S	—
Uses materials well		N

ATTENDANCE REPORT—Regular attendance is important. Frequent or long absence causes lack of interest in school work and retards progress.

	PERIOD	
	1	2
Days present		
Days absent	2	
Times late		1

HEALTH HABITS

	PERIOD	
	1	2
Takes care of personal appearance	S	—
Keeps objects from mouth	—	N
Sits, stands, walks correctly	—	N
Works and plays safely	S	—

WORK HABITS

Tries to do his best	S	—
Finishes work	—	N
Works well on his own	S	—
Listens and follows directions	—	N

SOCIAL HABITS

Works quietly	S	—
Is thoughtful of others	S	—

Figure 3.1.   First grade report.

EXPLANATION OF MARKS

A – 93-100 Superior
B – 85-92   Above average
C – 77-84   Average - Work done on grade level
D – 70-76   Below average
E – 65-69   Condition
F – Below 65 Failure

PERIODS	1	2	3	4	Year's Aver.
Religion	B	C+	B	B	B
Reading	B+'	B+'	A-'	A'	A
Language	A	B+	B	B+	B+
Spelling	A	A+	A+	A+	A
Arithmetic	C+	B+	B+	C+	B-
Writing	B	B	B+	B	B
Art	B	B	C+	C+	C+
Music	B	B	B	B	B
ATTENDANCE					
Days absent				2	2
Times tardy					

Although marks are given for all subjects, promotion to the first three grades is based mainly upon the pupil's ability to read, since this is the fundamental work of the first three grades. Hence the grade in Reading will largely determine whether or not the pupil is promoted.

NOTE: No report is given to children in the first grade until the end of the first semester.

EXPLANATION OF MARKS

A CHECK (√) MEANS THAT IMPROVEMENT IS NEEDED.

CHARACTER FORMATION	PERIOD			
	1	2	3	4
SOCIAL HABITS				
Is considerate in work and play				
Respects rights and property of others				
Observes school regulations				
WORK AND STUDY HABITS				
Begins and finishes work promptly				
Concentrates on task at hand				
Follows directions accurately				
Works independently				
Does required assignments				
Works to maximum ability				
PERSONAL QUALITIES				
Is dependable				
Exercises self-control				
Is neat and orderly				
Respects authority				
Accepts correction well				
Conduct	A	A	A-	A
Effort	B+	B+	B+	B+

Figure 3.2. Fifth grade report.

29

activities, doing his homework in a creditable manner, and receiving respectable grade reports (Figures 3.1 and 3.2).

When he entered junior high school, however, a noticeable change began to take place in the formerly personable, cooperative child.

Stan started coming to school unprepared for the day's work. He would answer with a surly "I don't know" when quizzed in class. He seldom brought pencil or paper with him, nor was he accompanied by his textbook. Since this was a new school, with different teachers and a much larger student body than his neighborhood elementary school, no one was aware that a change had taken place in the youngster. After a series of complaints had been lodged with the counselor concerning Stan's attitude and demeanor, the counselor pulled his elementary file. Discrepancies between the reports of former and current teachers prompted the counselor to contact the principal and sixth-grade teacher at Walter A. Fenton Elementary School. The following is an example of the anecdotal reports Stanton's initial file contained:

> Stan Bailey is a quiet, polite child. He does adequate work; however, he is capable of greater achievement. He likes to read stories about animals and nature activities, and bears the sole responsibility for the care and cleaning of the class aquarium. He once wrote a touching story about wanting a puppy. Stan needs, but doesn't seek, attention. He is tolerated, but not well liked by the other children. He does not initiate relationships.

The above report was written by Stan's fourth-grade teacher. The following one was contributed two years later:

> Stanton Bailey is an average child of average ability. He is best described as a "plodder." Socially he has few friends, but not for any detectable reason other than that he is introvertive. He likes to read supplementary materials having to do with nature and science. He will let his class assignments slide while spending his time on outside reading and projects. A conference with the mother offered no insight into Stan's personality. Mrs. Bailey was noncommital about her son's activities at home, his study habits, his achievement level, etc. It was almost as if she didn't know her own boy!

The junior high school counselor's conversations with the sixth-grade teacher and elementary school principal were very enlightening. According to them, Stan had never been a behavior problem. A motivation problem— yes, but that was a different matter. His attitudes toward school, his teachers, and classmates had always been of a positive nature. The counselor's current concerns about Stan reached disbelieving ears. No one knew where to place the blame for the difficulty. The counselor returned to Stan's current school setting with a determination to discover the cause for Stan's problems.

Stan's initial encounter with his counselor took place during a planning interview designed to outline his courses for the next two academic years. Stan was cooperative, but reticent about engaging in any casual conversation.

Additional sessions were planned and gradually Stan's guard began to slip.

In a counseling session, Stan, while very cynical and detached, did offer some insight into his home life. The following is a verbatim record of his comments:

> I don't get a hell of a lot of food or sleep. I just don't get hungry and besides there's never nothin' to eat anyhow. I stay out late to stay out of his way 'cause I can't stand the sight of him. When I come home I go straight to my room and slam the door. I think I'd kill him if he ever came in there. He knows it too 'cause he's never tried. When I can't sleep, I read lots—mostly magazines I pick up places. Yeah, I steal 'em sometimes—you know, like *Stag, Playboy, Male,* and stuff like that. Sometimes I read stuff like that all night, then sleep in class the next day. I hate school. I hate school because I have to be there when I'd rather be someplace else.

When Stan was asked where else he would like to be, he would not or could not answer. He abruptly terminated the interview.

The counselor, concerned about Stan's lack of academic achievement, lack of social success, and negative attitude in general, suggested that the Baileys seek psychological help for the boy. This suggestion has remained unacknowledged. An anecdotal record describes Stan's classroom behavior in this way:

> Stanton Bailey spent the major portion of class time with his head on his desk. No amount of cajoling, and no type of suggestion is sufficient to stir the boy out of his lethargy. I have talked to him about his reading interests and have encouraged his use of the library. To my knowledge, he has never made use of those facilities. Some days, on tests, he will do passing work, but his overall cumulative grade average is failing. At present, I am at a loss as to how to reach this boy.

Currently, Stan is failing in three of his four subjects. He has never passed a physical education course, primarily because of nonattendance. At this rate, he has little chance of successfully completing a high school education (Figure 3.3).

C. Emotional Development and Adjustment

Stan has had to become independent of family ties at a very early age. Finding his family relationships unbearable, he has struck out on his own and seemingly has built a shell around himself as a protection against further harassment and hurt. This independence itself may have afforded the boy a sensation of self-confidence. On the other hand, the self-confidence may have permitted him to become so independent.

Stan has changed from a "personable and cooperative" child into a sullen, unapproachable, uncooperative young man. He apparently is incapa-

Teachers	Subjects	Per per Wk.	Term 1			Term 2			Term 3			Term 4			Year	
			Mark	Qr Hrs.	Per Abs.	Mark	Qr Hrs.	Per Abs.	Mark	Qr Hrs.	Per Abs.	Mark	Qr Hrs.	Per Abs.	Total Qr Hrs	Total Absence
Haas	Eng.	5	D		15	F		14								
EZELL	HIST	5	F		15	F		12								
Miller	Voc.Ed	3	C-		1	C		1								
Danbury	P.E.	3	(F)		8	(F)		10								
		Days absent			15			14								
		Times tardy			7			9								

HOME REPORT

NAME *BAILEY STANTON*
Last Name First

HOME ROOM *323B*   GRADE *11*

An encircled mark indicates undesirable behavior or lack of cooperation in class.

Figure 3.3.   Eleventh grade report.

ble of profiting from any educational opportunities. If he could receive intensive counseling or therapy, perhaps the sources of his problems could be
aired and the cathartic experience would be beneficial.

This young man's emotional-control system is under severe pressure. We
have little evidence as to how he relieves his tensions. His defensive behavior
primarily involves escaping from reality.

D. Psychosexual Development and Adjustment

Stan experienced no difficulty as a child in accepting his male role. In
addition to his father, he had two older brothers with whom to identify. In
school he associated with boys and girls alike, but has never had any close
friends of either sex. Because of his small stature, he has never been active
in aggressively physical activities. As a child he sometimes watched televised
sports events with his father and brothers, but this habit was short lived. His
father used to chastise the boy for his lack of participation in sports and
games. "What's the matter with you, you sissy?" and other such challenges
were part of Stan's preadolescence. The boy's continual absence from the
home has made such harassment a thing of the past. The wounds, however,
apparently have not disappeared.

The high school physical-education instructor, disgusted by Stan's absence record, noted this on his report to the school officials; "Bailey, Stanton:
absent 10 days out of the past grading period. Seldom dresses for activities.
May be due to physical development, a problem which I can't solve."

Stan is not only short in stature, but is behind the majority of his peers in the development of secondary sex characteristics. As a result of a periodic, mandatory health examination provided by the school, the following report was filed:

> Stanton Bailey appears to be quite underdeveloped for his age. His arms, legs, and chest are relatively thin, and he still retains childhood fatty deposits in his hips and buttocks. He has not yet begun to develop adult male characteristics in terms of skeletal changes, musculature, voice range, or distribution of pubic, body, and facial hair. While there is probably no cause for concern, he is considerably behind most of his peers in physical development.

Stan's relationships in school give no indication of heterosexual interests. Lack of observable reactions, however, does not necessarily mean an absence of such interests.

E. Social Development and Adjustment

Stan's social development is almost impossible to chart. He is an isolate in almost every facet of his environment. With the exception of the boys with whom he associates through his part-time job as a delivery boy, he experiences no social relationships that are discernable. There would seem to be no "social-self," as Stan has had little opportunity to relate to others. He has no status anywhere.

The other delivery boys, when pressed, described Stan in monosyllables; "okay," "cool," "quiet," or simply confessed ignorance of any true impression of him. Several of these boys have had difficulty with the law because of drug abuse. One of the group was "busted" a week before the interview concerning Stan took place. This may partially explain the reticence to comment about Stan.

F. Interests and Recreation

Since Stan is such a social isolate, it would seem natural for him to have either a variety of individual interests or a few of considerable intensity. No evidence for either condition can be cited. By his own admission, he reads sexually oriented magazines which he "picks up places." Whether he reads other materials is unknown but doubtful. There is no evidence of reading material in the home. The family subscribes only to a daily paper and *Popular Mechanics*. The father took *Time* for one year but "got disgusted with it" and did not renew. Stan, who read enthusiastically in elementary school, apparently has lost interest in this activity.

Since Stan does earn pocket money and does not contribute to the family budget, he may spend his money on recreation or amusements.

A prognosis in this case is difficult. Stan's future will have to be what he chooses to make of it with very little, if any, help. He is undoubtedly hitchhiking to some randomly chosen location, where he intends to establish a life of his own. His ability to succeed will depend upon his willingness to exploit his mental capacity and his energies, and to overcome his withdrawal tendencies. Assuming that he learns how to relate to others, he may be able to get a job of some sort. Perhaps Stan has some latent interests which have not yet developed.

G. Ideology

Stan has developed a self-concept which cannot give him a great deal of comfort. He compares himself physically with his age-mates and the results are not favorable. Because of a cruel, insensitive father, he has been maligned for one reason or another most of his life. Neither parent has given him any reason to feel that he "belongs" anywhere. In the school setting, Stan has either chosen to isolate himself, or his personality characteristics are so unimpressive that he is relatively unnoticed by his peers.

Stan's underlying attitudinal system seems to be a negative one. He has become cynical and this is quite understandable. It is surprising that he has not struck out or struck back, in some way, at the world which has made him so embittered. Under the current circumstances, Stan has very little chance to become self-actualized.

Interpretive Questions

1. The description of Stan's physical appearance is not very positive. How do you think this affects his self-concept? How might he try to compensate for lack of physical attractiveness?

2. List all of the factors, physical and psychological, that Stan has working against him. What chance does he have to become self-actualizing? What avenues are open to him? Which ones are closed? What could he do to help himself?

3. What reasons, besides those of a physical nature, can you think of for Stan's "peculiar" eating habits? Do adolescents normally eat a "balanced diet"? At what stage in life are most food preferences established?

4. Many adolescent boys like to peruse magazines similar or identical to those mentioned in Stan's self-report. Accepting the obvious, what other reasons may they have for such reading tastes? Is this typical adolescent behavior?

5. Should a young man be allowed to purchase and bring such materials into his home? Would this discourage stealing, or surreptitious reading? Would this discourage interest in the material?

6. Parents and teachers have long assumed the roles of censors. Is this a realistic approach to encouraging wholesome interests and values? How can parents set the best examples in this respect?

7. Stan was described as "introvertive" in the sixth grade. Is this normal behavior at that age? How do most boys behave during preadolescence?

8. One elementary teacher described Stan as doing "adequate work" but being "capable of greater achievement." A later teacher termed him "an average child of average ability." What reasons can you suggest for this difference of opinion?

9. Is it possible that Mrs. Bailey "doesn't know her own boy"? Do you think Stan really knows his mother? His father?

10. What changes do you recognize as having taken place in Stan's life since his grade school experience? Can you identify some trouble spots that are unaccounted for by his former teachers?

11. Is Stan's junior high school in any position to help him at this time? What can the teachers do? What can his counselor do?

12. How do you feel about Stan's independence? Did it come about as a result of self-confidence or vice versa? Are independence and self-confidence mutually dependent?

13. In addition to the unfortunate parent-child relationships, what other things may be of concern to Stan?

14. How does Stan escape from reality? What dangers lie in this type of behavior?

IV. CURRENT STATUS; DIAGNOSIS AND PROGNOSIS; RECOMMENDATIONS

One week prior to the conclusion of this study, Mr. and Mrs. Bailey were summoned to the school because of Stan's unexcused absence. Several calls had been made to the home prior to the office notice delivered by an attendance official. These calls had not resulted in any satisfactory explanation. Mrs. Bailey was hesitant to talk with the school officials and told them on each successive call that "Mr. Bailey will talk to you tomorrow." Mr. Bailey never contacted the school. Upon closer examination of the situation, it became apparent that the Baileys had not seen their youngest son for two weeks. They showed very little concern about Stan's disappearance and were resentful of the "interference" of authorities. Neither of the older Bailey boys could or would shed any light on the subject. Merton was unaware of the situation, and Earl had not been cognizant of his brother's absence for several days, until he tried to find him "to borrow a little money til the end of the month."

The owner of the grocery store was unconcerned when Stan did not show up for work because "none of these guys are very regular." Only one of the other delivery boys had thought anything about Stan when he had not appeared that last Saturday. "I wondered if he really had taken off like he said he was going to," was his reply to inquiries.

Stan had mentioned "taking off" several times within the last month and had asked this particular boy if he wanted to come along. "I sort of thought about it, myself," Stan's associate explained further, "but my ol lady would be left alone and I just ain't ready to do that."

Asked where Stan intended to "take off" to, the informant was unable to specify. Apparently no true destination had been established. San Francisco, Denver, Arizona, and Texas had all been mentioned.

Because Stan had passed his sixteenth birthday, no legal action could be taken by the school on a charge of truancy. As long as he had remained enrolled, the school did have to assume some responsibility for his attendance record. A week after the investigation was completed to everyone's apparent satisfaction, Stan's folder was pulled and placed in the "inactive" file.

Stan has faced a crisis in his young life and has made an important decision. He has left what few ties he has in this world. This is typical of his usual pattern of seeking escape. He has given up his schooling, at least temporarily, but he was not profiting from the educational opportunities which were available to him anyway.

Armed with money he has undoubtedly saved from his earnings, and with a self-confidence of sorts, he has chosen to be truly independent of everyone and everything. Stan probably plans to find a job and remain employed, or perhaps to finish his high school education at night, and may eventually develop a self-concept with which he can live comfortably. Hopefully, Stan can pull himself out of the rut that so defeated him.

Realistically, there is also the possibility that this boy will remain trapped by everything that has operated against him, some of which was self-imposed. If he continues to withdraw from reality, and if he has been and continues to be involved with drugs, the future may become blacker than the past. He could eventually come to the attention of legal authorities, be returned to his home town, and/or be imprisoned for some antisocial act.

Interpretive Questions

1. Describe the ways in which Stan's environment has operated against him. How many of these factors might he have changed if he so wished?
2. How effective will Stan's running away from home be in solving his problems? What new kinds of problems might this action create?
3. How typical were the reactions of Stan's parents to the fact that he had left home? If Stan were your son, how would you have reacted? What steps would you be taking now, if any?
4. Describe Stan's emotional development in terms of his personality characteristics. How well does he control his emotions, and what methods does he use?
5. How important is adult physical development to teenagers of both

sexes? Are boys more concerned about this area than girls are? How are physical development and heterosexual adjustment interrelated during adolescence?

6. What evidence do you have of Stan's level of psychosexual development and adjustment? Would you describe him as "normal" in this respect? Attempt to predict his future adjustment and behavior.

7. Do you agree that Stan "has no status anywhere"? Does anyone in Stan's life care about him?

8. Stan is now completely independent. How well is he equipped to undertake the responsibility for his own life? Do you think that he will give up and come back home after a short time? Defend your answer.

9. In what ways have Stan's parents deprived him of independence, and in what ways have they given him too much freedom?

10. How well does Stan really know and understand himself? What is his basic motivation? Describe Stan as you think he might describe himself.

11. Stan seems to be facing an identity crisis. What does this term mean, and how does it apply in Stan's case?

12. How do adolescents discover their own identities? What factors have hampered this process in Stan's life? Is it too late to correct the situation? What positive steps could be taken?

Drug Abuse

The incidence of drug abuse in America is impossible to document accurately. Those statistics which do emerge cannot be trusted. Inaccuracy in compiling data is inevitable since much drug abuse remains undetected. Realistically, therefore one must assume that available statistics tell only a part of the story. One part of the story with which we are familiar, if we choose to be responsibly informed, has to do with the expenses involved in drug abuse. Every person who earns a taxable income contributes to the millions of dollars which are spent each year in an attempt to control drug usage and to rehabilitate those who have become psychologically or physically dependent upon drugs in some form or another. This expense does not even include additional millions which are lost or forfeited by those who, no longer productive, become victims of their addictions and, in turn, victimize their loved ones.

Drug abuse occurs as a result of ingesting certain drugs over a period of time in doses too concentrated and too frequent to be considered normal medication. Psychological dependence is caused by a need to prolong drug usage in search of the relief of anxiety or any other tension-producing sensation that causes emotional discomfort, or to obtain a temporary euphoria or feeling of well-being that may follow drug ingestion. Physiological dependence is caused by the continued use of drugs which affect the central nervous system. Narcotic abuse, for instance, produces both types of dependence, physical and psychological. Hallucinogen abuse, while not physiologically addictive, does often result in psychological dependence. Marijuana is a hallucinogen and is abused by more young people than any other drug.

Current research reveals that acquaintance with and extensive use of "grass," "joints," "pot," etc. is prevalent in all segments of our society, by the rich and the poor, by the young and the old. Most often, however, the users are individuals between the ages of 18 and 30. The lower limit of this age range is dropping dramatically with every year. Drug usage by high school, junior high school, and even elementary school children has become a fact of life. Drug abuse among these young people is not limited, however, solely to marijuana.

Whereas marijuana is not considered to be physically addictive, its most obvious danger involves emotional or psychological dependence, a natural trap for the immature, insecure, status-seeking person. Desiring social acceptance, wishing to escape from feelings of anxiety or depression, and relishing the thrill of the unknown or forbidden, the adolescent is often easy prey to the attractions of "blowing grass."

The psychological attractions of hallucinogens have long been glamorized in literature by such impressive names as Baudelair, Dumas, Poe, Aldous Huxley, and others. However, the young person today is far more impressed with current advocates, found in folk heroes here and abroad. Popular music, which plays an important part in the culture of adolescence in this country, also serves to glorify the use of drugs through the lyrics of many songs and the behavior of certain performers idolized by young people.

Marijuana is easily distinguishable from other hallucinogenic drugs such as LSD, mescaline, DMT, and STP. However, its basic effects are an altered state of consciousness with distortions of the senses and of the normal processes of perception which are similar to the effects of the other "mind-expanding" drugs, although less severe and prolonged. Because of a lack of concrete evidence concerning possible permanent physical or mental damage resulting from the prolonged use of marijuana, it is not viewed as a dangerous drug by many people. The scientific reports which appear from time to time present conflicting evidence which can be interpreted in various ways. Therefore the general public reacts to marijuana in much the same way as it did to the early reports about the dangers of smoking tobacco. In fact, those who favor the legalization of marijuana sometimes claim that cigarette smoking is a much more dangerous practice. It may be some time before science can provide us with a complete description of the effects of marijuana upon the human mind and body.

Until that time, many authorities, while acknowledging that marijuana does not appear to be physically addictive, are alarmed by the prospects of users shifting from "pot" to more lethal drugs. Since the average medicine cabinet contains the necessary ingredients for a bona fide "fix," accessibility is seldom a problem for a drug abuser. Young people can soon find themselves "hooked" on amphetamines, barbiturates, or opium derivatives as well as "acid." Ice water and peanut butter oil, among other substances, have been injected for a "fix." The lack of wisdom reflected in such acts can hardly be ignored or excused as "childish" or rebellious behavior. Addiction definitely is a physical and emotional problem.

Drug users are not a happy lot. While many exhibit a false sense of euphoria, close and continued observation reveals a much more unpleasant picture. Certain personality changes gradually become apparent. A listlessness, perhaps best reflected in a decreasing motivational level, along with a deterioration in standards of personal appearance and increasing difficulty in establishing and maintaining personal relationships are part-and-parcel of a drug abuser's world. Family life becomes painful, if not impossible. Non-drug-abusing peers become unappealing or unaccepting. School work becomes intolerable and classroom behavior and performance begin to drop noticeably in quality.

Extensive and expensive research has begun to provide facts and figures about individuals who have become addicted, in terms of the reasons for addiction, the personality of the typical user, and what eventually happens to most addicts. It is not a pretty picture, and yet millions of young people are still falling into the yawning trap of drug abuse. Marijuana is their primer. With this as a beginning, they continue to search for greater "mind expansion," bigger thrills, and far more serious problems.

It is natural for adolescents to experiment in seeking excitement, and to question and challenge those in authority, especially if their values and ideas seem "square" or passé, but this should be done on an intelligent, rational basis rather than a popular or emotional one.

Many drugs are available to the user and many can lead to dependence or addiction through abuse. Those most often abused can be divided into four categories: hallucinogens, including marijuana and LSD; stimulants, such as amphetamines, "pep" pills, or "uppers"; sedatives, involving tranquilizers, barbiturates, and alcohol; and narcotics; such as heroin, morphine, and codeine.

The facts concerning drug abuse are readily available from a number of different sources. Everyone working with adolescents, as well as the young people themselves, should become informed in this area so that they have a better understanding of this particular kind of behavior.

A Case Study of Suzanne Allen

The first shock came to Mr. and Mrs. Allen when they learned Suzanne had left her dormitory and was living off-campus with a boy named Curtis.

The second shock came as a result of their daughter's appearance. Her long dark hair was dirty and stringy and her clothing was disreputable. When they tried to find out what had caused these changes, they discovered that they could no longer communicate with Suzanne.

I. IDENTIFICATION OF SUBJECT AND SOURCES OF INFORMATION

Name: Suzanne Allen
Address: 2402 Haywood Court
Race: Caucasian
Sex: Female
Age: 18
School or Occupation: State University, freshman year
Sources of Information:
  1. Personal observation
  2. Interviews with subject
  3. Interviews with parents
  4. Interviews with former teachers
  5. Interviews with college counselors
  6. Interviews with residence hall counselors
  7. Interviews with roommate
  8. Interviews with peers
  9. Interviews with police
  10. Interviews with university medical personnel

II. THE FAMILY HISTORY

The Allen family consists of six members. Raymond Allen, the father, is 45 years of age and Priscilla Allen, the mother, is 42. The subject of this case study, Suzanne, is the oldest of four children. The sons, Harold and Roy, are 16 and 14 respectively. Lou Ann, the youngest child, is 13.

A. Health and Physical Characteristics

The family members are all of medium or "average" build. By most standards, the Allens would be judged to be in excellent health and physical condition. No one has suffered from any serious or debilitating illness nor suffered any significant injury. Abundant physical energy is characteristic of each family member, and this contributes to their exceptionally active existence. There is considerable participation in sports, because the Allens are all athletically inclined and tend to excel in their chosen activities.

Minor concerns regarding Mrs. Allen's tendency to put on "a few too many pounds" and Mr. Allen's excessive smoking are frequently discussed, but very little is done about either problem. Mrs. Allen tries to be a calorie counter, but she enjoys food too much to permit the retention of her once youthful, slender figure. She is usually just a few pounds overweight.

All of the Allens can be considered good-looking. Their healthy bodies and neat appearances make them an attractive family. All of their health and physical characteristics can be described in positive terms.

B. Educational Status

Education is important to the Allen family. Raymond, the father, obtained a law degree. Priscilla, his wife, earned a bachelor's degree and a teaching certificate. These parents are very determined that each of their children will excel academically and will obtain a college degree. Mr. Allen naturally has dreams of seeing his sons follow in his footsteps and prepare for a career in law. Neither boy has given any evidence of a crystallized vocational goal as yet. Mrs. Allen has expressed some concern about too much pressure from the father. She feels that the boys have every right to make their own decisions and follow whatever vocational path they find most attractive to them. Mr. Allen, quite obviously, is not this broad minded. Suzanne, the eldest, and already in college, has not been very definite about her vocational aspirations. Her mother and father both expect her to become certified to teach, whether she actually enters the profession or not. They feel that a certificate is "something you can always fall back on if another job, or financial matters, don't work out right." Mrs. Allen has never had to "fall back" on her own certificate and it, of course, expired years ago. Nonetheless, she insists that "that little piece of paper made me feel very secure." Suzanne's feelings about this are not known. She simply enrolled in a liberal arts course and does not have to declare a major for another academic year.

The boys are both in high school, while Lou Ann attends junior high school. All of the children have above-average academic records. Suzanne was salutatorian of her graduating class. The other children have seen their names appear on the honor rolls at their respective schools many times.

Raymond and Priscilla Allen are proud of the educational attainments of their children. While they encourage good study habits, they have never had to pressure any of the children in order to motivate them. Mrs. Allen commented, "I know we are very lucky in this respect. So many of my friends have a constant hassle in their homes about school work. I'm grateful that we have no problems of this nature."

C. Economic Status

Mr. Allen is a self-employed attorney. Mrs. Allen is a housewife. The economic status of the family is moderate. Mr. Allen initially was associated with a prominent law firm in the city. He became disenchanted with this position after three years of menial tasks and, impatient with the slow promotional practices, he severed his relationship with the firm. Mrs. Allen was terribly upset by this move and regrets that her husband took such "rash" action. She wonders whether he does not also regret this at times. His private practice has never seemed to give him either the personal satisfaction or economic rewards which he feels he deserves. Also, the family has never enjoyed the level of social status which both Raymond and Priscilla desire.

There are frequent arguments about such issues as the need for a newer, more expensive second car, more clothes for the girls, and housekeeping help for Mrs. Allen. The children all have what their parents believe to be "adequate allowances," but the boys, especially, are always "whining" about needing more money. Since Suzanne is now away at school, her frequent long distance phone calls are, more often than not, thinly disguised requests for additional funds.

D. Social Status and Adjustment

The immediate family consists of the two parents, four children and two grandmothers who live separately, but in the same neighborhood. The grandmothers both spend quite a lot of time in the Allen household. Mr. Allen's mother is very demanding of her son's and her daughter-in-law's attention.

The family life is not very harmonious. There is usually at least one argument under way at any time of the day or evening. Much of the dissension is the result of differing opinions regarding which child will be allowed to do what and when. Mrs. Allen is much more permissive than her husband, who is an arch-conservative in every respect. He is especially hard on the girls, expecting them to act and look like "ladies" at all times. Raymond Allen is much more lenient in his attitude toward his sons. This set of double standards causes children, parents, and grandparents to be at one another's throats a great part of the time.

In the neighborhood, the children are well known and well liked. The same is not true of their parents. Neither Raymond nor Priscilla have been active in any school or community groups. They have very few friends. As previously mentioned, they often express dissatisfaction with their social life, but seem to remain impotent regarding any solution to their problems.

E. Interests and Recreation

Mrs. Allen is an excellent seamstress and continues to make many clothes for her daughters, although lately, Suzanne has not been very appreciative of her mother's creations. Mrs. Allen, although somewhat hurt by this attitude, has tried to write it off as a part of "growing pains." Lou Ann is following her mother's example and is becoming quite accomplished at sewing and knitting.

Since all of the Allens are athletically inclined, sports participation plays an important part in the lives of all family members. Tennis, bowling, skiing, boating, fishing, and hunting are all family sports. Baseball, basketball, football, and soccer get the attention of Harold and Roy, while Suzanne and her younger sister have both participated in dance and gymnastic activities.

Reading is not a family pastime, perhaps because everyone is so active. Suzanne "caught a reading bug" during her senior year in high school, according to her mother, and read "everything in sight." This abrupt change in behavior and the seclusiveness which it involved was worrisome to Priscilla Allen, but she again attributed her daughter's behavior to "growing pains" and tried to ignore it.

There is not a great deal of social interchange among the family members. Conversations invariably result in arguments so they are held to a minimum. Mr. Allen had once proposed that discussions be held in a "round-table family council" type of setting and that all major decisions be made as a result of the democratic process. This plan was a dismal failure as all voting procedures disintegrated into battle with at least one, if not more, of the participants in tears. At the present time, all of the Allens operate as independently of one another as possible. This causes a rather confused home life as no one knows where anyone else is or what his or her plans may be. Mrs. Allen complains bitterly about this situation, but nothing is done about it. Now, with Suzanne out of the home, she simply has one less "body to worry about."

F. Ideology

Raymond Allen has set very conservative standards for his family. His wife is less rigid, but she defers, in most instances, to her husband's judgment. The basic philosophy revolves around a belief that everyone has the intellectual and moral responsibility to make "the right decisions" for himself, but as long as he lives under the roof of the Allen household, those decisions will be made by the father. Mr. Allen might be described as a benevolent dictator. He feels that he is "king of his castle" and no one had better cross him lest they bear the consequences of his wrath. The father has displayed his greatest preoccupation with the role of disciplinarian in his dealings with his older daughter. His relationship with Suzanne has always been tenuous, and more recently, visibly disintegrating.

Mrs. Allen finds herself in the precarious position of an arbitrator attempting to serve the needs and disregard the idiosyncracies of eight individuals who span three different generations. Suzanne, however, more and more, seems to represent a fourth generation all her own. Mrs. Allen moans that the "generation gap becomes wider with every day."

Interpretive Questions

1. All four Allen children have been academically motivated. What factors in their environment have influenced them in this respect?
2. In terms of Mr. Allen's initial work experience, what can you tell about his personality?
3. The Allens are frustrated by their lack of social success. How will this affect their children?
4. How are young people affected by engaging in or witnessing constant arguments about finances? Describe several expected reactions from "typical" situations.
5. Indicate several ways in which the father contributes to the dissension in his home.
6. What justification is there for a double standard in determining behavioral expectations for teenage boys and girls?
7. Are "growing pains" really causing Suzanne to be unappreciative of her mother's sewing efforts? What is the true problem?
8. Is it unusual for a girl of Suzanne's age to "catch a reading bug" and suddenly become seclusive?
9. Why did Mr. Allen's idea of a round-table family council fail? Have you heard of families which do operate in this way? Under what circumstances could such a plan work advantageously?
10. If you were in Suzanne's situation, how would you feel about the "generation gap?" Is such a gap inevitable? Do all parents and their teenage children experience this loss of communication at some point?

III. THE CASE HISTORY

A. Health and Physical Characteristics

Suzanne Allen is 5 ft. 4 in. tall and weighs about 120 lb. She is slightly taller than her mother and more slender. Her facial features favor her father as do those of her younger sister. The boys, however, resemble their mother.

Suzanne's birth was quite normal and she was a full-term baby. She walked at ten months and talked by her first birthday. She has had no serious diseases or injuries. A peculiar situation occurred during childhood when her hair mysteriously began to fall out. Various diagnoses were made, including suspected nutritional deficiencies, until a specialist suggested that Suzanne was pulling out her own hair. Her parents took turns observing the child during her sleeping hours and substantiated the diagnosis. At the age of three, Suzanne's curls were short, and until she was five years of age, her hair was never allowed to grow over half an inch long. By the time she entered kindergarten, her hair had grown to a reasonable length and her hair-pulling habit had disappeared. Other than this peculiar behavior, throughout childhood Suzanne displayed no observable nervous habits. At the present time, she admits to and presents evidence of frequent nail-biting tendencies.

B. Educational History

Suzanne began kindergarten at the age of five. She enjoyed her school experience from the very beginning. While many of the other children cried and clung desperately to their mothers those first few days, Suzanne left her mother with considerable aplomb and busied herself at the sand-table and in the toy corner.

Teachers in the primary and elementary grades all regarded Suzanne as a capable student, a friendly child, and a "joy to have around." A verbatim report of the fourth-grade teacher provides the following descriptive information:

> Suzanne Allen is a delightful and amusing child. Her sense of humor is precocious. The other children find her to be quite funny. She makes friends easily and definitely is a leader. Her mind is rather inventive and she is good in dreaming up projects or activities which she then procedes to direct.

Suzanne's academic records were always quite respectable. A copy of her sixth-grade record is included in this study (Figure 4.1). Suzanne attended parochial schools until her entrance into college. Her activities in high school revolved primarily around the dramatics club, of which she eventually became president, the Latin club, in which she also held office for three years, the school newspaper, of which she was business manager, and the school yearbook, which she edited.

Suzanne's high school teachers also found her to be amusing and capable of many leadership responsibilities. A college education was definitely encouraged, although Suzanne was advised to enter a small, private, religiously affiliated girls' school rather than the large State University which she ultimately chose. Her academic record was such that she would have received scholarship recognition and assistance at almost any institution she might have considered. The final decision, however, was made by Suzanne, with the approval of both parents. Suzanne enrolled as a freshman at the same university attended by her mother and father.

C. Emotional Development and Adjustment

Prior to the time when Suzanne left home to enter college, she had regarded herself as being relatively emotionally independent of her parents. This was not altogether true. While Suzanne outwardly displayed considerable self-confidence in the family situation, there were some self-doubts about being loved and wanted as much as her younger siblings. She did resent the fact that the boys and her younger sister were favored in most situations.

SUBJECT	ACHIEVEMENT				COMMENT			
	1	2	3	4	1	2	3	4
KNOWLEDGE OF CHRISTIAN DOCTRINE	a	a	a	a				
LANGUAGE ARTS								
Reading	B	a	a	a				
Word attack skills								
Oral reading								
Comprehension								
Spelling	a	a	a	a-				
Application in written work								
English	B	B	B	B				
Oral expression								
Written expression								
Handwriting	B	B	B	B				
MATHEMATICS	B	a	a	a				
Fundamental processes								
Problem solving								
SCIENCE - HEALTH	B	B	B	B				
GEOGRAPHY			a	a				
HISTORY	a	a						
ART	B	B	a	a				
MUSIC			B	B				
PHYSICAL EDUCATION								

Achievement Code	Comment Code
A Excellent achievement	1 Satisfactory in relation to ability
B High achievement	2 Unsatisfactory in relation to ability
C Good or average achievement	3 Fails to complete assigned work
D Low average achievement	4 Seldom participates in class
F Failure	5 Frequently fails to listen and to follow
√ Check mark in subheadings	directions
indicates area of weakness	6 Parent please see the teacher

Exponent in reading (remedial) indicates grade level

PERSONAL — SOCIAL DEVELOPMENT	1	2	3	4
Respects authority				
Respects rights and property of others				
Accepts and fulfills responsibilities				
Works well with others				
Is considerate and courteous				
Studies well independently				
Is a source of disturbance				

√ Check mark indicates area of weakness

Figure 4.1

She did not think that age differences could account for the many examples of preferential treatment that bothered her.

Suzanne is described by her mother as being very uncooperative as a teenager, refusing to help with housework, pestering her brothers and sister and "sassing" her parents on occasion. She started spending most of her time in her own room, which she had decorated to suit her own psychedelic tastes. Posters and mobiles were abundant. Suzanne and her mother argued about the condition of her room almost incessantly. One day Mrs. Allen discovered that Suzanne had removed all of the furniture, except for mattress and springs, and stored everything else in the basement and attic. Mr. Allen moved everything back in the room with the recalcitrant help of his sons and forbade Suzanne any further rearranging.

Mr. Allen, according to his wife, was visibly relieved the day they left Suzanne in her college dormitory. He was somewhat concerned about the fact that his daughter's roommate was a black girl, but his relief overcame his anxiety.

Both Mr. and Mrs. Allen had talked with the admissions advisor of the university and also with Suzanne's residence hall counselor. They were assured, on the basis of their daughter's previous academic records and character references, that she would "thrive in the campus environment."

D. Psychosexual Development and Adjustment

Suzanne had always assumed a feminine role with considerable ease. Although an accomplished athlete, Suzanne had graceful bearing and demeanor. An attractive girl, she dressed well and appropriately for her age. Neither her mother nor father regarded favorably the current clothing fads, so Suzanne dressed conservatively out of necessity rather than by choice. Until she entered college, her school apparel was a required uniform.

Having always attended a girls' school, Suzanne's relationships with the opposite sex were restricted to her brothers and several boys whom she encountered through coeducational activities shared with a nearby boys' school. There had been numerous dances and parties during her high school years which she attended with an acquaintance. She never truly had a specific "boyfriend."

E. Social Development and Adjustment

Suzanne has always enjoyed successful peer relationships. As a child and teenager, she has been popular and has exuded self-confidence in the social setting. This young lady has been, for the most part, extrovertive and aggressive in her social pursuits, but introvertive to the point of being seclusive at home.

Having been a natural organizer and leader, she was naturally expected by friends, teachers, and parents to continue the same patterns of social behavior once she became familiar with her new and more extensive, and perhaps more challenging, campus environment.

As might be expected, Suzanne had no difficulty meeting the academic demands of college courses and began, with considerable finesse, to acquaint herself with college life outside of the classrooms. Through an acquaintance in biology class, Suzanne met a young man who lived off campus. Curtis was a college drop-out who had been drafted and had spent six months in the army before he was discharged because of an allergy. Although it had been over a year since his return to the campus, he could not quite "get with it" and had not, as yet, reenrolled. Suzanne, her friend from biology class, and her boyfriend spent a great deal of time in the apartment Curtis shared with another young man. There was much discussion, "rapping," listening to records, and eventually sharing of marijuana and drugs.

Suzanne's parents found it difficult, if not impossible, to reach their daughter by phone on numerous occasions, even late at night. Mr. Allen confronted the dormitory counselor with this information and was informed that Suzanne had signed in every night but that obviously bed checks were unfeasible in a hall which housed 350 men and women. Mr. Allen was incensed and made an appointment to see the Dean of Students. During this interview, Mr. Allen learned that the university was no longer in a position to serve *in loco parentis* and in fact, the Allens had specifically allowed Suzanne to reside in a coed dorm, with no special restrictions on her comings and goings. They had signed "blanket permission cards," which meant that their daughter could come and go as she pleased as long as she signed in and out according to dormitory regulations. Mr. Allen admitted that he had had no reservations about allowing Suzanne to live in a dormitory where men lived on every other floor. "After all," he commented, "she is a good girl and I know we can trust her good judgment."

On this same visit to the campus and to the Dean of Students' office, the Allens scoured Suzanne's dormitory inquiring about her whereabouts. After several frustrating and unsuccessful hours, Suzanne's roommate appeared. She told the Allens that "Susie was with Curtis." Under considerable duress, the roommate was persuaded to tell Suzanne's parents who Curtis was and where he probably could be found. The Allens went straight to the apartment which was several blocks from the campus. Curtis and Suzanne were somewhat surprised by this unexpected intrusion.

The Allens were appalled. They forced Suzanne to leave with them and literally shoved her into the office of the Dean of Students. During this encounter, the Allens learned that Suzanne had "blown pot" long before she left for college. She had "tripped" several times before her high school graduation so, she informed her parents, Curtis most certainly could not be blamed for what was happening. She also admitted, rather belligerently, that she was "taking the pill," that she had been "sleeping with" and "having sex" with Curtis for some time and "he isn't the first either." Mrs. Allen left the room at this admission.

Mr. Allen, badly shaken, agreed to terminate the session on the promise that Suzanne would make an appointment at the Student Counseling Service. Suzanne agreed to this suggestion and quickly exited, ending the uncomfortable encounter. She also promised to go home the following weekend so she and her parents could "talk this out."

It was on this visit and subsequent ones that the Allens became aware of many changes in their oldest child. Suzanne's appearance had changed drastically. Her long, dark hair had become stringy and ragged. Her clothes were "disreputable" and she obviously did not wear a bra. While at home,

Suzanne spent most of her time in her room, asleep. She would appear for meals, upon prodding, but never exhibited her former enthusiasm for food. Her mother despaired at the very sight of her. Mrs. Allen began experiencing long periods of depression after her daughter's visits.

Becoming more and more desperate because of this deteriorating situation, Mr. Allen found himself less able to cope with family problems. He and Mrs. Allen argued bitterly about their respective responsibility for their daughter's rebellion. The two grandmothers inevitably chimed in with their unsolicited opinions, sides would be chosen, battles won and lost, and the wounds became more serious with every encounter.

Mr. Allen, in contact with the counselor whom Suzanne was seeing, got permission to join Suzanne during a counseling session. Suzanne had explained to the counselor the futility of this plan because "I've never been able to talk with him, why should I now?" Her permission, however, was obtained and the session involved the following confrontation:

> **FATHER:** Why are you doing this to us? What on God's earth have we done to you that you want to hurt us this way?
>
> **DAUGHTER:** It's my life, isn't it? I can do with my life anything I want. I'm not doing anything "to you." I'm just doing everything for me. For 18 years I've done everything you've asked, even those things I didn't believe in or want to do. Now I'm free. I'll do anything I want for as long as I want. As usual, you're thinking only of yourself and what I'm doing "to *you.*"
>
> **FATHER:** But Suzanne—you're ruining yourself, your life. The drugs, the drugs will wreck your body and your mind. Why must you ruin everything? How can you possibly enjoy this destruction? You are such a bright girl—you're too smart to be taken in by that hoodlum—that bum—that degenerate who feeds you this contamination . . .
>
> **DAUGHTER:** I'm off speed now, so it can't hurt me, and pot is harmless. Just read everything about it and you'll see it's harmless.
>
> **FATHER:** I have read everything and it isn't harmless, there are studies . . .
>
> **DAUGHTER:** Studies, studies, all that crap—there's nothing conclusive, and besides, he's not a hoodlum, I love him, I need him . . .
>
> **FATHER:** But you're breakin' the law—marijuana is illegal. You could go to jail. Do you want to go to jail? You couldn't be with that creature in jail—you'd have to be there without him.
>
> **DAUGHTER:** So what's so bad about getting 'busted?' I know lots of kids who have—so what?

The remainder of the conference was very repetitive and neither Mr. Allen nor his daughter felt that anything could be accomplished. Suzanne did agree, however, to continue seeing the counselor on a weekly basis.

During subsequent counseling sessions, Suzanne willingly described her drug experiences. She was almost enthusiastic in admitting her involvement. The following is a typical comment: "I loved for people to see how high I was. I loved to sit around and hear people say, 'Boy, look at Suzanne, she's really stoned'."

The extent of her involvement is apparent in her familiarity with and use of such terms as "barbs," "goofballs," "copilots," "bennies," "wake-ups," "speed," and "main-line." No needle marks were visible on her arms although she freely admitted "shooting up" under her tongue. Suzanne reemphasized time and time again that she was "off of speed" and did not like "acid," that all she currently used was "pot." The counselor feared that "the young woman doth protest too much." Suzanne's physical appearance belied her reports of abstinence. She was observably nervous, found it difficult to sit still, often perspired profusely during the interviews even though the room was not overheated, her eyes were blood-shot, and her skin in poor condition.

According to her parents, their formerly articulate, intelligent daughter had become incapable of speaking coherently or much beyond the level of monosyllabic speech. Of course Suzanne never did talk much at home, but the change was still an obvious one. Since she no longer associated with any of her old friends, it was impossible for them to make any viable comparisons. One of her former high school classmates also attended State University and lived in the same dorm, but she had little information to add to the record of Suzanne's metamorphosis. She did remark that she and Suzanne "no longer had anything in common" and that she had long ago "given up having anything to do with her because she spends all of her time with some weirdo."

F. Interests and Recreation

Suzanne has lost all interest in her former favorite activities. She no longer reads plays nor has any desire to become involved with any of several dramatic groups on campus. Her proclivity for sports and dance has dissipated. Her reading has dwindled off to virtually nothing but textbooks and those not very diligently.

She spends every available minute with Curtis in what her mother describes as a "perfectly filthy place." Her friends are few and are of similar interests, namely "turning on," listening to records and tapes, and doing as little studying as possible, "just enough to stay in school."

G. Ideology

Suzanne has been attracted by the philosophy of a subculture which she has adopted for her own. Surrounded by young people who revile the values of their parents, and who go overboard in their assertion of emotional independence (though not financial independence), she takes pleasure in rebelling and rejecting everyone and everything from her background.

Having always been successful and therefore self-confident in her social relationships, it is peculiar that she must or wishes to seek attention through drug usage. ("I love for people to say, 'Look at Suzanne, she's really stoned'.")

Her self-concept, once well-established and undoubtedly self-accepting, may be less stabilized at this time than it was prior to her most recent experiences. Her relationship with Curtis may confuse her or cause some feelings of insecurity.

Suzanne is really still trying to find a "self" with which she is comfortable.

Interpretive Questions

1. Would you have predicted that Suzanne might display behavior of this kind if she attended a large university rather than a small private college? Would her behavior be the same if she were living at home and going to college? Defend your answers.
2. Explain Suzanne's changed life-style as you think she sees it, and as it appears to her parents. How might a psychologist interpret her behavior?
3. How widespread is this life-style among college students today?
4. How much of the "blame" for Suzanne's present situation should be placed upon Curtis and his friends? Who else shares the responsibility?
5. What factors led to Suzanne's excellent high school record? What has happened to these factors?
6. Would you describe Suzanne's psychosexual development as "normal"? How do you explain her present behavior in this area?
7. Why do you suppose Suzanne was attracted to drugs? What purpose are they serving in her life? Is this consistent with the reasons most college students give for drug usage?
8. What is Suzanne trying to say by her changed appearance? Is this a cry for help, an act of defiance, or simply another form of conformity?
9. Suzanne seems to think that she has become a real nonconformist. Has she? Defend your answer.
10. How typical is the conversation between father and daughter recorded in this study? Are they really communicating with each other at all? Is either one of them honestly trying to communicate with the other? Explain your opinions.
11. Evaluate the arguments presented by Suzanne and her father. Who is closest to the truth? Could either one ever convince the other? Why, or why not?
12. Why does Suzanne apparently enjoy having other people observe her when she is "high"? What unmet need does this situation satisfy? Why does this need exist?

13. Describe Suzanne as seen through the eyes of Curtis, one of his friends, and one of her former classmates.
14. Has the change in Suzanne been a positive or negative one? How did you arrive at your decision?

IV. CURRENT STATUS; DIAGNOSIS AND PROGNOSIS; RECOMMENDATIONS

This case study represents a crisis in the life of a young woman. Suzanne is experiencing many conflicts and, while she has the native intelligence to deal with these on a rational level, it is doubtful that she can do so emotionally. Further complications have arisen as a result of Curtis's arrest during spring vacation for pushing drugs. Interestingly enough, he told the arresting officer, "I don't need the money—I just want to feel important." Suzanne asked her father to help with money in posting Curtis's bond, but her father refused this request. Suzanne displayed a fit of hysterical temper and hid in her room for days, coming out only at night to get scraps of food from the kitchen.

The Allens want Suzanne to seek psychiatric help. However, so far she has refused. At this point it is doubtful that Suzanne will return for the next academic session. Her grades have dropped precipitously during the spring semester. Mr. Allen has told Suzanne that he will refuse to finance her education if she is not willing to stop seeing Curtis and start applying herself to her studies. At the present time, there is a relative stalemate in the Allen household, and Mr. and Mrs. Allen are beside themselves with worry and despair.

Hopefully, Suzanne will eventually be willing to accept help from a psychiatrist. The Allens are aware that such treatment can be very extensive, and therefore expensive. Mr. Allen will spend "whatever it takes to bring her back to us." The next few months may indeed be the most important in Suzanne Allen's life.

Interpretive Questions

1. The author of this study describes Suzanne's friends in an extremely negative way. How accurate, in your opinion, and based upon your own experiences, is this description?
2. Do you feel that Suzanne is trying to find her real "self" in her current behavior pattern? If the answer is yes, how successful is she likely to be?
3. How do you explain Curtis's remark to the officer who arrested him?
4. Evaluate Mr. Allen's decision to withdraw his financial support unless Suzanne stops seeing Curtis.

5. What reasons may lie behind Suzanne's insistence that she is "off speed and acid"? Do you believe she really restricts her usage to marijuana? Why?
6. Do you agree that psychiatric help will solve many of Suzanne's problems? What other kinds of treatment or therapy might be employed?
7. What is your prognosis for Suzanne's future? What suggestions would you make in order to resolve the present situation?
8. What different actions and reactions by Suzanne and her parents might have resulted in a vastly different adolescent from the one described in this study?
9. Many people would say that Suzanne is "wasting" or "spoiling" her life. Would you agree or disagree, and why?
10. How accurately can most adolescents evaluate the possible effects of their behavior upon their future life?

5

Social Maturity

During the transition from childhood to adulthood, certain developmental tasks pertaining to social relationships are encountered by the individual. We expect the adolescent to leave behind the social immaturity of the child as he learns new relationships with his peers.

The adolescent is much more dependent upon peer relationships than is the child, whose sphere of operation still centers around the home and its family members. The adolescent, as a result of, or in conjunction with, the predictable surge for independence, finds that the emotional ties with parents are becoming more flexible, if not less binding, and begins feeling the effects of peer or social pressures to a greater degree. These pressures can have tremendous influence in affecting a young person's behavior, attitudes, appearance, and outlook on life. The need for conformity has already been discussed; however, the need for social acceptance deserves some additional attention.

At no other point in life does the peer group exert as much influence as it does during adolescence. In many instances, parents inadvertently contribute to a young person's vulnerability to social pressures. It is a natural wish on the part of a parent for the son or daughter to be popular among age-mates and to be a social success. Some parents, trying to relive or vicariously outdo their own social pasts, unmercifully push their offspring into social situations which may be inappropriate in terms of the child's maturity and sophistication or, at least, in terms of his interest. Mothers, terrified that their daughter may become a "wallflower" or their son a social drag, often promote numerous social activities and relationships while entertaining unrealistic expectations which lead to frustration and unhappiness for everyone concerned. A great deal of agony is endured by youngsters who are pushed and shoved into social arenas for which they are not emotionally prepared. A more concrete example of such forced precocity is the very young lady, who, in order to be properly attired, is encouraged to wear makeup and trappings far too mature for her years, including articles of underwear for which she has no possible physical justification. Some parents "use" their children socially and this is particularly apparent during the adolescent period.

Parents can retard as well as attempt to accelerate a child's social development. Rather serious conflicts can occur within the home when parents realize that the influence of the peer culture offers some stiff competition with regard to the establishment of codes of acceptable dress, hair styles, language, reading matter, curfews, use of the family car, ad infinitum. Considerable mediation and compromise may be necessary. The mutual respect which does or does not exist between parents and adolescent will determine how much of a battle occurs and what constitutes a victory. The adolescent who has the greatest ego strength, the most emotional maturity, and who is less dependent upon either parental or peer dictates, will evaluate both viewpoints and, upon the basis of rational judgment, will form his own opinions and develop his own values without being seriously troubled by the opposing sides.

In various studies of peer groups, three types of relationships tend to emerge: crowds, cliques or gangs, and friendships. Each of these relationships serves in some way to help the adolescent in his socialization process. The crowd offers the attraction of organized activities: dances, parties, spectator sports, and other interpersonal settings. The clique, a smaller and more closely knit group, involves a great deal of communication (much telephoning) and many informal, unorganized social encounters before and after school, during lunch hour, and in homework study sessions. The category of friendship implies a degree of intimacy and, in fact, involves an intensity that is not likely in the previous social categories.

Because adolescence denotes a period of adjustment to a changing physical and psychological self, a friend can serve as a buffer between the "self" the adolescent wants to be and the person he really is. A friend can often support a faltering ego, buoy up a sagging self-image, and because of an honest and open relationship, help the adolescent keep everything in the proper perspective, both the good and the bad. A friendship, like other social relationships, can be a learning situation, providing the adolescent with a sounding board upon which to try out new values, ideals, and modes of behavior. According to Diogenes, "When Zeno was asked what a friend was, he replied, 'Another I.' " Zeno might well have been an adolescent at the time of this statement (circa A.D. 200).

Few individuals, young or old, male or female, can face lack of social acceptance with any degree of equanimity. Most adolescents, who base much of their self-concept upon their acceptance by others, are particularly vulnerable in this respect. There is a gnawing need "to belong," and some adolescents will take dramatic, if not drastic, steps to assure that "belonging" occurs. The reader can no doubt cite numerous examples of an adolescent's desperate and sometimes futile attempts to win social acceptance from peers of both sexes.

A young person's heterosexual interests naturally expand during the adolescent period. We expect the individual to begin to cross childhood sex lines, so to speak, lines of deliberate, arbitrary delineation separating boys and girls. Once the social barriers are down, and heterosexual relationships are acceptable within the immediate peer group, then social relationships become primarily date-oriented, at least as far as crowd and clique activities are concerned.

Unfortunately, the individual who is not accepted socially, who is seen as an outcast, and who feels rejected, has tremendous difficulty in reversing this set of circumstances. Rejected because of lack of social poise or self-confidence, he or she has little chance of rectifying the situation since these qualities develop in the presence, not the absence, of social acceptance. Personal immunity to lack of popularity is seldom observed in the human being and even more rarely in the adolescent. There are some exceptions as there are in most situations. In a very few cases, a young person of unusual, if not phenomenal self-confidence, whose adolescence has been devoid of the usual conflicts, doubts, and social interests, will not experience the magnetic pull of peer pressure. One wonders, however, if this individual does not miss part of the essence of adolescence. In addition, there is no guarantee that adult life will be any richer, or even as rich, as a result of this omission of an important developmental task.

A Case Study of Linda Wilson

Since Linda has been enrolled in college, she seldom goes home. While her classmates are running in and out of town with frenzied frequency to visit their homes, other campuses, or just going into the city, Linda stays well-planted in her dormitory room. She has received no peer acceptance, but then she has never given anyone a chance to know her.

I. IDENTIFICATION OF SUBJECT AND SOURCES OF INFORMATION.

Name: Linda Wilson
Address: 714 St. Moritz Towers
Race: Caucasian
Sex: Female
Age: 19
School or Occupation: Headrow College for Women, sophomore year
Sources of Information:
1. Personal observation
2. Interviews with subject
3. Interviews with mother
4. Interviews with classmates
5. Interviews with teachers
6. Interviews with dormitory counselor

II. THE FAMILY HISTORY

Linda Wilson is the only child of William and Laura Wilson. A male child was stillborn five years after Linda's birth, and Mrs. Wilson was advised against any additional pregnancies.

A. Health and Physical Characteristics

The family members are healthy and physically fit with one noteworthy exception: the father has experienced three kidney stone attacks over the past six years.

Mr. Wilson is of average height; Mrs. Wilson, however, is above average in this respect and is two inches taller than her husband. Linda, at the age of 19, has reached her peak height of 5 ft 10 in., an inch taller than her father.

Except for the stillborn child, Mrs. Wilson has had few physical or medical problems. She is, however, extremely nervous and is under medication prescribed by her psychiatrist, whom she sees twice a month.

B. Educational Status

Linda comes from a family which is very concerned about education. Both parents have baccalaureate degrees. William Wilson began his career as an engineering consultant with a large manufacturing corporation, in which he now serves as vice president in charge of production. Mrs. Wilson has a degree in fine arts, but she has never been employed. Linda is in her second year of college, preparing to be an elementary school teacher.

C. Economic Status

The Wilsons, from a relatively modest beginning, have progressed rapidly up the socioeconomic scale. William and Laura married the summer after their graduation from college and, shunning all offers of financial aid from both sets of in-laws, began their married life under very frugal circumstances. Mr. Wilson's drive and perseverance quickly came to the attention of his superiors and promotions came in rapid succession. Moving from their initial apartment to a larger one, then moving again and again to increasingly better accommodations, the early years of marriage found the Wilsons constantly trading in furniture and neighborhoods with little regard for either. After Linda's birth, the momentum was suspended for a time, only to resume again when the second child was lost. Linda was shunted from one school to another for several years until the inevitable decision to place her in an exclusive private school was made.

The Wilsons currently reside in a new condominium apartment house, considered to be the most exclusive address in the city.

D. Social Status and Adjustment

Socially, the elder Wilsons are very active. Mrs. Wilson is involved with many women's groups and their numerous charitable activities, and rushes from meetings to receptions, from banquets to concerts, and frequently attends conventions in other cities. Mr. Wilson, heavily involved in his business activities, encourages his wife to busy herself as much as possible so that she will not "get bored" or "resent his preoccupation." While the elder Wilsons have adjusted to each other's separate social needs, Linda has been known to express her dissatisfaction with this modus operandi.

E. Interests and Recreation

The Wilsons share no recreational activities. The parents previously belonged to several bridge clubs at various times, but their frequent moves and improving socioeconomic status necessitated the abandonment of successive groups of friends. While this apparently was accomplished with considerable ease on the part of William and Laura Wilson, their daughter was a victim of short, unstable, and abruptly terminated friendships. When she complained about missing so-and-so or wanting to invite a long-lost playmate to a new residence, Linda was reprimanded with comments like, "Don't be silly, you don't want to play with *her* anymore."

The interests of Mr. and Mrs. Wilson are simply "business comes first" for William and "social activities are the raison d'etre" for Laura. Very little time is spent together, and there are few common interests shared by all family members.

F. Ideology

If there is a bona fide family philosophy, it must be to do whatever is necessary to get ahead, and to let nothing stand in the way of economic and social progress. Personal relationships are not important, except in the very shallow sense of leading to further and perhaps more profitable associations.

The Wilsons expect their daughter to obtain a superior education, marry a suitable young man at the appropriate time, and live a life that meets all of the standards her parents have set for themselves.

Interpretive Questions

1. Now that you are familiar with the social background of William and Laura Wilson, what might you suspect about their daughter's attitudes toward her parents in this respect?

2. Describe the psychological atmosphere within the home as it might be seen from Linda's perspective.

3. The Wilsons have provided Linda with every conceivable material advantage. However, in your estimation, has this girl experienced a deprived childhood and early adolescence? Support your answer.

4. At the age of 19, Linda is in the throes of dealing with numerous developmental tasks. List those which have become apparent from the information presented thus far.

5. How might Linda's experiences at home have been different if she were not an only child? Would the presence of a sibling be to Linda's advantage or disadvantage? Why?

6. Since there are no common interests or recreational activities in this family, what effect will this have upon the development of Linda's interests, attitudes and values?

III. THE CASE HISTORY

A. Health and Physical Characteristics

Linda was born under normal circumstances. Delivery was accomplished while the mother was under local anesthetic. According to Mrs. Wilson, "Linda thrived in every respect and was a precious darling from the beginning." The baby babbled at an early age and began to say single words at about nine months. Mrs. Wilson, eager for her child to be precocious, encouraged Linda to express herself verbally. The baby was constantly exposed to various types of stimuli in the hope of provoking a verbal response. In later years, when Linda pleased her mother with recitations and other performances, usually before guests, she was rewarded with candy or sometimes coins for her piggy bank.

Linda completed the developmental stages which eventually led to her ability to walk unassisted. She crawled, scooted, crept, balanced herself upright, took several shaky steps while clutching an adult's hand, and finally took her first solo steps at 11 months.

Linda sucked her thumb at night and when she took her naps. She was never given a pacifier because the pediatrician advised against this. Much later, Mrs. Wilson learned that the use of the pacifier probably would have been wise. Linda always took a teddy bear to bed with her, and to this day she sleeps with some sort of stuffed toy. Linda took forced naps until she was seven years old. She was sent straight to her room after arriving home from school. No protest was accepted by Linda's mother. Linda reports that she would lie there, stroking her teddy bear and staring at the ceiling, until she was allowed to get up. She had difficulty sleeping at night also. Today, as a college student, she is seldom in bed before 1 or 2 A.M. As a result, she is always "exhausted." She attempts to justify her unreasonable sleeping habits by "the need to study." Linda is an inveterate time-waster but she seldom studies in the wee hours of the morning. More than likely, she is daydreaming instead of night-dreaming. Linda reports that a great deal of her time is spent fantasizing. Her teachers in high school attest to Linda's propensity for day-dreaming. An anecdotal record from Linda's ninth-grade folder makes the following revelation:

> If only this child could apply herself, for she has considerable potential, but no motivation. I feel as though she has thrown up a wall between herself and the teachers. She looks interested in the lessons but when asked a question, she obviously has been paying no attention.

Linda was the victim of several childhood illnesses of a minor nature—measles, mumps, and chickenpox. She was usually left in the care of a household servant during these illnesses. The child experienced no physical difficulties throughout her childhood. Her first menstrual period came at the age of 12 years, six months. Her preparation for this event involved the reading of a pamphlet, produced by a sanitary napkin manufacturer, at the suggestion of a friend of her mother's whose daughter had brought it home from school. Linda had also seen a movie, produced by the same manufac-turer, in her health class. At the end of the movie the teacher had asked, "Are there any questions?" According to Linda, no one said a word. She had not really understood much of the movie, but she would not have dreamed of displaying her ignorance to others.

B. Educational History

Linda entered nursery school at the age of three-and-a-half. The next year she went to kindergarten in another school. She entered the first grade and remained in the same school for two consecutive years. After that, the moves were frequent until the ninth grade when Linda was sent to Country Day School. She remained in this educational setting until she graduated from high school.

Her grade reports at all levels were satisfactory, but barely so. Her only A's were in deportment, citizenship, and cooperation. Achievement in subject matter was usually reflected by B's and C's. Receiving very little encouragement at home, Linda exhibited little motivation. She simply had no competitive instinct and since her parents expressed so little interest in her school work, she did the minimum amount of work needed to get a passing grade. Her father never once looked at her report cards, and her mother signed them with a great deal of detachment. "That's fine dear, do better next time," was all she ever heard at the end of a grading period.

Since she did not study a great deal, and fortunately was bright enough so that she did not need to, much of her time was spent immersed in casual reading. She was an avid reader of almost anything. Having read everything to be found on the untouched shelves of her father's study, most of which was much too adult for her years, she found the school library a complete bore. One of her proudest possessions was her very own library card which gave her access to the treasures of the public library. Fortunately the person in charge of the checkout desk was no self-appointed dictator of Linda's tastes. Recognizing the girl's appetite for literary challenge, the librarian steered her away from the sweet-sop of most fiction aimed at the adolescent and allowed her to partake of more sophisticated material. Once in a while, a casual, "Oh Linda, maybe not that one; how about this instead?" was enough to encourage tasteful and wholesome reading. Linda is still an avid reader and looks forward to directed individual study for which she will be eligible during her junior and senior years. Under these circumstances, she can engage in independent reading, which is more to her liking than attending classes.

C. Emotional Development and Adjustment

Linda, at the age of 19, can best be described as a "loner." She has very little self-confidence about relating to other people and, as a result, she does not try. She is content, or at least appears to be, to stay in her dormitory room, surrounded by her best friends (books) and out of the general stream of things. She has not entered into any dormitory or campus activities. She was asked by a residence hall counselor to serve on an advisory committee for freshmen students, but she declined. The counselor had hoped to "draw Linda out" but had no success. The following written report describes the circumstances:

> Linda Wilson was approached with the suggestion that she serve as a sophomore representative on the dormitory advisory board. The duties were explained in considerable detail in terms of helping freshmen students adjust to dormitory and campus life. It was hoped that, once having accepted a responsi-

bility of this sort, Linda would "come out of her shell." Unfortunately, she would not accept the appointment.

Linda, the loner, has faced very few challenges to her life-style. She is concerned about student-teaching responsibilities, realizing that she will have to relate to her cooperating teacher and, of course, to the children she teaches. She is not as concerned about relating to her pupils, as children do appeal to her, hence her vocational choice. She has had conferences with several members of the faculty of the Department of Elementary Education, who have criticized her reticence to respond in class or to participate in activities such as the elementary education club. Linda feels these things are "Mickey Mouse" and totally unnecessary, particularly when they are basically unappealing to a given individual with a given personality. In other words, Linda feels that the individual is more important than the situation and that the latter should adjust to the former. She feels that this philosophy will not hinder her in her prospective vocation as children are malleable and she will simply set her own stage once she has her own classroom. This may well be a facade, for Linda rarely exhibits independence of any sort, in any degree. She may simply see her "own classroom" as another refuge, much like her dormitory room, or her room at home where she surrounded herself with the books she considered to be her "friends."

Linda has succeeded in isolating herself so well from her peers that it is almost impossible to get an objective description of her personality characteristics. Those who know her best, which is very casually, offer such adjectives as "quiet," "introspective," "moody," "aloof," and, of course, "a loner." The justification for the label of "moody" is difficult to track down. Linda's inability or refusal to relate to people may be mistaken for sullenness or depression. Since it is difficult to discover how Linda spends much of her time in seclusion, it is impossible to determine whether she uses this time constructively, or indeed is given to "moods" of a negative sort.

Linda has engaged in some attempts to express herself in writing. Her ability to communicate in this manner is reflected in the excellent grades she receives on written assignments. Her "verbal ability" is exercised at least in this respect, even though a willingness to converse is absent.

Linda has kept a diary, of sorts, for some time. The contents are primarily concerned with her reactions to the many books she reads. At various intervals, original poems are inserted. These poetic attempts come closer to revealing Linda's innermost thoughts than any other aspects of her personality. The following poem is representative:

> I saw my soul just standing there—
> alone, afraid, unsure—wanting love, needing love
> but only a love that's pure.

In this instance, we see a young woman, seclusive by choice, revealing her loneliness, her lack of self-confidence, and her need for emotional attachment.

D. Psychosexual Development and Adjustment

By circumstances and/or by choice, Linda has been isolated from the opposite sex. From the time she was placed in a private school, she has been separated from boys of her age. Having had no brothers or sisters, sharing only brief and sporadic childhood friendships, and deprived of coeducational experiences, Linda has grown up in a one-sided world—a feminine one.

Linda's father never bothered with Linda because of his constant preoccupation with business matters. The absence of an influential male figure in Linda's early developmental stages may have affected her ability to relate to boys in general, although the circumstances of her life make this impossible to prove.

During Linda's first year in college, a traumatic incident occurred. A "mixer" was held in conjunction with a nearby men's college. The policy of Linda's school was that every girl in the dormitory was "assigned" a date at random. Linda refused to appear at the appointed time, so another student went to Linda's room and dragged her to the drawing room where the introductory rituals took place. The forced small-talk and social niceties were confusing to Linda, but once the dancing began, she started to enjoy the festivities in spite of herself. The young man was personable, nice-looking, and extremely polite and deferring to his "date." A week later, he returned with two of his buddies to take Linda and several others to the movies. After the show they went to a drive-in restaurant for the usual snack and then headed back to the campus. On the way, the driver pulled into a rest-park along the highway and the usual type of necking activities began. Linda was stricken. She did not know how to act, but she was intrigued by the sights and sounds from the front seat. When her own date became more aggressive, she responded. Flourishing in the physical indications of affection being given to her for the first time in her life, and fascinated by her own emotional and physical reactions, she abandoned herself to the delights of what she supposed to be "love." However, when her date started making more intimate advances, she panicked—she screamed, she cried, and she begged to be taken back to the dorm. The pleasant evening had turned into a nightmare for Linda and an embarrassing and unpleasant one for her companions. Needless to say, the young man was never heard from again.

Since this incident occurred some time ago, it is difficult to tell whether Linda still bears some emotional scars. She has not dated since and one wonders whether or not she would, were the opportunity presented.

E. Social Development and Adjustment

Linda's social isolation has already been established. Linda has received no peer acceptance, but then she has never given her peers a chance to know her. The superficial acquaintances she makes in the dormitory are established solely on the basis of proximity. The girls in the neighboring rooms, and those with whom Linda sits during the evening meal, which is served family-style at assigned tables, are truly the only people with whom Linda associates, if even that term applies. Conversation is at a minimum, although Linda is always polite and never refuses to respond when greeted or plied with the usual queries of, "How's it going?", "What's new?", or the inevitable "How was your weekend or vacation?" Linda's usual reply to the latter is, "Oh— great, just great, thank you," and one wonders what "great" really is for such an isolate.

Linda operates under considerable pressure from home because of her social aloofness. Mrs. Wilson constantly harangues about "associating with the right people" and being "socially active." Since Linda has been away at college, she seldom goes home. While her classmates are running in and out of town with frenzied frequency, to visit their homes, other campuses, or just going into the city on excursions, Linda stays well-planted in her single dormitory room. Although her father's company has an executive airplane which flys a regular schedule between a nearby town where a plant is located and Linda's home town, she uses this only on prescribed holidays, when her college dormitory closes and all its inhabitants go home for Thanksgiving, Christmas or Spring Vacation. On these occasions, Linda retreats into the sanctity of her room in her parents' apartment, and exposes herself to her family only when it cannot be avoided. Since her parents are seldom home, especially during the heavy social schedule surrounding holidays, she is left mostly to herself, just as she prefers.

F. Interests and Recreation

With the exception of reading voraciously, and writing poetic compositions, Linda's recreational habits and/or forms of amusement seem nonexistent. She has an expensive stereo record player/tape recorder in her dormitory room. However, no one recalls ever hearing it in use.

Linda has taken part in the compulsory physical education program, but has never participated in intramural activities. She is an excellent swimmer and a proficient tennis player, but no amount of cajoling could get her to volunteer for the dormitory teams.

She attends various dramatic productions on campus, probably as a reflection of her literary interests, but she never could be convinced to join the drama club. Linda, in her chosen life-style, perfers to be self-entertained.

G. Ideology

Linda must have an unattractive view of the world at large. If this is not the case, why would she be compelled to shut herself off from as much of the view as possible? As far as her place in the world is concerned, she has wrapped herself in the security of seclusion, thereby protecting herself from disappointing circumstances. Her "friends" are her books, which, after all, do not give her a great deal of trouble. If a certain piece of literature should threaten her in any way, she can banish it from her room, and from her mind. One does not deal with real friends so easily.

Linda probably views herself as someone who was miscast for a given role. Failing to live up to the expectations of her mother, in particular, she may blame the casting director instead of herself. This, at least, is inferred from her previous statement: "The individual is more important than the situation." Perhaps resentful that few, if any, situations have been sacrificed to her individuality, she simply removes herself from that conflict by withdrawing into what has become her secret self. She observably belies the words of John Donne, one of her favorite authors, who stated in 1624, "No man is an island, entire of itself; . . .," unless she rationalizes that her books and her projected career indeed prevent her from an insular existence.

Her chosen occupation presents another enigmatic situation. Why, when her preference is obviously to be left alone, independent of the influence of others and vice versa, has she chosen a highly extrovertive occupation? Her failure to relate to anyone may carry over to the children who are her charges. Yet Linda is not impressed by what she reads and hears in terms of personality characteristics typical of successful teachers in the elementary grades. Her confidence in this respect may reflect a determination that has served her well in the past. Whenever Linda sets a goal for herself, she does succeed; the only problem is that the goals are few and far between and must be self-imposed.

Interpretive Questions

1. According to the mother's report, was Linda precocious with regard to verbal and motor development? What effect might this have upon an individual's personality?

2. Linda still sleeps with a stuffed toy. Is this typical of a person her age? Why does Linda do this? Is it simply an archaic behavior pattern?

3. What reasons can you think of to explain Mrs. Wilson's failure to prepare Linda for the physical changes of adolescence? How might this be affecting Linda's attitudes about herself as a woman?

4. What else, besides offering Linda a committee membership, might the dormitory staff have done to "bring Linda out of her shell"? Why, in your estimation, does Linda not relate to other people?

5. Do you agree or disagree with Linda's philosophy that "the individual is more important than the situation"? Why do you suppose that she feels this way? How realistic is this philosophy in terms of Linda's proposed career?

6. In view of Linda's personality and behavior, teaching seems to be a rather strange vocational choice. Why might Linda have selected this occupation? Assuming that she does become a teacher, how successful do you think she will be in this career?

7. What purpose does writing poetry serve for Linda? Is this fairly typical behavior for adolescent girls? How healthy is it in Linda's case?
8. How important is a good father-daughter relationship in terms of its influence upon psychosexual development? Describe Linda's experiences in this area.
9. What are Linda's chances for normal heterosexual adjustment at this point? Attempt to predict her future behavior and adjustment in this area. Is there any feasible source of help for her?
10. When Linda says "just great" in response to inquiries about her weekends and vacations, how would you classify her response? Does she really mean what she says? Defend your answer.
11. Is Linda's reclusive behavior a natural outgrowth of the family situation, or have other factors contributed to her personality as well? How else might an adolescent react to socially aggressive parents?
12. Describe Linda as you think she might describe herself. How much insight do you think she has about her own behavior and the reasons for it?
13. Why did Linda react so violently during the date described in this study? What was the real threat to her in this situation?
14. If Linda could find a friend, would her situation improve any? Would it be even better if her friend were a male? Defend your answer.

IV. CURRENT STATUS; DIAGNOSIS AND PROGNOSIS; RECOMMENDATIONS

Linda Wilson, age 19, faces two more years of college before she becomes vocationally, and thereby financially, independent of her family. This is a situation which she looks forward to with unusual intensity. Linda was offered her own car, any model of her choice, for her 18th birthday. Linda never chose her gift. Her parents, especially her mother, send gifts of money and clothing to Linda at frequent intervals. Linda deposits the checks and leaves the clothes in their wrappings. She wears nondescript sweaters, jeans, and sneakers, no makeup, and her hair long, unstyled, but always neat and clean. She has mortified her parents by arriving home in this apparel and has been publicly chastised in front of guests. Linda seems unconcerned by her parents' attitude toward her appearance. Mrs. Wilson has stopped dragging Linda from her room when guests are in the home because of the embarrassment that would ensue. This, of course, is exactly what Linda wants: to be left alone.

Linda will graduate from college with no academic distinction, but neither will she have any difficulty in achieving this goal. Assuming that she can get a teaching position in a field which is becoming more competitive with every year, in spite of what may be negative comments from faculty advisors and supervising teachers, Linda will try to "set her own stage." How successful she will be as a classroom teacher will depend upon her willingness to bend with the wind. She may learn, though rather painfully, that although she may continue to wish that "the individual is more important than the situation", in reality, this is seldom the case.

So far, Linda has assumed very little responsibility of any sort, other than apparently keeping herself on an even keel in spite of uncomfortable and uncompromising circumstances. One can admire, in certain instances, her perseverance. However, her total lack of resiliency will be to her disadvantage.

The next two years in college will not change Linda perceptively. Perhaps increased maturity will positively influence some of her personality characteristics. At this point, however, Linda is an island unto herself.

Interpretive Questions

1. List the defense mechanisms that Linda has invoked. Is the use of a defense or behavior mechanism limited to maladjusted individuals? What dangers lie in the habitual and long-term use of such mechanisms?
2. Why does Linda reject the money and gifts from her parents? Is this typical adolescent behavior in view of her home situation? How might someone else in similar circumstances handle such gifts?
3. Although Linda attends a very fashionable girl's school, her likes and dislikes reflect total disdain for the accoutrements typical of most of her peers. Is this a sign of independence, of rejection, of individuality, or of something else?
4. How might Linda be described from her faculty advisor's point of view? Would this advisor be justified in making negative comments about Linda's potential as a teacher? How might Linda react to such comments?
5. How well can a teacher really get to know a student like Linda? Is there any possible help for her from this source? If you were Linda's teacher, would you feel that she needs help? What would you attempt to do?
6. Is there any occupation for which Linda is better suited than teaching, taking her interests, abilities, and personality into account?
7. Do you admire Linda for her "perseverance"? In what ways has she displayed this quality? Would you be tempted to call this behavior by some other name? What, and why?
8. The case-study author infers that Linda is lacking in resiliency. Do you agree? What other qualities does she lack? Can you think of any ways in which she has exhibited flexibility?
9. Is Linda likely to become more outgoing with maturity? What changes in her life will either encourage or continue to prevent this from happening? Describe the kind of adult you see Linda becoming.
10. Is Linda a happy person? Defend your answer. Would she be happier if certain changes were made in her life or personality? What changes would you advocate?

11. Linda's parents have had no apparent influence upon her choice of a career. Is this statement really true? How might Linda have reacted if her parents had disapproved of her choice, or made other suggestions?
12. Most people would feel that Linda is a poorly adjusted adolescent. What is your evaluation of her personality? How typical, in terms of most teenagers, is her behavior?

Independence and Parental Conflict

Among the many developmental tasks with which an adolescent must contend is one which also exerts considerable pressure upon the entire family. Achieving independence from one's parents is not a painless process, and having to create a distance between oneself and a mother and father with whom one has such close emotional ties can cause considerable distress, particularly if one or both parties are not prepared. Most parents have, at some point during their son's or daughter's adolescent period, wondered to themselves, "What have I done to deserve this?" The disagreements, shouting matches, tears, and other examples of a stormy relationship are resented by the adult who takes such treatment very personally. Parents need to be assured that the adolescent is looking for a fight, in fact he needs one, and therefore continually carries a chip on his shoulder. Actually, the young person is fighting with himself, although this is difficult to believe from a parent's perspective. The fight ensues because the conflicts the adolescent is experiencing make him very susceptible to emotional outbursts, hence the constant "chip on the shoulder" attitude. Recall, also, the lack of inhibitor mechanisms and the powder keg emotional condition this guarantees. These conflicts are often caused by the emotional struggle between the child and the incipient adult, both of whom reside within the adolescent. Wanting very much to be treated as an adult, but still needing some support and direction from parents, the adolescent resents his psychological state of limbo. Actually being neither boy nor man, girl nor woman, this emotional "no-man's land" is very unsatisfying. The adolescent, consciously or unconsciously, places the blame for this inevitable discomfort right in the laps of his parents.

Wanting very much to be regarded as an adult and awarded appropriate privileges, the adolescent may not be mature enough to assume the adult responsibilities which accompany them. Failing at this, he resents having his limitations or deficiencies brought to his attention, as they inevitably will be. The result is quite predictable: an adolescent/parent confrontation.

To tell parents that the best way to endure these unhappy experiences is "to grin and bear it," is perhaps oversimplification. However, it is a means of survival. A greater understanding on the part of parents regarding the inherent need for revolt on the part of their child will make the revolution less painful and perhaps less extensive for all concerned. Assurance that their situation is not unique and that virtually every family goes through a similar process will also ease the pain. The "what have I done to deserve this" feeling is quite universal, so some consolation may be found in this realization. Perhaps such knowledge will remove some of the guilt which parents feel, quite unnecessarily, when their son or daughter exhibits rude, tyrannical, or otherwise unacceptable behavior. In most cases, it is not the parent, as an individual, who is at fault, but the drive on the part of the adolescent to separate himself from the parental figure and assume the status of an independent adult.

Some parents inadvertently contribute to their own misery during this period of mutual turmoil. The neurotic mother or father who cannot face growing older may try to inhibit the passage of time by keeping their son or daughter a child in spite of impending or on-going adolescence. The overprotective parent, who unreasonably restricts social activities, who punishes overt displays of incipient independence, or who refuses to encourage a psychological "cutting of the cord" impedes a young person's social development and encourages unhealthy and prolonged dependence upon the parent. The anxiety-producing thoughts of "an empty nest" threaten parents and sometimes cause them to react irrationally to their child's assertive behavior.

The quality of the new relationship between parents and adolescent which must emerge before the younger person can attain adult status is determined by all of the parties involved. Everyone must assume his or her share of the responsibilities, and this can best be accomplished by a "we're in this together" attitude. Less personal friction will ensue, and the battles will be less bitter and less debilitating. Perhaps the survival of this psychological revolution might best be referred to as a mutual developmental task.

A Case Study of Irving Lee Katzman

Irving's ambivalent feelings about his relationship with his parents have caused him to become depressed and anxious. While he still relies upon his mother and father to make decisions for him, he resents their overprotective tendencies and constant interference in his life. At present Irving is trying to shake off his apathy, find himself, and identify his own goals. He finds this an unfamiliar and threatening process.

I. IDENTIFICATION OF SUBJECT AND SOURCES OF INFORMATION

Name: Irving Lee Katzman
Address: 2731 University Court, Apt. 520
Race: Caucasian
Sex: Male
Age: 20
School or Occupation: City College, junior year
Sources of Information:
1. Interviews with subject
2. Subject's diary
3. Interviews with parents
4. Interviews with friends
5. Interviews with teachers
6. Interviews with psychologist

II. THE FAMILY HISTORY

The immediate Katzman family includes the father, Marvin, age 45; the mother, Esther, age 43; Irving, age 20; and his two younger sisters, Marcia age 16 and Deborah, age 12.

A. Health and Physical Characteristics

Mr. Katzman is shorter than average and has a stocky, but not fat, physique. Irving resembles his father in this respect. Mrs. Katzman and her daughters are also short and tend to be somewhat overweight.

Both parents have difficulties with varicose veins. Mrs. Katzman had hers stripped three years ago. The father often suffers from nervous indigestion. He has subjected himself to a complete gastrointestinal X-ray series on four separate occasions. No diagnosis of an ulcerous condition has ever resulted. Mr. Katzman has changed physicians (internists) four different times. The last doctor told him the problem was that "he swallowed too much air" and this was causing his discomfort. Mr. Katzman, sincerely hoping this is the cause of his trouble, has consciously tried not to swallow air for six months. He is still having difficulty, however, and plans to consult yet another physician.

Mrs. Katzman had a benign tumor removed from her left breast two years ago.

None of the children has ever suffered from any serious ailment or disease. Typical childhood illnesses are part of each child's medical history. The incidence of mumps caused the greatest family drama, because all three children and their father were infected concurrently. Mrs. Katzman reports to this day that she "nearly lost her mind" during the family's incarceration.

Mrs. Katzman and her daughters are constant weight-watchers. Their efforts, so far, have been observably futile. Irving also had weight problems during early adolescence, but seems to have outgrown this difficulty.

There has been a considerable incidence of cancer on both sides of the preceding generations in this family. For this reason, the parents, in particular, are very cancer-conscious. Mrs. Katzman has yet to recover from the scare caused by her tumor operation. Mr. Katzman has grudgingly given up smoking. He relates that this self-denial was "absolutely the most difficult accomplishment of his life." He harbors an insidious fear that his digestive problems are caused by some malignant condition.

All members of the Katzman family tend to be somewhat hypochondriacal. The physical condition of each individual is a constant topic of conversation. Irving has begun to find this both boring and embarrassing. He resents this trait in his parents and sisters. "My God, all they talk about is their dumb bodies," he remarked in one interview. In the same session, he admitted that his own concern about his physical being was probably "overworked."

B. Educational Status

Mr. and Mrs. Katzman are both college graduates. Marvin Katzman has a law degree from Harvard and Esther Katzman graduated from City College with a degree in fashion design. The parental attitude toward education is a positive one. The Katzmans expect all of their children to attend college, and furthermore, to excel in their studies. Irving is to attend graduate school in the area of his choice, preferably law or medicine. His often-expressed interests in architecture and city planning have never received any encouragement. According to Irving, "No one would ever even listen" when he tried to discuss such vocational aspirations. "As far as they (parents) are concerned, there's no such profession," Irving reported remorsefully.

Mr. and Mrs. Katzman have always encouraged, if not pressured, their children to reach for excellence in their academic pursuits. Fortunately, Irving and his sisters, for the most part, brought home report cards that seldom gave either parent reason to be disappointed. Irving's grades in college, however, have not resulted in any parental accolades, but this will be discussed in more detail later in this study.

C. Economic Status

Mr. Katzman is the owner-manager of a wholesale diamond business. He has been self-employed since the death of his father-in-law, who established the company. The business has been very successful and has allowed the family to live on a very comfortable socioeconomic level.

Mrs. Katzman has never been employed. She married the day after her graduation from college and has devoted her time and energy to her home and family since that day.

Irving has worked for his father during vacation periods. He has been allowed to spend his earnings as he wished. Mr. Katzman has encouraged him to "make some wise investments," believing that one "cannot begin too early" in this respect. Irving reluctantly purchased some airline stock which, unfortunately, has never earned him any money. In view of this initial disaster (from his perspective), Irving admittedly spends "every dime" he earns.

The Katzmans live in a well-to-do residential section in a fashionable suburb of the city. There are four cars in the family. Each parent has a car, the girls share one, and Irving has his own at school.

Mrs. Katzman, as a result of her own proclivities and college training, has taught all of her children to be clothes conscious. Almost no expense is considered too great when it comes to purchasing wearing apparel. Irving, while enjoying his mother's encouragement and financial assistance in establishing and maintaining a "flashy wardrobe" during high school, encountered some peer disapproval once he entered the university. As a result, his subsequent habits of dress have been somewhat altered.

No economic limits have ever been placed on the Katzman children in terms of their material desires. Every possible cultural advantage has been theirs for the asking. Music, art, dancing, and riding lessons, parties, camp, travel, museums, and concerts have contributed to the childhood and adolescent experiences of all three children.

Mr. and Mrs. Katzman have always tried to give their children every possible advantage and enrich their lives in many ways. The children, while not effusive with their gratitude, are appreciative of all the opportunities and possessions which have been afforded them.

D. Social Status and Adjustment

The elder Katzmans have always been active socially and have participated in many school, synagogue, and community activities. Mr. Katzman belongs to several fraternal groups as well as remaining an active alumnus of his college fraternity. Esther Katzman is active in several organizations for Jewish women as well as a bridge club, a book review club, and a matinee musicale. The Katzman girls each belong to several clubs and organizations for young people. They are especially active in the programs of the Jewish Community Center. Irving, now that he no longer lives at home, has given up his community activities and replaced them with various campus involvements.

As a family, the Katzmans are highly regarded by their neighbors and social and business associates.

There is one rather serious adjustment problem that is of concern to each family member. The paternal grandparents are very possessive about their son. They, in a sense, have never allowed him to "grow up" and still try to control his life as much as possible. They are demanding of his time and attention. They almost disowned him when he went into the diamond business instead of opening a law practice. For three years they refused to communicate with either Marvin or his wife, of whom they did not approve because of her father's business. This schism was very hard on Marvin Katzman because his family had been very closely knit. This problem caused Esther Katzman to "feel very guilty," since she naturally assumed most of the blame for the estrangement. Although the elder Katzmans eventually softened their attitudes toward their son and his family, they are still very critical of him, his wife, and their children. This does not, however, affect the demanding and possessive characteristics of their parent-son relationship. Irving's father is constantly being chastized about his business connections and maligned for "neglecting" his parents and ignoring their advice regarding his life and that of his family.

E. Interests and Recreation

Every member of the Katzman family has his or her own social life independent of the others in the household. There is, therefore, a certain attitude of "to each his own life." In addition, there are several hobbies and interests which are shared. Music, for instance, is a common interest. There are four stereo sets in the home, one in each of the girls' rooms, one in the master bedroom, and another in the den. A built-in speaker and intercom system makes it possible to play music throughout the house. Irving, of course, has his own stereo-recorder in his campus apartment. The Katzmans have an impressive record-tape collection ranging from classical to popular contemporary selections. All three children have had music lessons. Irving studied piano for seven years, but showed no true talent. The girls both started with the piano, but Marcia has since switched to violin and Deborah currently is interested in voice lessons. If this desire persists, a voice teacher will be retained beginning with Deborah's 13th birthday.

The Katzmans are all avid readers. The children have always been encouraged to purchase whatever books struck their fancy, assuming, of course, that they were wholesome. Each child has been provided with bookshelves in his or her room and as a result, each has an extensive personal library. The den of the home is shelved from floor to ceiling and the book collection is not only expensive and tasteful, but well-read.

Every member of the family is somewhat athletically inclined and they have participated in numerous sports, both individually and as a family.

E. Ideology

Philosophically, Marvin and Esther Katzman are very conservative. They live a very affluent life and have no sympathy for those of lower socioeconomic status. Feeling that anyone who wants to "make it" can do so, Marvin Katzman thinks welfare recipients are "lazy, good-for-nothings who don't deserve a penny of an honest man's taxes." He describes himself as "being sick and tired of handing out money, hand-over-fist, to a bunch of parasites who do nothing but loaf and have each other's babies." Mrs. Katzman, who always agrees with her husband, exhibits a similar attitude. Irving's parents are extremely prejudiced against minority groups since, according to them, "most of them are on welfare." Both are often heard remarking that Jews have always been victims of discrimination, "but you don't find them on welfare." Irving confesses that he is sick and tired of hearing "that kind of junk" coming from his parents. He once told them so, in so many words, and was chastised for being a "smart aleck." Complaining that "I can't open my mouth about anything, even baseball averages, without having my old man jam his opinions down my throat," Irving, having rented an apartment of his own, spends as little time as possible in his parents' home. Except for religious holidays when his presence is demanded, Irving avoids confrontations with his parents.

While Mr. and Mrs. Katzman maintain high-level interest and active participation in their religion, Irving seems to be less and less interested in his religious heritage. He feels the same may be true of his sisters, who, while still under the watchful eyes of his parents, may only feign interest in religious convictions.

Interpretive Questions

1. On the basis of the parental vocational biases described in this study, what problems may Irving encounter in formulating his own vocational goals?
2. Many prepubescent boys have weight problems which they carry with them into adolescence. What are the major reasons for this?
3. What personality problems can arise out of a weight problem? Whom is it likely to bother the most, a boy or girl?
4. Is the attitude of Irving's parents regarding education surprising or expected? What is stereotyping? How could the tendency to stereotype ruin the objectivity of a psychologist or anyone else who studies human behavior?

5. What sorts of "lessons" in economics has Irving been learning throughout childhood and adolescence? How might he be affected in terms of making an eventual vocational choice?

6. In terms of Irving's "flashy wardrobe," what resistence do you think he encountered once he entered college? What pressures began operating on him that were not present in high school?

7. Describe the educational advantages which Irving enjoys as a result of his background that are denied a child of less affluent parents.

8. How might a young person who experiences a minimum of these educational advantages compensate for the lack of his opportunities as compared to Irving's?

9. Certainly environmental factors have significant influence upon the level of academic achievement, but what other factors also play very important roles?

10. What, if anything, can you predict about Irving's parents allowing him to "grow up"? Are they going to be possessive, following the pattern of the paternal grandparents? How do you think Irving will react to any parental attempts to "control" his life?

III. THE CASE HISTORY

Irving Katzman, age 20, is the eldest of three children. Currently enrolled in his junior year at the college level, Irving lives away from home in his own campus apartment.

A. Health and Physical Characteristics

Birth was normal and development proceeded at an expected rate. The child walked at approximately one year of age and talked lucidly at the age of two. There were some early digestive problems and difficulties with formulas. The mother refused to breast-feed the baby. After several periods of weight loss, the infant's digestion stabilized.

The usual childhood diseases posed no serious problems except the inconvenience of and wear and tear on the mother.

Irving displayed a high level of physical vigor throughout childhood and early adolescence. Some of this physical energy was attributed to "nervousness" by his mother, who explained that her son "never could sit or stand still." During the pubescent period, Irving developed a weight problem. In spite of his physical activities, he could not lose excessive poundage. Attempts at dieting were not successful. Irving's appetite was always a healthy one and Mrs. Katzman, while wanting her son to slim down, could not bear to see him "starving himself." Mrs. Katzman, who also has a weight problem, is perhaps overly sympathetic in this respect. Both daughters are also overweight for their age and height. By the time he was 16, Irving had lost what he refers to as "baby fat" and developed a normal, well-proportioned physique.

There was some concern about complexion problems, but these too have been resolved. Irving's mother was constantly admonishing her son about "eating all that junk which makes you break out like a flower garden." Irving reports that "life was pretty damn miserable" in those days. His mother was constantly "nagging" him about something. There was, in his words, "no peace."

At the age of 20, Irving is still active physically. He has played in some intramural sports and presently is very enthusiastic about the formation of a new soccer league. He feels his health is "good," and except for being "very nervous," feels fine most of the time.

B. Educational History

Irving Katzman began his schooling at the age of five upon entrance to kindergarten. He relates that he was always being chastized for mischievous behavior, but does not recall misbehaving. As a result he "developed a persecution complex."

Irving's educational progress was normal and satisfactory to him and his parents until the last two years of high school, when his grades began to drop. In spite of constant admonitions and generally critical comments from his parents, especially his father, Irving could not be stirred from his newly developed apathy. He graduated, but not with honors, from the college preparatory high school. His father berated him for not being eligible for a college academic scholarship. The grandparents joined in the continual harassment.

Irving's relationships with his teachers have never been too rewarding. His "persecution complex" may have contributed to this. A grade-school teacher described the boy as "having a chip on his shoulder." Another explained that "the Katzman boy has a tendency to withdraw and be sullenly reserved with me." Irving relates that until high school he had regarded all teachers as wise and unchallengeable. After that time, however, he began to recognize their frailties and had less fear of and less respect for them. He seems to resent the fact that most college professors are "standoffish and seem to prefer it that way." "Perhaps they wouldn't be such bad guys if they'd just let down a little bit." When asked if there were any particular professor he really admired, he named a young member of the faculty who has enjoyed considerable fame, if not notoriety, as a "far out liberal." Irving felt that "if more guys like him would go into teaching, then school would be a ball!" Sometime later, when this particular instructor did not return for the academic year, it was discovered that his contract had not been renewed. This caused considerable furor on the campus and Irving was in the midst of it. The newspaper carried a picture of a group of students storming the administration building to protest the instructor's dismissal. Marvin Katzman arrived at his son's apartment, newspaper in hand, and threatened to cut off any further funding of Irving's education if he didn't "stop acting like such a jackass and grow up." The furor was not long-lived, as it was soon revealed that the former faculty member had been there under false pretenses, had used fake credentials, and legally and professionally did not have a leg to stand on. Irving admitted he was hurt and resentful because the man he had most admired had turned out to be "a phony after all."

Irving's college academic record is no more commendable than that of high school. He admits to apathy, to "not getting with it," and a depressed feeling because of this attitude. Labeled an "underachiever" by earlier teachers, Irving was sent to a psychological center for mental testing. He was informed of his approximate academic potential (I.Q. 125) and this only depressed him further.

C. Emotional Development and Adjustment

As a child, Irving displayed a high degree of dependency. He remembers comments about "mama's boy" during childhood. Looking back, he realizes that although he was not a "clinging" child, the presence and attention of his parents was very important to him. Even during early adolescence, feelings of dependency were very prevalent. Now, having moved from his parents' home, he finds it difficult to assume much independence. Even though he is not around his mother and father, he feels his actions are more often directed by their attitudes than his own. He frequently experiences guilt and feels that he is not living up to his obligations.

Irving describes himself as "lacking self-confidence until recently." His "persecution complex" was accompanied by an "inferiority complex" which, apparently, still gives him some difficulty. Lately he has been trying to convince himself that he is capable of doing good college level work, and that he had better "get with it." He is also discovering that he can make friends and takes pleasure in being more outgoing and receptive in social situations than ever before.

Irving's feelings about his parents are ambivalent. On one hand he loves them very much, while on the other hand he senses their overprotective tendencies and resents this to the point of rage at times. He wants them to understand that "they have their lives to live and I have mine, and no one should be too demanding upon another."

In describing his own personality, Irving related: "I'm one hung-up guy. I'm depressed almost all the time. Really, I'm kind of a masochist. Sometimes I think I really enjoy being depressed 'cause sometimes I don't even know what's depressing me."

Irving explains that one of the reasons why he is so active athletically is that this is an acceptable means of relieving the tensions under which he is operating.

At one point, his depressive state was so overwhelming that he sought psychological consultation at the university counseling center. "It was nice to talk to someone who seemed interested," he reported, "but nothing seemed to do me any good so I quit going."

Irving also describes himself as being anxious. This, he feels, was true even in childhood when he would awaken, screaming because of a nightmare. He still experiences nightmares which "reflect anxieties." Irving was not willing to reveal the contents of his dreams. His "day-to-day" anxieties involve conflicts about school, vocational choice, and his parents. He suffers from a severe, "maybe unreasonable" fear that no one does or ever will love him.

Overall, Irving sees himself as "hyper-emotional," "moody as hell," "apathetic," and "scared out of my mind."

D. Psychosexual Development and Adjustment

Irving has always shown a willingness to accept his male role. As a child and as an adolescent he has shown typical masculine characteristics and interests. In late grade school, he went through the normal period of rejecting all females as unworthy of his attention. In high school, having emerged victorious from the trials of pubescence and obesity, Irving was relatively popular with both sexes. Any lack of success was due to his retiring ways rather than to lack of physical attractiveness or social graces. Irving simply preferred, for the most part, to be a loner. He began dating as a junior in high school. There was no difficulty in getting dates, but there was difficulty in getting him to ask for one. Several young ladies appealed to Mrs. Katzman for help. Irving's mother, needless to say, was an eager "matchmaker."

Irving relates that he "really got hooked" on a girl in his freshman year. They were inseparable all summer and into the next academic year when she, according to Irving, "got shook, she got scared, and wanted not to go steady anymore." Irving could not accept the new relationship and the rejection that it meant for him. "It really strung me out. I thought I was going to die," he related in retrospect. It was at this point that he, at the urging of several friends, sought psychological help. Although considerable time has passed and Irving has begun dating again, he still entertains a "faint hope" that the young lady will reconsider. They date occasionally but Irving is always so "uptight" that the relationship is a strained and uncomfortable one. Irving feels that he can never truly be interested in another girl.

E. Social Development and Adjustment

Irving has already been described as retiring and withdrawn. In his own eyes, Irving Katzman sees himself as "shy and lacking self-confidence." He tries to avoid group activities, except when playing a team sport. He feels that "no one has ever gone out of their way to be friendly" to him. Irving feels the only recognition or acceptance he has ever received has been due to his athletic prowess. During his senior year in high school he made "quite a name for himself" running track. When asked why he did not continue this activity in college, he replied, "I just wasn't good enough."

Irving Katzman sees himself as a follower rather than a leader. If he disagrees with a leader's philosophy or interests, he "just drops out." He has never had any desire to assert himself or "take over." He refers to himself as a "nonconformist," as he has a tendency to do what he wants to do when he wants to do it, ignoring the influence of others.

As far as how others see Irving, he feels that he is "well-liked," is known as a "faithful friend," and is sensitive to the feelings of others." He does not like to see his friends "depressed" and tries to "cheer them up."

F. Interests and Recreation

As a child, Irving was as happy, if not more so, playing by himself than he was when involved with other children. Childhood and adolescence introduced him to baseball, touch-football, hockey, and track, all of which he enjoyed, and his interest in sports continues.

Besides building stamp and coin collections, Irving occupied himself as an avid reader. Reading was encouraged in the home and this has developed into a continuing interest. Irving relates that he keeps up with current novels, has read the "Great Books," is interested in existential writings and other books with "intellectual appeal."

G. Ideology

Irving Katzman admits that he is "in a state of terrific confusion." He does not know exactly what his wants or his needs may be. Basically, he is self-accepting and considers himself a "good individual," but is not sure if others feel this way about him. His lack of confidence is very worrisome. He feels that he must find some way to prove his individual worth.

At times, when self-confidence is at its peak, he tries to convince himself that he has the ability to do "anything at all." During these intervals, he tries to picture himself as a physician with a "big and lucrative practice." When confidence wanes, he wonders if he really has the "drive to complete medical school."

Irving expresses fears regarding the possible necessity of going into his father's business. His concerns are reflected in the following statement:

> If I don't somehow find myself, that's exactly how I'll end up and it scares the hell out of me. I don't even know if I can accept the so-called middle-class existence as a way of life. I'm basically a far-out liberal, but I can't stand a hippie way of life either, I'm too conservative for that. What am I going to do?

Interpretive Questions

1. What influences in Irving's life may have affected his motivation from his last two years in high school until the present? Why haven't his relationships with teachers been very rewarding?

2. What is an "underachiever"? Would you place Irving in this category? If so, what factors would you cite to support your opinion?

3. What reasons can you give for Irving's involvement in the protest over the dismissed professor? How do you think he felt when the truth was revealed?

4. In what ways was this whole episode representative of many of Irving's basic problems?

5. Which developmental tasks of adolescence has Irving already mastered? Which ones are still giving him trouble?

6. Describe the ways in which Mr. and Mrs. Katzman have prevented Irving from achieving independence. What might be some of the reasons for their actions?

7. What steps, if any, has Irving taken to achieve independence from his parents? How well has he succeeded or failed, and why?

8. Why do the Katzmans have such strong feelings about Irving's choice of a vocation? How might this situation best be handled?

9. Is it common for a young person to feel guilt in terms of not living up to parental expectations? Under what circumstances does an individual "outgrow" this?

10. Irving's feelings toward his parents are described as "ambivalent." What evidence can you cite to support this statement? Is such ambivalence "normal," or typical of adolescence? Why, or why not?

11. Several of Irving's attempts to describe himself have been included in this study. He refers to himself as being "hung up." Would you agree? If so, what is he "hung up" on?

12. Little mention has been made in this study of Irving's sisters. What kinds of problems might they face when they reach his age? Is it easier for boys or girls to achieve independence from parents? Defend your answer.

13. This young man, because of hurt and disappointment, feels that he will never be interested in another girl. How common is such a feeling among adolescents? What reasons provoke such reactions?

14. Why might this experience have been particularly traumatic for Irving? Does it have any connection with his quest for independence?

15. How do you think the parents would react if Irving wanted to marry a girl of a different religion? What would Irving do in this situation?

16. Irving describes himself as a nonconformist. Is this an accurate description, or just wishful thinking on his part? Defend your answer.

IV. CURRENT STATUS; DIAGNOSIS AND PROGNOSIS; RECOMMENDATIONS

Irving Katzman is a nice-looking, well-mannered young man who is suffering from an identity crisis. While he is fair-minded and accepting of others, he is very critical of himself. He is suffering from certain self-inflicted anxieties which cause him to frequently experience a depressed state. This depression may be preventing him from exploiting his academic and social potentials.

Since his vocational goals have not crystallized and probably will not until he becomes more self-actualizing, Irving has been playing academic musical chairs. He has switched from college to college within the university and from program to program within each college until his transcript is a mishmash of confusion. Currently he is enrolled as a psychology major, with pre-medical training as his intent. However, Irving expresses continual doubts about this being the proper course for him to pursue.

Basically, Irving wants to remain dependent. He panics in the decision-making process. He is still relying on his parents to determine his course of action. Perhaps, had he been encouraged to pursue his expressed interest in architecture and city planning, he might have found himself before this.

Reasonably self-accepting in terms of his intellectual capacity, he is incapable of experiencing any motivating forces. Irving's psychological records do not picture him as a lazy person, but primarily apathetic. He just does not seem to care enough about anything or just can not identify any acceptable goals toward which he might direct his energies. In the meantime, he has stagnated and slipped into a rut of depression and loneliness.

Irving should be encouraged to seek additional psychological help. He is in the process of finding himself, but has been lost for so long that he has no bearings. A counseling situation could encourage him to identify and set a true course for himself.

The loneliness and depression are, hopefully, only temporary. Once he gains more self-confidence, he will be encouraged to seek relationships with others. The fact that he feels "no one has ever gone out of their way to be friendly" is significant in that Irving has neither sought nor encouraged any friendships, except in the case of the young woman who hurt him with her rejection.

Irving needs help in identifying and dealing with all of the sources of his depression. His relationships with his parents need to be brought out into the open and analyzed rather than continue to be repressed.

Assuming that Irving does receive help and can develop insight into his problems, considerable improvement in his attitude should take place. This young man would seem to have every potential for academic and professional success, if he can just emerge from the cloud of uncertainty which surrounds him.

Interpretive Questions

1. What is meant by an identity crisis? What psychological authority is most often associated with this term? Do all adolescents experience such a crisis?
2. What developmental tasks are most closely associated with elements of identity crisis?
3. Are Irving's anxieties primarily "self-inflicted"? What defense mechanisms does he employ to combat anxieties?
4. Do you agree that Irving's depressed state prevents him from "exploiting his academic and social potentials"? Why?
5. What is self-actualization? Which should logically come first, self-actualization or vocational choice? Can it work either way? Give examples.
6. Had Irving been allowed to pursue his original line of interest, would he be better off now? In what respects?
7. Assuming that Irving would be willing to seek help, how might a counselor or psychologist aid him? Should a person be forced to seek help? Why or why not?
8. Do you agree that Irving's loneliness and depression are "temporary"?
9. How would you advise this young man to help himself?
10. What is your prognosis in this case? Even if Irving can change his own attitudes, is there any chance of a change in parental behavior?
11. How might his parents be helped to understand Irving's problems and assist in their resolution?
12. Why is independence from parents one of the most widespread and frequent problems facing adolescents today?

7

Prolonged
Education

One of the basic facets of the "American dream" is that any child can grow up to become whatever he wishes. The device which makes this dream a reality, according to parents, is education, and lots of it. Until quite recently, it has indeed appeared that parents were correct in their assessment of the situation, for increased technology demanded higher and higher levels of formal education, the shortage of qualified teachers was acute, business and industry required at least a bachelor's degree for managerial positions, and doctors and lawyers could expect to command fantastic incomes. It was indeed the heyday of the college graduate; sought after, pampered, and courted by numerous potential employers.

The historical reasons for this great emphasis upon the importance of formal education in America are quite simple to trace. Better educational opportunities for their children was one of the basic desires of the huge number of immigrants that poured into this country during the last century. Once established here, primarily in "blue collar" jobs, these parents quickly noticed that the "white collar" jobs were held by those who possessed more education. Since higher economic status was accompanied by higher social status, the obvious way to ensure a better life for one's children was to see that they got enough education to enable them to fill a "white collar" position. At approximately the same time, free public education in America and compulsory school attendance were being extended to cover longer and longer periods in a child's life.

These two factors, in combination with the greater educational needs previously cited, created the huge demand for formal education which now finds our colleges and universities bulging at the seams, desperate for classroom space, money, and adequate facilities. These same factors have also meant that large numbers of students go to college because their parents expect them to obtain a degree, because all of their friends are going to college and they do not want to appear "dumb," because they learned no vocational skills in high school and do not know what else to do with themselves, or, until quite recently, because they want to escape military service. Two current trends in higher education, the general studies program and the core-curriculum, or common two years, are made to order for these students, who really do not want to be in college, and have no idea of what subjects they want to take.

What adolescents are experiencing at present is a great deal of parental and societal pressure to obtain at least a bachelor's degree, on the assumption that this will enable the young person to maintain or surpass his parents' social status. Therefore the vast majority of adolescents troop obediently off to college, whether or not they possess either the interest or the aptitude. High school counselors busily search out a college which will accept even the poor student, in the hope that he is a "late bloomer," and to be enrolled in a vocational or general program is akin to social oblivion. Since program decisions of this sort must be made before entering junior high school, and thus well before most children can entertain any realistic vocational ambitions, our young people are practically committed to college at the kindergarten level.

Meanwhile, interesting things have happened at the other end of the educational process. Since almost everyone has a bachelor's degree, one must now have a master's degree or a doctorate to stand out from the crowd. Great numbers of young people now find that their education cannot stop at the end of four years, but must continue for two, four, or six years more. While these perpetual students pursue their advanced degrees, they discover that life is passing them by. They hang suspended in an academic limbo, no longer adolescents, but unable to assume the full responsibilities of adulthood because they are still students. These young people face an unhappy choice between prolonged adolescence and part-time adulthood, and neither alternative generates a great deal of self-esteem.

However, the picture does seem to be changing. Some experts are calling for a change in vocational perspective and the return of dignity and worth to the "blue collar" job. Teenagers are beginning to realize that many of their older brothers and sisters have been educated right out of the job market, and that a college degree is not necessarily a passport to vocational and social success. Even parents and educators are beginning to suspect that not everyone should go to college, or at least not go directly to college from high school. More emphasis is being placed upon vocational training and technical schools as an alternative to college. Perhaps, in time, these ideas will become widely accepted and America's educational pattern will change. Until that time, however, large numbers of perpetual adolescents will continue to fill our colleges and universities.

What kinds of problems face the individual who goes to college without really knowing why? He usually feels a sense of alienation from those of his peers who are pursuing definite vocational goals. He does poorly in his academic work because nothing seems relevant to him, and he has little or no motivation to succeed. While physically an adult, to his parents and society in general he is still a child because he is usually not self-supporting and therefore independent of his parents. Having no idea of his own future, he may turn to drugs, alcohol, sex, or radical behavior in an attempt to find some meaning in life. He may fail, or drop out, after one or two years of college, still vocationally unprepared. He may eventually discover an area in which he has ability and become a successful student. He may hover on the academic fringes for four years, graduate, and still be vocationally unprepared or unable to find a job. He may go to graduate school and begin the cycle all over again.

Every adolescent in America today, at one time or another, must face the issue of how much education, and what type of education, is right for him. It is probably one of the most crucial decisions a teenager makes.

A Case Study of Michael Carson

While Mike is 20 years old, his life is similar to that of an elementary school child and Mike seems to be perfectly happy with the situation as it is. At least he shows no outward signs of rebellion against the status quo. It might be healthier if he would stand up on his own two feet more often, instead of refusing to assert himself in any way. Perhaps Mike still thinks of himself as a child, despite his age.

I. IDENTIFICATION OF SUBJECT AND SOURCES OF INFORMATION

Name: Michael Paul Carson
Address: R. D. #3, Box 42
Race: Caucasian
Sex: Male
Age: 20

School or Occupation: Winston Junior College, sophomore year
Sources of Information:
1. Interviews with subject
2. Interviews with parents
3. Interview with high school counselor
4. Interview with college advisor
5. Interviews with teachers
6. Interviews with peers
7. Interviews with subject's girlfriend

II. THE FAMILY HISTORY

Michael Carson is the youngest child, and only son, of Fred and Alice Carson. His two sisters, Bernice, age 28, and Sally, age 26, both married immediately after their graduation from high school and now live in other states.

A. Health and Physical Characteristics

For the past eight years, the Carson family has consisted of the father, Fred, age 52, the mother, Alice, age 50, and Mike. Since the family lives on a farm, there has always been plenty of fresh air, good, simple food, and vigorous exercise. As a result, all of the members enjoy good health, except for Mike. He has always been rather listless and underweight, despite his mother's constant efforts to "fatten him up."

Fred Carson is a large, hearty man with a shock of bushy, graying hair and a skin deeply tanned from long hours in the sun. His wife, Alice, is of medium height, with a tendency toward plumpness which does not worry her unduly. Both parents have enjoyed exceptional health and rarely even catch colds. Fred's amazing feats of strength when younger are still something of a legend in the community, while Alice's cooking formerly won many prizes at the state fairs.

The two daughters seem to have inherited the robust physiques of their parents, for both are tall, sturdy girls who have experienced only the usual childhood illnesses. Mike, by contrast, is the only short, thin member of the family. Before the girls were married, strangers who saw the Carsons all together sometimes asked if Mike were an adopted child.

Mr. Carson's father was also a farmer. He was killed in an accident when the tractor he was driving flipped over and crushed him. Mrs. Carson subsequently remarried and, upon her husband's retirement, moved to Florida. She now has little contact with her son's family. Alice Carson's parents live in the same small rural community. Her father runs the local hardware store, and while he often talks of retirement, Mrs. Carson believes that he will never do so. Both maternal grandparents appear to be vigorous and healthy, although they are in their early 70s.

B. Educational Status

Fred Carson was 16 when his father was killed. His older brother was serving in the army, where he was subsequently killed in action, and there were two younger sisters still at home. Fred immediately dropped out of high school and assumed his father's place as head of the family. With the help of a hired hand, Fred ran the farm. The people of the community admired Fred for his courage, and his lack of a high school diploma has been no handicap.

Alice Carson, however, graduated from high school. She spent several months working in her father's store, then accepted Fred's proposal and married him shortly thereafter. Both sets of parents seemed pleased with the match, although Alice's mother may have felt that her daughter could have done better.

Neither of Fred's parents went to high school. Alice's mother and father both have high school diplomas. Fred's sisters were able to finish high school, and one, Sandra, completed an additional year of secretarial training in the city and now helps her husband run a small business. Joyce, the other sister, married a local boy who became a career army man. They are currently living on a base in Texas.

Both Fred and Alice insisted on a high school education, but no more, for their daughters, feeling that too much education makes a woman dissatisfied with her basic roles of wife and mother. They do not particularly approve of careers for women and feel that the women's liberation movement is "ridiculous." However, their plans for Mike are quite different. Surprisingly enough, Mr. Carson feels that four generations of farmers in the family is enough, and he wants Mike to go to college and learn a profession. His thinking may be based upon the fact that he had to drop out of school, and consequently has known very little besides hard manual labor for most of his life. The longest trip Fred has ever made was to Florida to visit his mother and father-in-law two years ago. The trip was a brief one since the farm could not be left for very long.

Mrs. Carson agrees with her husband's plans for Mike, but for somewhat different reasons. She feels that Mike is not strong enough for farm work, and indeed he shows very little interest in, or aptitude for, farming as an occupation. Mrs. Carson would like to see Mike "make something of himself and marry a nice, refined college girl." Since finances do not seem to be a problem for the Carsons, there will be enough money for Mike to complete four years of college. Being the youngest child, and the only boy, all of the parents' hopes and dreams seem to center around Mike, and they expect him to achieve things which were impossible for them.

C. Economic Status

The Carsons live in a substantial farmhouse which has been completely modernized for many years. There are several other buildings on the 250-acre farm, and all are kept painted and in good repair. Mr. Carson keeps a herd of dairy cattle in addition to his basic crops of corn and soybeans. Mrs. Carson is in charge of the chickens, as well as a substantial garden which supplies most of the family's fresh vegetables all year long, as the summer surplus is either canned or frozen. Fred runs the farm with the help of one hired man and numerous pieces of modern farm machinery. Mrs. Carson has never had any help in the house, because the girls assisted until they left home, and now that they are gone, there is much less work. Mike does very little to help either parent, and spends most of his free time watching television or "just hanging around" in town.

The house is modestly but comfortably furnished. There is a large color television set and a relatively new radio. Neither of the parents enjoys reading or music, so they have no phonograph, and few books are in evidence. The family subscribes to the local newspaper and several farm journals, but no popular magazines.

The family owns two cars. One is a late model pickup truck, and the other a new compact station wagon which Mike takes to school during the week and Mrs. Carson uses for weekend shopping trips. Neither of the parents owns very extensive wardrobes, since they rarely entertain and their social contacts are limited to church affairs, which they attend regularly. Mike's sisters were always well dressed, by community standards at least, for they made almost all of their own clothes. While his sisters favored more conservative styles, Mike has a taste for flamboyant outfits and bright colors. He has a rather large wardrobe of the latest male clothing fads, and is the envy of younger boys in the town. His college peers, however, think he tends to overdo it, since their tastes run more toward blue jeans and tee shirts.

The Carson family is obviously in a solid financial position. The farm continues to show a profit every year, due to Fred's careful management and hard work. The parents spend very little money on themselves, and whatever is left after expenses is put away for Mike's education.

D. Social Status and Adjustment

The Carsons are very well thought of in the small rural community where they live. Both families have lived in the same area for several generations, and are known as thrifty, hard-working, solid people. Since almost everyone in the community farms, there are very few social events, except for those sponsored by the Baptist Church, to which the Carsons belong. The church holds an annual fish fry in the fall, and monthly socials during the year. Fred and Alice can be counted on to take an active part in these events, and to appear regularly every Sunday at worship services. Other than this, their social life consists of having the maternal grandparents for dinner every Sunday and on holidays, and an annual trip to the state fair.

Neither parent seems to feel a need for more social contact with other people. They are both small-town people, and therefore accustomed to the relative isolation of rural life. While they have been known to come to the aid of a neighbor in an emergency, they prefer to work hard and mind their own business. Their only regret is that the two daughters live so far away and cannot come home for frequent visits.

E. Interests and Recreation

The Carson's work-filled days leave little time for outside interests. Mr. Carson is usually up at dawn and retires shortly after dark. His only hobbies seem to be reading farm journals and trying to improve the yield of the farm. He enjoys discussions with other farmers on his trips to town and at church affairs.

Mrs. Carson usually watches television in the evening. Her hobbies are crocheting, canning, and making jelly. Both she and Fred used to exhibit at the state fair, but in recent years it has become "too much trouble" to do so.

Neither parent is interested in politics or current events. Family conversation centers around events on the farm and in the community, small-town gossip, the latest letter from one of the girls or Fred's mother, and Mike's activities.

F. Ideology

Fred and Alice Carson are honest, hard-working, unsophisticated farm people. They believe in minding their own business unless someone needs help. They ask very few favors, preferring to stand on their own two feet and achieve what they want through their own efforts. A strong belief in God, hard work, and the inherent goodness in people forms the basis of their philosophy of life.

While they appear to be satisfied with their own lives, like most parents, they want more for their children, and particularly for Mike. They seem satisfied with the paths their daughters have chosen, especially since each has produced a grandchild, but have elaborate plans for Mike. Although they have not specified any career, they would probably be delighted if he were to become a doctor or lawyer. At any rate, they definitely feel that the city holds more of a future for Mike than the country does. They sometimes talk of selling the farm and going to live in the city, "to be near Mike after he establishes himself."

Interpretive Questions

1. Describe the physical self-image Mike might have when comparing himself with the rest of his family. What effect could this have upon his personality?
2. Evaluate the reasons given for the Carsons' desire to have Mike go to college. Can you think of any other reasons why they feel so strongly about this?

3. Why did the parents have such a different educational philosophy concerning their daughters? How common is this kind of thinking to-day?
4. What would have been the reaction of the parents if one of the girls had insisted upon going to college? How might the community have viewed this proposal?
5. Do you think that the Carsons believe that education is the key to success? If so, are they correct? Defend your answer.
6. The Carson family appears to take very little interest in the outside world. What kinds of attitudes has Mike probably developed as a result? Might the home situation be a handicap to him in any way?
7. What do Mike's tastes in clothing reveal about his personality? What must his college peers think of his wardrobe? Why might he shy away from their styles of dress?
8. Cite indications that Mike may have been somewhat spoiled by his parents.
9. Describe the role model Mr. Carson presents for his son. Evaluate this model, as seen from Mike's perspective.
10. Judging from his experiences with his mother and sisters, what might Mike think of women?
11. Why is Mr. Carson so unconcerned about Mike's lack of interest in farming? How would he react if Mike decided to become a farmer?
12. Fred and Alice Carson talk of selling the farm and moving to the city. Would this be a wise plan? Defend your answer.

III. THE CASE HISTORY

A. Health and Physical Characteristics

Mike's two older sisters were born at home, under the supervision of the one doctor in the community. However, Doctor Johnson retired shortly before Mike was born, and so Mrs. Carson checked into City Hospital in order to produce the family's only son. It was well that she did so, for Michael was a breech birth and therefore a somewhat more complicated delivery. Although the two girls had been successfully breast-fed, Mike developed an allergy to his mother's milk and was eventually put on a formula. Mrs. Carson grew more and more upset at having to remain in the hospital, because she was concerned about her husband and two small daughters at home. Although the neighbors took turns looking after the children, both Carsons hated to ask favors of their friends.

Mike was an average-sized baby at birth, but did not gain weight very rapidly in subsequent months. As a child he was shorter and thinner than other boys his age, and at the age of 20 he is only 5 ft. 6 in. tall and weighs 130 lb. While he is not a "picky" eater, according to his mother, he just does not eat enough to "keep a growing boy alive." He has displayed the same lack of interest in food since childhood.

As the only boy in the family, Mike generated a great deal of interest when he was brought home from the hospital. His sisters were enchanted with their new baby brother, and would take turns helping their mother take care of him. In fact, they continued with this pattern long after Mike was able to do some things for himself. As a result, Mike was slower than the average child in learning to walk and talk. With two extra "mothers" available whenever they were not in school, Mike soon learned more about giving orders than about self-reliance, and quickly became rather spoiled. Unfortunately, the girls usually let Mike have his way because he was the youngest. Mrs. Carson gave in because he was a boy. Mr. Carson, instead of insisting that his son become more independent, tended to spoil him also, on the grounds that Mike would have to "work hard enough when he grew up." As a result, Mike virtually had his own way until he was old enough to start to school.

As a small, consistently underweight child, Mike caught virtually every bug that his sisters were exposed to, including some that never got a foothold on the girls. He also seemed to have more than his share of coughs, colds, and sore throats. Even the removal of his tonsils at the age of six did not seem to help this problem. While various doctors have been unable to supply a reason for his low resistance, Mike continues to suffer from these minor ailments. At present Mike is a short, thin young man with a rather pale complexion, moderately long, dark hair, and brown eyes which seem enormous in his thin face. In high school, one of the teachers discovered that Mike was having trouble seeing the board, and suggested that his vision be checked. This examination revealed that Mike was nearsighted, and he now wears steel-rimmed glasses. The vision problem did not disturb Mike because, as he remarked to his mother, "I'm not a big athlete or the school movie star. Glasses won't interfere with anything I do."

Mike recalls being teased about his small size when he was in elementary school. Rather than fight with the other boys, Mike admits that he attempted to become the "teacher's pet" so that he rarely was punished in class, while the other boys were. Most of the teasing stopped when Mike was in high school, although a few of the biggest boys still called him "Shrimp." His parents and sisters always assured Mike that he would "shoot up and fill out" as he grew older, but Mike has given up all hope of this.

B. Educational History

Mike started school at the age of six, since there was no kindergarten in his rural school district. The first few months were rather traumatic, for he had been master of his small world at home, and suddenly found himself in competition with a number of other children for the teacher's attention. The school bus, the strange children and adults, the big building, and the long hours all combined to make Mike very frightened and withdrawn. Mrs.

Carson reports that Mike would leave in tears and come home in the same state almost every day. The family was quite perplexed, since neither of the girls had experienced similar difficulties.

Mike's attendance became quite sporadic. He complained of sore throats, earaches, stomach pains, caught several colds, and came down with measles and mumps. He also had his tonsils removed at the suggestion of the family doctor. All in all, Mike missed so much school that his teacher felt that Mike should repeat the first grade. The Carsons agreed with this decision.

Mike's second encounter with formal education went much more smoothly. Perhaps he decided to bow to the inevitable, or perhaps he was now mature enough to cope with the situation, but at any rate, there were no more tears and stomach aches. In fact, Mike soon began to look forward to school, because his learning of the previous year gave him a great advantage over the other students. Mrs. Carson suspects that Mike might have become somewhat "bossy" because he continually reported how he had gotten the other children to line up for recess or to quiet down at dismissal time. His mother cannot recall that Mike made any special friends during this year.

The consolidated school which Mike attended contained grades one through eight, plus a four-year high school. Thus Mike stayed with approximately the same group of students for the entire 12 years. His progress through the grades was steady, but not spectacular. Mike's report cards show mostly "B's" and "C's," with an occasional "A" or "D." His parents recall that he showed some interest in art in elementary school, but refused to pursue the subject in high school because it was "sissy." Mike displayed no particular aptitude for any subject, and seemed to dislike physical education, probably because of his size. His elementary school teachers remember Mike as a child who liked to be the center of attention, with a tendency to sulk when he did not get his own way, and generally average academic ability.

Mike's high school, being relatively small, offered three different courses of study; vocational, general, and academic. Since it had always been understood that Mike was going on to college, he enrolled in the academic track. Again Mike displayed no particular interests or aptitudes, and his grades fell slightly, so that he graduated with a straight "C" average, and a position of 125 in a class of 203 students. His high school teachers describe Mike as an average student, neither outstandingly good or bad in any subject. His physical education teacher felt that Mike never really tried in his subject, and was almost constantly finding excuses to avoid dressing for class. He reported that Mike seemed afraid of many class activities, and showed interest only in wrestling where the boys were matched according to size.

Mike was a member of the school newspaper staff for two years as a cartoonist, but lost interest and dropped out. In his junior year he joined the dramatics club. However, when the advisor suggested that he would be perfect for the part of a young boy in a forthcoming production, Mike also dropped out of that group. "I should play a 12-year-old! Wouldn't the kids love that?'' he remarked to his mother. To add to Mike's disgust, the part was eventually given to a girl.

Mike's high school counselor describes him in the following way:

> Michael Carson was a very difficult student to get to know. It was almost impossible to tell what he was thinking or feeling. While he was only an average student, he was adamant about going to college, but had absolutely no plans concerning a major field or future vocation. I gave him both the Strong and Kuder tests, but no definite patterns emerged. I finally suggested that he enroll in a two-year college until he had more concrete ideas about what he wanted to do with his life. It almost seemed as though he had no interests at all.

Mike took his counselor's advice and enrolled at Winston Junior College, which is a 45-minute drive from the farm. His parents are very enthusiastic about this plan, because it enables Mike to live at home while he attends college. Mike is taking a general studies program, which involves a number of different areas and no major field of concentration. His grades remain ''C's'' for the most part, and while he does not particularly dislike any subject, there is nothing he really likes either. When pressed, he says he enjoyed art history the most. However, the teacher of this subject was unaware of any special interest on Mike's part, and some of his teachers from last year have trouble in remembering Mike at all. His English and American history teachers of this year describe Mike as a quiet student who rarely participates in class discussions, but who is always prompt in turning in assignments. He appears to them to be an ordinary, average student.

While the college extracurricular activities are somewhat limited, Mike has not joined any groups on campus. He explains this by saying that his long drive does not leave him any time for clubs. In effect, Mike's college experience has been almost a duplicate of high school and elementary school up to the present.

However, Mike is approaching the end of his sophomore year at Winston, and will graduate in June with an associate's degree. At this point, some decision concerning at least the next two years must be made. Mike definitely plans to transfer to a four-year college in the city and complete a bachelor's degree. He must decide whether to live on the campus or to commute an even greater distance than he does now. He can choose to continue with the last two years of a general studies program, which will not prepare him for any vocation, or he can select a major area leading to some vocation. The latter would probably mean that Mike would have to go to summer school or in some other way make up the required courses he has not taken for a major field. Perhaps the biggest problem of all will be for Mike to decide on which major to select, since he does not appear to have any special interests or aptitudes.

Mike's college academic advisor sums up the situation in the following way:

Mike Carson is typical of a number of college students today, and perhaps especially typical of junior college students. These young people feel that going to college is required of them, either because their parents say so or because all their friends are going. However, they really have no idea of what courses they want to take or what goals they want to reach. Many of them have only minimal academic ability and barely scrape by with "C's" and "D's." Some of them drop out; some graduate from here and find that they still don't know where they're going, two or more years later. Some, like Mike, are going to spend four years in college and still not be prepared for anything . . .

I've had five conferences with Mike, and we never seem to make any progress. He simply doesn't know what he wants to be. His folks talk about law or medicine, but Mike really doesn't have the academic ability to pursue either of those programs. His I.Q. scores, College Entrance Tests, and present grades indicate only average ability. Besides that, he shows no interest in these fields, or related fields that do not require as much education. The general studies program is designed to help people like Mike "find themselves," but in his case it hasn't seemed to work. Some of these students really blossom when they get to college, but Mike appears to be following his old high school pattern. We just can't seem to find any area which really appeals to him. I admit that I don't know what to suggest at this point.

Mike himself does not appear to be very concerned about his future, although a decision must be reached within the next six weeks so Mike can transfer to his new college in time for fall registration. He has narrowed down his alternatives to a choice between continuing in general studies and majoring in history. The history major is the suggestion of his girlfriend, Elaine Wilson, who would like to see Mike go to graduate school and become a college professor.

C. Emotional Development and Adjustment

From all reports, Mike was rather spoiled as a child. Until he started to school, he was accustomed to having his own way in almost everything. Mike was rarely punished, perhaps because he could do little wrong in the eyes of his family. When punishment was administered, usually by Mrs. Carson because her husband was out working, it consisted primarily of sending Mike to his room for a period of time. Mike's repeated illnesses and the attention they generated also served to reinforce the idea that Michael Carson was a very important little person.

Mike's first school experiences must have been quite a shock to a little boy so ill-prepared to deal with this radically different situation. Sulking and pouting, which had operated so successfully at home, were no longer effective, even though several of his elementary school teachers remember this tendency. This sudden loss of importance, coupled with a lack of initiative and independence, were probably responsible for Mike's intense dislike of school. Being a year older than his peers, when he repeated the first grade, was a helpful factor in Mike's case. However, he still wanted to be the center of attention, and attempted to secure this position by "bossing" the other children around. As he progressed through school, Mike seemed to realize that he simply had no outstanding abilities which would enable him to hold the spotlight. Even athletic prowess, which many boys use successfully, was denied to Mike because of his small size. As a result, Mike seemed to resign himself to the idea of being a nobody. "Average" and "quiet" are the two words used most frequently to describe Mike.

From a child who displayed his emotions quite openly, Mike has grown into a very self-contained, rather emotionless adult. He is rarely excited or enthusiastic about anything, but neither is he moody or depressed. He just drifts on from day to day in much the same manner. Elaine, his girlfriend, finds this one of his most appealing qualities. "You can always count on Mike to be just the same," she comments, "not up one minute and down the next, like most of the kids are." However, one wonders just how happy Mike really is, and whether his lack of emotion is merely a defense against an outside world which labels him "average" and refuses to give him the attention he had as a child.

There is no doubt that Mike loves his parents and sisters, although he never uses the word. His parents are "swell," and there seems to be no generation gap in the Carson family. He "likes Elaine a lot," but they have no plans to be engaged or married. Mike has never been a discipline problem or showed any signs of emotional disturbance, unless his lack of enthusiasm and interest is an unhealthy sign.

D. Psychosexual Development and Adjustment

Being a farm child, Mike was exposed to birth, death, and the facts of reproduction at a very early age. He reports that he has never discussed sex with his parents, as they are somewhat "old-fashioned" about the topic, but rather supplemented his own information with bits of knowledge contributed by the other boys at school and several books on the subject. Neither Mike's school nor his church conducted any classes in sex education, perhaps because of the rural setting. As in so many other instances, Mike does not seem particularly interested in the subject of sex.

Contrary to the attitudes of many young people his age, Mike holds rather conservative views about sex. He does not believe in sexual experiences before marriage, in liberalized abortion laws, or in fewer restrictions on pornography. He believes that homosexuals should be arrested and punished. While his opinions can be attributed to his small-town background and religious upbringing, it is also possible that Mike has felt some inner doubts about his own masculinity. His small size has prevented him from being very successful at sports and games, and thus he has had little opportunity to demonstrate his maleness in the usual manner. He has relatively little contact with his father, does not work around the farm, and at best would have difficulty in identifying with Fred Carson. Mike never brags about his sexual adventures as the other boys do, and it may be that he has never had any to talk about.

According to Mike's medical records, his sexual development has proceeded normally. Although his voice will never be deep and booming like his father's, it is definitely masculine in pitch and quality. According to his mother, Mike was greatly pleased a year ago when he began to shave regularly. As far as one can tell, Mike has had little, if any, sexual experience.

E. Social Development and Adjustment

Until he started to school, Mike had very little contact with other children. Few visitors came to the farm, and they were usually adults. Thus he was somewhat at a loss as to how to make friends. During the first grade, his "bossy" attitude did little to make him popular with his peers. Gradually, however, Mike did begin to make friends. He never had a great many friends, but rather seemed to establish a few lasting relationships. He has had the same three friends throughout elementary school and high school. All three boys are very much like Mike. They are relatively short in height, average in ability, and generally unremarkable. Mrs. Carson describes them as "just nice boys from nice families." None of the other boys has gone on to college. One works at the local feed and grain store, and the other two are helping their fathers farm.

Mike's friends have been male, even when he was young. Perhaps he felt that he got enough female attention at home, or maybe he just felt more comfortable with boys his own age than with girls. Mike went through the stage when all females were taboo, and emerged successfully by learning to tolerate his sisters again. By this time the girls were teenagers and not terribly interested in the activities of their younger brother, so Mike found himself, except for his mother, in a predominantly masculine world.

Mike's high school peers describe him as a boy who hovered on the fringe of things rather than being in the center. He certainly was not a member of the "in crowd"—the popular boys and girls who dominated the social life and activities of the school—but he was not a loner who was always by himself. After school he and his friends spent their time hanging around the drugstore in town, looking at magazines and drinking cokes. Mike still spends much of his free time at the drugstore, talking with the younger boys who are still in high school. Mike is something of a hero to these boys because he goes to college, and they seem to admire his flashy clothes and the air of sophistication which he assumes.

Until he met Elaine at Winston, Mike never had a real girlfriend. He went on occasional double dates with his buddies, and asked a girl from his church to the senior prom, but that was the extent of his social activity. Elaine is a preeducation major at Winston and plans to transfer to City College with Mike and become an elementary school teacher. This probably explains why she would like Mike to become a college professor.

Elaine is a rather shy, quiet girl who comes from a broken home. Her parents were divorced when she was small and she has very vivid memories of her father's terrible temper and the heated arguments which preceded the divorce. She confesses that she had to "pursue" Mike and make a number of overtures to get him to notice her. He finally began to invite Elaine over to the Student Union for coffee after class, and eventually asked her for a date. Since then they have drifted into a fairly steady relationship, and go out almost every weekend. Elaine comes from a small town near Winston, where her mother works in the local bank. The Carsons like Elaine, but feel that Mike should not commit himself to any girl until he has finished his education. Mrs. Carson is sure that Mike will meet a number of more attractive girls when he goes to City College. Elaine is short, rather plump, and not at all what she has in mind for Mike's wife.

F. Interests and Recreation

Mike appears to have very few specific interests. He has never helped with the farm chores, partly because of his size and health, and partly because Mr. Carson wanted to spare him from hard work. Therefore Mike did not belong to 4H, as most farm boys do, and never developed hobbies related to farming. As a child, he made a few sporadic collections, only to lose interest and turn to something else. He is not particularly fond of reading, and spends no more time than is absolutely necessary on his school work. He watches television for hours every night, and goes down to the drugstore in town from the time classes are over until dinner. These activities, and his dates with Elaine, seem to be the things he does for recreation.

Mike's only apparent interest centers around his personal appearance and dress. He is very fond of the current hair and clothing styles for men and always looks like something out of a fashion magazine. While Mike may be using clothing as a means of gaining status among his peers, so far his system has worked pretty much in reverse. In both high school and college, the trend among his peers has been toward blue jeans and other casual dress styles. Many of Mike's peers at Winston refer to him as "the funny guy who comes to class all dressed up." Sam Foster, a boy from Mike's home town, who sometimes rides to school with Mike, is probably his closest male friend at Winston. Sam reports that he has tried to get Mike to dress more like the other guys, but Mike refuses to discuss the subject. The high school boys at the town drugstore, however, think that Mike is a real fashion plate.

G. Ideology

It is very difficult to determine Mike's ideology, since he is so hard to get to know. He is somewhat conservative by present adolescent standards, yet certainly not a complete conformist. He really appears to have few concrete goals, and just seems to drift from day to day, letting events shape his life with little control on his part. However, the time is rapidly approaching when Mike will have to snap out of his apathy and make some decisions. Although Mike is 20 years old, his life is similar to that of an elementary school child, and Mike seems to be perfectly happy with the situation as it is. At least he shows no outward signs of rebellion against the status quo. It might be healthier if Mike would stand up on his own feet more, instead of refusing to assert himself in any way. Perhaps Mike still thinks of himself as a child, despite his age.

Interpretive Questions

1. Describe Mike's self-concept as you think it might be at this point in his life.
2. Which of Mike's experiences have been most critical in forming his self-concept?
3. What combination of factors contributed to Mike's being spoiled?
4. How well has Mike learned to accept his physical self? Defend your answer.
5. How do you reconcile Mike's early desire for attention with his current apathy? Does he really believe that he is just "average"?
6. Speculate as to the reasons for Mike's short-lived interest in art and dramatics. Do you think he entertains some doubts about his masculinity? Cite evidence to support your answer.
7. How wise, all things being considered, was Mike's decision to go to college? What other alternatives were open to him? Was Winston a good idea?
8. Why does Mike hesitate to become involved in outside activities at Winston, and prefer to hang around a drugstore with younger boys?
9. How typical is Mike of college students today, in terms of his lack of direction? Defend your answer.
10. Evaluate Mike's two possible courses of study at City College. Which should he take? Would you suggest any alternative plans for his consideration?
11. Describe the kind of relationship which seems to exist between Mike and his father, and Mike and his mother.
12. Advance possible reasons for Mike's conservative attitudes toward sex. Do you feel that he is out of step with his contemporaries on this topic?
13. Describe Mike as he must appear to Elaine. How well do you think she really knows him? Why does she feel attracted to him?
14. Do you think that Mike is still very much of a child? If so, what factors have led to this situation?

IV. CURRENT STATUS; DIAGNOSIS AND PROGNOSIS; RECOMMENDATIONS

Michael Carson is a young man who seems to be drifting through life. While he has not encountered any of the traumatic problems facing many of his adolescent peers, he has rarely asserted himself in any way or made any important decisions. He attends college because his parents wish him to do so, but he has no real interest in his studies nor any goals toward which he is working. His steady date is a girl who is primarily responsible for their relationship. He has few friends, and seems to prefer the company of younger people who admire him for rather superficial reasons. Although he goes through the motions, Mike seems to be a spectator at his own life.

Mike appears to be using prolonged education as a means of escaping adult responsibilities. However, he cannot drift much longer without making some decisions. It is highly probable that he will take Elaine's advice and major in history. This will enable him to spend at least three more years, and possibly more, in college. He may then be able to secure a teaching position, despite his apparent lack of interest and aptitude. Such a career will probably have some appeal for Mike, because he can thus continue to "hide out" from many of the realities of life.

It would be much better for Mike to leave school at this point and do some growing up. He needs to get out on his own, see some of the world, and learn to make decisions. His entire life so far has been centered around academics, a situation in which he has only average ability. Instead of accepting himself as average, which in his heart Mike really does not believe, he should try to find some other field of endeavor in which he does possess ability. Mike needs to try his hand at some different kinds of jobs, or perhaps enlist in some branch of the service and give himself time to grow up. So far he has had very little experience upon which to base decisions and plans.

At the very least, Mike should plan to live away from home for the next two years. This will enable him to mix with other young people, gain some new perspectives, and discover just how immature he really is. Unfortunately, Mike has just enough academic ability to stay in school. If he were to flunk out, he would be forced to grow up. As matters stand now, however, he will continue to drag out an undistinguished academic career. Unless something happens to break this pattern, Mike will probably marry Elaine, become a teacher, and continue to plod along for the rest of his life, vaguely unhappy but powerless to do anything about it.

Interpretive Questions

1. Do you agree with the author's prognosis for Mike's future? Why, or why not? Are there any points you would like to add?

2. Do you feel that Mike is an unhappy person? Defend your answer.
3. Evaluate the suggestion that Mike leave school at this point and work for a few years.
4. Evaluate the suggestion that Mike join some branch of the service until he grows up.
5. Are there any other alternatives to the above suggestions which might be more helpful to Mike?
6. How does an adolescent go about growing up?
7. If nothing happens to change the present situation, describe Mike as you think he will be at the age of 40.
8. What kind of a teacher do you think Mike would be?
9. Would staying in school, but living away from home, be a good plan for Mike?
10. What problems typical of adolescence might Mike have to face as an adult?

8

Responsible
Sexuality

Several of the developmental tasks of adolescence directly relate to the assumption of an adult sexual role, namely: achievement of new and more mature relations with age-mates of both sexes, achievement of socially approved masculine or feminine role, and acceptance of one's physique and the effective use of the body.[1]

Assuming that these tasks are successfully accomplished, the young person is confronted with tasks more characteristic of adulthood, for instance: selecting a mate, learning to live with a marriage partner, and starting a family.[1]

Naturally, for reasons previously discussed in Chapter 2, namely prolonged adolescence, there is a considerable amount of overlapping between the developmental tasks of the adolescent and adult periods.

The pace at which a young person encounters each respective task is influenced by many things: culture, socioeconomic status, religion, degree of

[1]Robert J. Havighurst, *Human Development and Education* (New York: Longman, Green, 1953).

social acceptance, and rate of physical development, to name but a few. In some locales and in some social classes, early marriage is the rule rather than the exception. In other areas, even pairing off into couples for dating purposes is delayed because of social pressures.

Some young people, whose sex education has been limited, if not nonexistent, are inhibited in their psychosexual development simply because of ignorance or lack of sophistication. Others, more knowledgable and casual about sexual matters, may exhibit precocious and sometimes socially unacceptable sexual behavior. The road to achieving responsible sexuality can be a rough route to travel and the adolescent needs all of the wholesome help available in order to proceed comfortably and wisely.

It was once widely believed that an individual's sexuality suddenly began exerting its influence as a behavior determinant at the onset of puberty. Prior to this dramatic event, the individual supposedly was totally innocent and devoid of any sexual influences. A more modern and realistic approach to human sexuality acknowledges the fact that the boy or girl is a sexual being from the time of birth, or to be truly precise, from the moment of conception. Data regarding one's sexuality is accumulated by the individual from the beginning of his or her existence and continues to collect throughout a lifetime. Sex education, per se, is a life-long process and one that cannot begin too soon.

An individual's sex education comes from a variety of sources: familiarity with his or her own body and information concerning the physical characteristics of the opposite sex, the role models within the family setting, the facts provided by parents, peers, teachers, books, etc., and most important of all, the individual's personal perception or interpretation of all of these types of data.

The adolescent period is recognized as that stage in life when, particularly for the male, the biological sex drive is so strong that sexual activity and capacity reach their peak. A similar apex in sexual behavior does not occur for the female until sometime later, normally during the late 20s and early 30s. This disparity, although dramatic, does not seem to affect heterosexual relationships very seriously. Because of this surge of interest in the opposite sex during the adolescent period, the boys begin to pay attention to and, in fact, may pursue the girls. The girls, who were interested in their male counterparts long before this attraction was reciprocal, glory in their new status and love every minute of it. The one conflict which can occur is that imposed by the "double standard" regarding appropriate behavior for the girl as compared to that expected of or accepted for the boy. In spite of a current trend which encourages the relaxation of certain restrictions on the sexual role of the woman, many young women experience severe conflicts when attempting to assume responsibility for their own behavior. Being pursued is one thing; being pressured is quite another.

Cohabitation without benefit of a legal marriage license has become more commonplace. Whether these alliances are as happy or happier than those maintained by married couples is a matter for conjecture, as no extensive research has, as yet, provided a definite answer. Realistically, we should acknowledge the fact that no marriage certificate can guarantee adjustment or happiness, but the man or woman who is sexually responsible has a headstart over anyone for whom such responsibility seems unnecessary or remains unobtainable.

Sexual mores, and the interpretation of what kinds of behavior constitute responsible sexuality, are socially determined. Thus different codes apply in different cultures, or in the same culture at different periods. There is little doubt that at present the moral code which exists in the United States is in a process of transition. Thus adolescents are learning to operate under a set of standards different from those of their parents. This difference, which may range all the way from openly doing what the parents have been secretly doing to behavior which parents simply cannot conceive of, frequently is a basic source of conflict between the generations. While it is too soon to evaluate the changing moral values of our society, most parents experience a negative reaction when confronted with evidence of sexual behavior on the part of their children. Such behavior emphasizes the fact that the child is rapidly approaching adulthood, and will soon leave the parental nest. It may also reactivate unresolved sexual problems in the parents, or simply remind them of advancing age or decreasing control over the life of their child.

However, the fact remains that today's teenagers are being exposed to a moral code vastly different from the one their parents grew up with. Factors contributing to this new code are newer methods of birth control, more explicit sexuality in the mass media, more sex information and education given to children at an earlier age, and perhaps the general state of our society at the present time. Those who view this change with favor praise a more honest approach to sex, sexual equality and the disappearance of a double standard, and trial cohabitation as a means of reducing an astronomical divorce rate. Critics point to the statistics which reveal that venereal disease is on the increase among adolescents, the number of unwed mothers is rising, and sex crimes are a major problem in every city.

Whether or not the changing moral code is a prelude to the demise of our society remains to be seen. It will depend to a great degree upon how well adolescents handle the amount of sexual freedom which seems to be theirs. The typical teenager is bombarded on all sides by an overemphasis on the importance of sex. How well he handles this aspect of his life depends upon the example set for him by his parents and the kinds of attitudes he has developed while growing up. In the final analysis, each person bases his standards for sexual behavior upon the kinds of moral premises which have been built into his life. While most sexual decisions involve only a small number of people, the accumulated decisions of adolescents will have a telling effect upon the future course of our society. Never before has the concept of responsible sexuality been so vital in the adolescent period.

A Case Study of Anne Mathis

Anne had her first sexual experience when she was 13. Today at the age of 19 her relationships with men, in spite of her promiscuity, do not seem to be based upon a sexual attraction, or at least not a conscious one. Her sexual relationships are unfeeling and therefore unsatisfying. Unless she can bring herself to take an initial step toward making some changes in her life-style, her treadmill existence will take its psychological toll.

I. IDENTIFICATION OF SUBJECT AND SOURCES OF INFORMATION

Name: Anne Mathis
Address: 5083 Rose Avenue
Race: Black
Sex: Female
Age: 19
School or Occupation: Typist
Sources of Information
   1.   Interviews with subject
   2.   Interviews with mother
   3.   Interviews with peers
   4.   Interview with former school counselor
   5.   Interview with employer
   6.   Interview with co-workers
   7.   Interview with family physician

II. THE FAMILY HISTORY

Anne Mathis is the only child of Marie and Oscar Mathis. Anne's mother is 36 years of age. The father, who no longer resides in the home, is 45.

A. Health and Physical Characteristics

Marie Mathis married at the age of 16 and on her 17th birthday gave birth to a baby daughter. During the next four years she had three miscarriages and was informed by her physician that any additional pregnancies would endanger her life. Oscar Mathis was disturbed by the fact that his wife could have no more babies. The couple began to experience their first serious disagreements about this time. Eventually the estrangement became unresolvable and Oscar Mathis left his wife and child.

Marie is a striking woman. Her height, 5 ft. 10 in., and slender build, weight 120 lb., contribute to her attractive appearance. Since her physical difficulties caused by the miscarriages were remedied by an eventual hysterectomy, she has enjoyed good physical health. However, she describes herself as "highly excitable" and complains about "being nervous all the time."

Oscar Mathis was well known for his athletic prowess during his high school years. He ran track and played baseball, basketball, and football. He won letters in all four activities. His physique is characteristic of an athletic build. He is 6 ft. 2 in. tall and fluctuates between 175 and 185 lb., depending upon the amount of physical activity he engages in over a period of time. His physical health has never been a problem to him; however, he has been known to drink heavily at infrequent intervals. Since he no longer resides with his family, information is lacking in some details.

Grandparents on both sides of the family are all still living. Marie's mother and father, now in their 70s, live nearby. Marie and Anne pay frequent visits to the older couple. The grandfather, Alvin Cooper, suffered a stroke two years ago and is confined to the house. His wife, Alberta, is physically able to care for her husband and accepts no help other than an occasional ride to the supermarket. If no rides are available, she goes on her shopping trips by taxi.

The paternal grandparents, who live in another city, have never been close to the Oscar Mathis family, so there is nothing to report other than the fact that they are living. No information is available concerning their states of health.

B. Educational Status

Marie and Oscar Mathis both graduated from high school. Marie completed her senior year after she was married. Her marital state was kept secret until pregnancy made revelation imperative. Marie was asked to leave school when her condition came to the attention of school authorities. The school rules forbade any pregnant student to attend classes, regardless of her marital state. Most girls in Marie's school who encountered such a ruling simply dropped out. There was a minimal educational program offered at the local home for unwed mothers, but few girls took advantage of it. Because Marie was a good student and probably because she was indeed a married woman, she was allowed to complete her courses by correspondence and graduated with her class. She was told by her senior class advisor that if she "hadn't been so foolish and gotten married," she would have been eligible for a PTA scholarship and could have attended college, at least for one year. Marie would have liked to attend college; however, her decision to marry Oscar, she knew, would end any chances for further education.

Oscar Mathis was an average student and had no aspirations which involved a college education. He shifted from job to job after graduation but had settled into his job of postal clerk in a dependable, if uninspired, way by the time he married Marie.

None of the grandparents attended high school. All but one completed at least eight years of elementary school. Neither parents nor grandparents have ever expressed any hopes that Anne might attend college. Anne has never indicated any interest in further education.

C. Economic Status

Marie and her daughter live in a small apartment in a large housing complex. Oscar Mathis sporadically contributes to the support of his wife and child. Marie and Anne Mathis are both employed. Now that Anne has passed her 18th birthday, Oscar is no longer legally obligated to provide for her. He still sends support payments to Marie and, infrequently, some additional sums which are specifically intended to be given to Anne.

Marie is a receptionist in the office of a black physician. She has held this position for 10 years and is highly regarded by her employer. At one time she was encouraged to enroll in a practical nursing course. Although she never took the course, Marie now handles many paraprofessional tasks in the medical office.

Anne and her mother feel no true financial pinch. They have a car of medium price range and of recent vintage. They both dress very well, believing that you "lose money when you buy cheap clothes." Since Marie wears uniforms during her working hours, her major expenses involve clothing to equip her for a very busy social life. Anne and her mother wear the same size, so they can share their extensive wardrobe. Anne wears well-made, attractive clothing both to work and on social occasions.

The Mathis apartment, though small, is adequate and tastefully decorated. When Anne started working and contributing to the household income, she and her mother completely redecorated their home. New draperies, carpet, and furniture were purchased and all of the rooms were repainted. Anne and her mother each have their own bedroom and share the bath. There is a very small kitchenette. The dining area is at one end of the living room. The apartment is on the ground floor. There are double glass sliding doors leading to a small yard and patio. Anne and her mother both have an interest in gardening. Their small yard is a profusion of colorful blooms from spring to fall.

D. Social Status and Adjustment

Marie and Oscar Mathis have been separated for 10 years. Neither one of the parents sees the need for divorce. Marie has often been heard to comment that she never intends to marry again. In the event that she did divorce Oscar and remarry, his financial obligations would be obviated. Oscar's desire for freedom, in this sense, has never made itself apparent. Although Anne's father has never had a close relationship with her, she feels that he does love her and this may be one reason why he does not sever all family ties.

Anne's mother, young and very attractive, has not been deprived of male companionship in spite of the breakup of her marriage. She is constantly sought after and dates heavily. There have been many male visitors in the home, and Anne is quite accepting of her mother's popularity. Anne has a complicated social life of her own which will be discussed later.

Marie has had several affairs over the years. Her desire not to remarry is probably the direct result of the disillusionment which is the aftermath of the failure of her marriage. According to her own admission, she becomes "physically but not emotionally attracted," although emotional involvement usually follows if the affair is not casual or of short duration.

E. Interests and Recreation

When both parents lived in the home, many activities involved the whole family. They often attended drive-in movies in Oscar's convertible. Oscar belonged to a bowling league, but he also took his wife and daughter bowling every Sunday afternoon. Now Anne and Marie belong to their own, separate leagues.

Marie is an inveterate reader and if she does not go out in the evening, she reads. She subscribes, through the office and therefore at a reduced price, to *Life, Time, Ladies Home Journal, Ebony, Vogue,* and *Reader's Digest.* She belongs to the Book of the Month Club and in addition purchases many paperback books which she shares with Anne. Oscar purchased his daughter a stereo-phonograph for her 16th birthday. Anne and her mother both make use of the record player, although their tastes in music are somewhat different. Anne buys most of the new selections, although she often buys suitable records for her mother for her birthday and for Christmas.

F. Ideology

Marie Mathis is somewhat cynical. She was hurt badly by the breakup of her marriage. She does not place all of the blame on her husband, however. She explains this by saying, "It takes two to tango and two to tie up." She does feel considerable resentment about Oscar's reaction to their limited family. Oscar, having four brothers and three sisters, could not accept a one-child family of his own. He took out his frustration on his young, physically weakened wife who fought back the only way she knew. The bitter arguments, the tears, and shouts which became their way of life destroyed the understanding which caused them to fall in love in the first place. Marie's frantic attempts to bear Oscar another baby, which resulted in illness and additional disappointment, eventually led not only to the ruin of their physical relationship, but of their marriage as well.

Since she has lived a single existence, and especially now that Anne is really grown and financially independent, Marie makes no pretenses about her relationships with men. Although she does not blatantly flaunt her sexual freedom, neither is she hypocritical about it. She feels that "Anne is old

enough to face life; after all she's known the facts of life for some time now."
Marie explains Anne's sophistication in this way:

> I told her all about everything when she was 10 years old. Already she was
> beginning to grow into a woman. Her little body began blooming in all directions.
> So I told her about men and women, about her Daddy and me. I didn't scare
> her like my momma scared me. I just told her it can be beautiful if you want it
> to be or it can be ugly if everything isn't right. I didn't tell her to wait til she got
> married because nobody waits anymore. I didn't tell her she'd go to hell if she
> had sex without being married because if that were true, everybody would go
> to hell. I just told her the truth like I wish someone had told me.

Marie Mathis believes that "everybody has to look out for himself because nobody does anybody many favors in this life. Make a good living at
an honest job, keep your nose out of other people's business, and do unto
others, that's my philosophy."

Anne and her mother seem to live according to this ideology. Both earn
a comfortable living, are respected by their co-workers and employers, and
are well liked by their neighbors, who see them as "quiet but friendly folks."

Interpretive Questions:

1. Anne's mother is described as "cynical." What incidents in her life have
   encouraged this cynicism? What effect, if any, may this have upon her
   daughter?
2. How do you explain Oscar's reaction to his limited family? Could
   coming from a large family cause a bias so strong that it could lead to
   the breakup of a marriage?
3. Describe the relationship which exists between Anne and her mother,
   and between Anne and her father. How has Anne been influenced by
   these role models?
4. Marie Mathis has described, in some detail, Anne's sex education.
   Discuss the mother's approach in terms of the age at which this information was given, the impact it may have had, and the philosophy it
   imparted.
5. Early marriages often fail because of unfulfilled ambitions, immaturity
   on the part of one or both of the partners, inability to accept adult
   responsibilities, the immediate arrival of children, financial problems,
   and a host of other difficulties. How many of these factors operated in
   the lives of Anne's parents?
6. This family appears to be middle-class black. In what ways are their
   values and attitudes the same as middle-class whites? In what ways are
   they different?
7. Explain Marie's decision to get married rather than attend college from

her point of view. In view of subsequent events, was her decision a wise one? Defend your answer.

8. Discuss possible reasons for Marie's failure to divorce Oscar and marry again.
9. How may Anne's attitudes toward men, sex, and marriage have been shaped by her mother's attitudes and behavior?
10. What different effects might the family situation have had upon a male child?
11. How do you think Oscar feels about his daughter? How does Anne feel about him?
12. Would you agree that Anne must be "sophisticated" about sex?

III. THE CASE HISTORY

A. Health and Physical Characteristics

Anne Mathis is an attractive young woman. She favors her father, which she considers somewhat of a disadvantage because she regards her mother as being "beautiful." Anne is tall, 5 ft 8 in., slender, 118 lb., and well proportioned, 38–26–36.

Anne's history of development and records of health all reflect normal progress and absence of serious illness or injury. A bout with tonsilitis resulted in the usual minor surgical procedure. Anne has some difficulty with hay fever but it is only a seasonal irritant rather than a disability.

Childhood interests reflect an enthusiasm for physical activity—kick-ball, hopscotch, roller-skating, and all the usual games played with youngsters in the neighborhood. As a teenager, Anne continued the bowling she once enjoyed with her father plus dancing and ice-skating. There have never been any economic restrictions placed upon her recreational activities so Anne has been able to try out her interests in all types of sports activities. She is agile, well coordinated and excels in whatever interests she pursues.

This young woman does exhibit some signs of nervous tension. Her nails are bitten to the quick and often even the skin around her finger tips looks chewed. She has frequently complained of severe headaches but no medical treatment has been sought. These incidents have been attributed to "nerves" by her mother and are passed off as such. Anne has never had any difficulty with her menstrual period and thinks girls who have cramps are "putting on." She has no sympathy for anyone who cannot or will not go swimming, bowling or anything else "because of her period."

Anne has some difficulty maintaining her figure. She loves food and has a healthy appetite. Unlike her mother, who subsists on one full meal a day, Anne eats heartily at all meals and sometimes in-between. Sporadically, she must go on a crash diet to keep her waist line "within reason." Her weakness for sweets does not help matters. She loves hot fudge sundaes, cheesecake, marshmallows, and rich cookies and breakfast rolls. Aware of her weight-gaining propensities, Anne has remarked, "If I ate everything I wanted to, I'd be as big as a house!"

Anne's work attendance record is unusual for someone who exhibits and enjoys such good health. She misses one, sometimes two days out of every month. Since she is part of a typing pool, these absences do not affect the office procedure. Anne knows that someone else will take care of her work if she is not there. One wonders what her attitude would be if she were in a position in which she bore the primary responsibility for getting a job done. When asked why she misses so much work, Anne replied, "Oh, I'm just too tired sometimes to go in there and hack it." When pressed as to why she is so tired, Anne explains that she had been out late or "There was this really cool party." Anne's attitude about her work record does not reflect that of her mother. Marie Mathis never misses a day of work. The dissimilar natures of their respective positions may explain this difference.

B. Educational History

Anne's school records reflect a better than average performance throughout her educational experience. She began school at the age of five when she attended Peter Pan Kindergarten in her neighborhood. She adjusted well and enjoyed the company of other children. Elementary school found Anne an eager and capable student. She was soon bringing books home "to read" before her reading instruction was actually initiated. A teacher in the primary grades offers this description: "Anne Mathis is a cooperative child. She conducts herself with self-confidence. Her motivation seems to be self-induced. She is a pleasure to have in class and is well liked by her classmates."

Anne made the transition from an all-black elementary school to an integrated junior high smoothly. This move meant that she no longer could walk the two blocks to school, but had to catch a bus three blocks away and travel for half an hour to the new and bigger school. Her social environment expanded drastically, but Anne took this in her stride. At the end of the ninth grade, Anne was encouraged to pursue a college preparatory course. However, having no interests in higher education, Anne chose a commercial course. She excelled in her studies, winning several prizes and earning special recognition at her graduation exercises.

C. Emotional Development and Adjustment

Anne's early childhood was disrupted because of her mother's frequent illnesses. Often Anne was taken to her grandmother's quite unexpectedly and left there for considerable periods of time. These upheavals frequently would happen in the middle of the night. Anne would be snatched from her bed by a nervous father or anxious grandmother and taken to her grandparents' home. Once there, she would be placed in a bed that seemed huge to her and left in a big, dark room all alone with her doubts and fears.

When her mother was scheduled for major surgery, Anne moved in with her grandparents on a long-term basis. She stayed with them for over a year while her mother recuperated. Upon her return to her home the child witnessed the abrasive atmosphere created by her parents' disintegrating relationship. Marie and Oscar made no attempt to shield their daughter from their emotional upheavals. Marie has explained that in the small apartment which became the arena for marital battles "there was no place for Anne to hide or get away from the fights."

Anne reports that her most vivid memories of her father involve the ugly scenes that took place during the family arguments. She remembers seeing him strike her mother on several occasions. She recalls many instances when her mother, crying hysterically, would throw anything within reach, books, dishes, framed pictures, small chairs, etc., at her husband. Anne often withdrew to her bedroom and hid under the bed. No one ever came to look for her. Caught up in the maelstrom of family discord, Anne was ignored by her parents.

Although Anne was academically and socially adaptable in school, at least one teacher mentioned some concern about Anne's withdrawal tendencies. This report was filed approximately six months after Oscar Mathis left his wife and child. Anne was then enrolled in the second grade.

> Anne Mathis is a quiet, sometimes preoccupied little girl. Although she always completes her work, she spends a great deal of time staring into space. She has a nervous habit of biting her nails. Her mother was informed of this, but she didn't seem to be concerned. The father has never attended any conferences or school affairs. Mrs. Mathis has never referred to her husband. The school is uninformed about any family situation which may be affecting Anne. This child may have need for psychological support. If her withdrawal tendencies intensify, she should be referred to psychological services.

It is interesting to note that this identification of symptoms was made rather early in Anne's life. No further mention was made of any psychological difficulties until junior high school when Anne's behavior came to the attention of the assistant principal.

> Anne Mathis, Home Room 209, was interviewed regarding her attendance record. She had missed 15 days out of the second grading period. Anne's grades have not suffered. Her attitude regarding the absences was nonchalant. The girl, although outwardly polite, is rather aloof. She stared out of the window much of the time and had to be forced into making responses. Her teachers have mentioned Anne's docility in the classroom. In the company of her peers, however, Anne is more outgoing. She is very popular, especially with boys.

D. Psychosexual Development and Adjustment

Anne's physical development was precocious when compared to that of her female peers. Her first menstrual period occurred at the age of 11. She reflects that the onset of puberty was "no big thing." She feels that she was adequately prepared for her physical changes and was not significantly affected by them, nor was she bothered by being ahead of her friends. If anything, she enjoyed the respect, if not awe, which was expressed by the other girls when they realized Anne had "graduated" from undershirts to adult lingerie. Anne's first bra caused quite a sensation in her social set. She recalls much "giggling and snickering" on her account, but she was not embarrassed; in fact, she enjoyed the attention, particularly from the boys. There was much "pushing and shoving" on the buses Anne took to and from school by boys who fought to win a seat next to Anne. A lot of "feeling" and "pinching" took place in those days and Anne admits allowing considerable exploratory behavior. She was flattered by the attention.

Anne had her first sexual experience at the age of 13. She normally spent many evening hours with other youngsters in the apartment complex. There was a social room provided for the residents and it was well used by the youngsters. They played cards, Ping Pong, and danced every night of the week. Anne's mother was seldom at home. One night, Anne, another girl and several boys discovered an empty apartment in the complex and gained entry through an unlocked window. Once inside, play activities became less innocent. Necking led to heavy petting as the boys took turns with the two girls. Anne was asked if she "would do it" and she reports thinking, "Why not?" Anne had some semblance of sex relations with all four boys while the other girl watched. The next day, Anne did not go to school as she felt somewhat chagrined. This embarrassment was not long-lived, however, and she returned to school more popular than ever.

The group sex scene was never repeated. Anne began dating, however, and never wanted for male attention. Depending upon her frame of mind, she would or would not "put out" on her numerous dates. Her "sex by whim" behavior perhaps made her all the more fascinating to the young men who sought her favors.

Anne's school attendance continued to be sporadic. At one point she was summoned by the counselor at John Marshall High School while she was enrolled in the 10th grade. The counselor asked Anne about her health and quizzed her about any physical problems. Anne merely replied that "some days she just didn't feel well." The excuses which her mother wrote for her were just as vague. The counselor suggested that Anne have a physical examination. Anne felt no need to follow this advice. She reports, however, that her absences were caused frequently by headaches or that she just "didn't feel like going to school or seeing anybody." When asked if she were depressed on those days, she replied with a simple "yes." She would not elaborate as to the cause of her depression.

E. Social Development and Adjustment

Anne Mathis has never experienced any difficulty winning the acceptance of her peers. As a child, she was always cooperative and well behaved and while no leadership qualities have ever emerged, she has maintained a high degree of popularity. Her social acceptability has probably been height-ened by her physical attractiveness and, in later years, by her sexual freedom. None of her female peers evidence any jealousy on their part because of Anne's popularity with boys.

Anne's mother has never placed any restrictions upon her daughter's social activities. She feels that Anne is a "good girl who knows what life is all about and can take care of herself." Marie Mathis has explained the necessity of birth control to her daughter, and this early and thorough sex education has spared Anne from the stigma of unwed motherhood. Several of Anne's classmates, who were not as cautious, have dropped out of school and given birth to illegitimate children. One girl, according to Anne, has had two abortions. Marie Mathis blames these unfortunate "accidents" upon mothers of girls who "don't know the facts of life and do something about them."

At work, Anne is pretty much of a loner. The other women in the typing pool are either married or much older. Anne dates several of the men who work in the same building. She recently broke up with one because she discovered that he was married. A co-worker started a whispering campaign about Anne and this man, who is white. Anne was not upset about being the subject of gossip; however, her curiosity about the man's marital state was piqued and upon inquiry she discovered that he had a wife and three chil-dren. She abruptly ended her liaison with him.

F. Interests and Recreation

Anne Mathis is a bright girl who has never exploited her academic potential. She reads avidly, but seldom anything of quality. She buys confes-sion magazines on her lunch hour and usually gets bored with the stories before she finishes them. She does not take them home because she feels her mother would disapprove of such "trash." When asked why she persists in reading this material when it seems to bore her, the vague reply was, "I don't know."

Her interests revolve primarily around a desire "to have a good time." She loves to dress handsomely and "go out" with a variety of men. Her escorts are chosen from men who are willing to spend money freely, who enjoy a "night on the town," and who will take her to "nice places." She feels that going to bed with a man is one way of "thanking him for a nice time." When asked if she enjoys these physical relationships, she responds enigmati-cally, "No, not really, but what difference does it make?" When asked if she has ever fallen in love, Anne replied with considerable emotion, "What's love? Anyhow, there isn't any real love anymore!"

G. Ideology

Anne Mathis seems to find life a rather "flat" experience. Constantly seeking a "good time," one wonders if she ever finds it. Her relationships with others are very superficial. Her attraction to men, especially her promiscuity, does not seem to be based upon a sexual attraction, or at least not a conscious one.

This young woman, at present, has no desire to get married. She wishes her mother and father could reconcile their differences or face up to the necessity of a divorce. Anne feels that she truly never had a father and feels sorry for other children in the same predicament. One reason why she does not wish to marry, is that she would not want to have children and possibly put them through what she experienced as a child.

She worries about her mother, realizing that, should Marie not remarry as she grows older, her social life will diminish and eventually disappear.

As far as her own future is concerned, Anne is unmotivated to change her status quo. Outwardly satisfied with her nonchallenging job, she seems content just to make a living.

Interpretive Questions

1. A changing body normally involves a changing self. What are Anne's attitudes about her "physical self"? Cite examples.
2. Anne has difficulty retaining her slim figure. What physical and emotional factors are involved in adolescent weight gain?
3. Describe the most influential determinants of Anne's psychosexual development. How would you describe her adjustment in this aspect of her life?
4. Speculate as to the causes of Anne's periods of depression. Decide whether or not she needs to seek help and, if so, suggest several logical sources.
5. Discuss the attitude of Anne's mother regarding her daughter's sexual freedom. How has the behavior and "advice" of Marie Mathis affected Anne's emotional development?
6. Anne seems to have very little in common with her co-workers. Having always been very popular with her peers, why has her social status met with change now that she's out of school?
7. Do you agree that Anne finds life to be "rather flat"? If so, why is this the case? What is missing from Anne's life? What is she really looking for?
8. Evaluate the reasons Anne gives for her frequent absences from school, and more recently, from work. What might her real reasons be?
9. Anne seems to feel equally comfortable in liaisons with black and white men. Discuss possible reasons for her attitude.
10. Why do you suppose Anne objects to having an affair with a married man? Is it a matter of morals, or do other factors enter the picture?

11. How typical were Anne's early sexual experiences? Were her responses as you would have predicted? Why, or why not?
12. What conditions in her home have contributed to Anne's decision not to marry and have children? Do you consider this a "normal" reaction to her early experiences?
13. Advance some possible explanations for Anne's lack of ambition and unwillingness to try to "better herself" in any way.
14. Describe Anne's future as you see it. Will she ever marry, have children, or advance to more responsible jobs? Will she ever find fulfillment in life?
15. Anne's attitudes and behavior are thought of by many as "typical" of blacks. How accurate is this kind of thinking in Anne's case? Would her attitudes and behavior be any different if she were white?

IV. CURRENT STATUS; DIAGNOSIS AND PROGNOSIS; RECOMMENDATIONS

The subject is an unhappy young woman. Her life, while on a virtual social merry-go-round, is unsatisfying to her, yet she appears unmotivated to change it.

Anne's position as a typist provides no challenge and thereby offers her nothing except a living wage. A higher-paying job does not seem to be appealing and therefore a driving-force, as she does not experience a need for additional funds. A job with greater responsibility would be more stimulating and consequently afford her greater satisfaction, if she could be encouraged to extend herself in this direction.

Anne's depression may be the product of repressed guilt feelings. On the other hand, since her sexual freedom has never been challenged either by her family or friends, guilt may not be an ingredient of her unhappiness.

Anne has assimilated her mother's cynicism and nurtured from it a sense of futility. Deciding, because of her unfortunate childhood experiences, that "there is no love in this life," Anne does not know how to become emotionally involved with anyone. This psychological deficiency has prevented her from developing any sensitivity regarding human relationships. She uses, rather than enjoys, other people and she allows them to use her. Her sexual relationships are unfeeling and therefore unsatisfying.

Unless Anne can bring herself to take an initial step toward making some important changes in her life-style, her treadmill existence will take its psychological toll. Conceivably her periods of depression will become longer and deeper. The sense of futility will intensify. Her relationships with others, now primarily with men, will deteriorate to an even more superficial, if not degenerate, level.

Anne Mathis needs help.

Interpretive Questions

1. List those steps which Anne might first take to get off the "treadmill."
2. What sort of help does Anne need? If you were in a position to advise this young woman, what would you recommend?
3. Does Anne have feelings of guilt? How do young people usually react to guilt-producing stimuli? What are some typical physical and psychological reactions?
4. What is responsible sex behavior? What are its prerequisites? How many of these were present during Anne's development?
5. What changes would have to occur in Anne's life to alter her feelings about marriage for herself? Why does she want her mother to remarry, under the circumstances?
6. American society is often characterized as experiencing a sexual "revolution." Does Anne Mathis typify such a cultural phenomenon? In what ways?
7. Why does Anne continue to drag out an existence from which she apparently derives little real satisfaction, rather than attempt to make some changes in her life?
8. Are there any ways in which Marie could help her daughter? How would Anne react if her mother should remarry, or ask Anne to leave home and strike out for herself?
9. Most adolescents are eager to break away from parental ties. Why has Anne been content to live with her mother?
10. Might Anne have more ambition if she were less secure financially, or would she simply allow welfare to support her? Defend your answer.
11. Does sexual freedom inevitably lead to boredom and promiscuity, as it has in Anne's case? Discuss the pros and cons of this issue.
12. Describe Anne's life as it would be if her attitudes toward sex were more traditional. Do you think she would find life more, or less, attractive under these circumstances?

Suicide

Self-destruction, the ultimate form of withdrawal from reality, is one of the most disturbing types of adolescent behavior. It is extremely sad to note that suicide is one of the major causes of death among the youthful segment of our population, second only to accidental loss of life.

As is often the case with any type of aberrant behavior, no single cause can be identified which begets the desire to end one's life, and no single pattern emerges from the grim statistics. The self-destructive urge is not unique to our own culture. Suicides occur all over the world where adolescents and adults comprise an extensive list of individuals who have sought and achieved an end to their existence. Even some children throw their lives away for often inexplicable reasons. The statistics, disturbing as they are, do not tell the full story, for many suicides are not detected nor recorded as such.

Almost every imaginable method of self-destruction has been employed; however, with the increase in the incidence of drug abuse, the overdose of drugs has made a horrifying contribution to the adolescent and adult mortality rate. More deaths, intentional and accidental, occur as a result of an overdose of barbiturates than from the ingestion of any other substance. Here is another example of how statistics can be misleading, for many overdoses recorded as accidental could have been induced purposely and vice versa.

Frequently, the young person who is suicide-prone experiences a lack of social success. Described psychologically in terms of "progressive isolation from meaningful social relationships," this phenomenon may be experienced at all ages.[1] As we have seen in previous chapters, the desire for social success during adolescence can be a driving force motivating behavior, which affects the development of the self-concept and which, unfortunately, can become a matter of life or death.

Lack of social success can establish a reaction pattern characterized by a vicious circle. Having desired and consciously sought peer acceptance and found rejection, the adolescent may tend to withdraw and avoid additional contacts which could lead to further rejection. This behavior makes acceptance and recognition impossible, so the stimulus for further and prolonged social isolation is presented, reinforcing the initial tendency to escape from additional rejection. The isolation and loneliness experienced by the immature, irrational, and highly sensitive young person may become unbearable. If the individual's misery comes to the attention of no one, if help is not available, the youngster's depression can so distort his thinking that he seeks a dramatic and often final solution to the problem.

There may truly be a myriad of causes of suicide. Guilt feelings which become unbearable are another frequent contributing factor. Perhaps the adolescent has exhibited behavior known to be totally unacceptable to parents or to society in general. Perhaps he has only had thoughts or feelings known to be grossly out of line and so disturbing that death is self-inflicted as a form of punishment. Female suicide, for example, is frequently attributed to real or imagined pregnancy.

Whatever the true cause, suicide is the result of a person's perception of his or her situation. When that situation becomes unbearable, or if it seems that no help in altering the situation or the individual's perception of it will ever be available, suicide often becomes the only apparent solution. It is unfortunate that any individual, of any age, should feel so alone or cut off from other people with whom he might share his problems that he seeks to end his life. However, statistics indicate that such is frequently the case, and an alarmingly high proportion of such individuals are adolescents.

Not everyone who attempts suicide is successful, and frequently those who make such attempts really do not want to die. Attempted suicide can be an extreme way of asking for help or calling attention to one's troubles. In such cases, the motivation behind the suicidal behavior is not to end one's life, but to induce someone to care enough to intervene.

Fortunately, new developments and greater public sophistication in the areas of mental health have led to the establishment of many suicide-prevention centers. "Hot-lines" and free clinics are frequently available to the indi-

[1] Jerry Jacobs, *Adolescent Suicide* (New York: John Wiley and Sons, Inc., 1971).

vidual who is aware of their existence. It is hoped that these and other developments will lead to a reduction in the number of suicides and attempted suicides at all age levels in our population.

A Case Study of Christina Ann Malcolm

There I was, staring at that frantic face in the mirror and wondering whose it was. I realized that I was that pathetic girl with tears running down her fat, red cheeks and I hated her. I began swallowing the pills as fast as I could. All I could think of was the desire to get out of my disgusting life.

I. IDENTIFICATION OF SUBJECT AND SOURCES OF INFORMATION

Name: Christina Ann Malcolm
Address: 2372 Larkspur Lane
Race: Caucasian
Sex: Female
Age: 17
School or Occupation: City College Preparatory School, senior year
Sources of Information:
1.   Interviews with subject
2.   Interviews with parents
3.   Interviews with siblings
4.   Interviews with high school counselor
5.   Interviews with family physician
6.   Interviews with art teacher

II. THE FAMILY HISTORY

Helen Malcolm, 52, and Alfred Malcolm, 60, are the parents of three daughters: Alicia, 22; Melba, 20; and Christina, 17.

A. Health and Physical Characteristics

Mrs. Malcolm is a tall, 5 ft. 10 in., slender, 135 lb., attractive woman. Her perfect posture and graceful bearing add to her impressive appearance.

Mr. Malcolm, also tall, 6 ft. 2 in., weighs 185 lb. His fair complexion compliments, rather than detracts from, that of his wife, who is very dark. The Malcolms are a very handsome couple.

Neither parent has suffered from any serious disease. Mrs. Malcolm is frequently incapacitated by migraine headaches for which she is under a physician's care. Mr. Malcolm has been hospitalized on two occasions by a spastic colon. He must watch his diet very carefully. Mrs. Malcolm is very rigid about her husband's food consumption. She watches him very carefully since he should not eat many of the dishes which she prepares for the family meals. Mr. Malcolm is expected to report to his wife, in infinite detail, the food he has eaten during the day while he is away from home.

Alicia Malcolm had appendicitis at the age of 13 and underwent surgery to correct the problem. Melba Malcolm broke her leg in a horseback riding accident. It had to be reset several times because of its failure to mend. She walks with a slight limp. All three girls have experienced the common childhood illnesses of measles and mumps and were quarantined for four weeks with successive cases of chicken pox and scarlet fever. Mrs. Malcolm recalls that siege with horror, commenting that "I very nearly lost my mind."

The older girls resemble their mother in terms of body proportions and other physical characteristics, including coloring and facial features.

Christina, the "baby," takes after her father. She is fair, has ash-blonde hair, a ruddy complexion, wide-set eyes, and heavy eyebrows. Her mother and sisters, by comparison, have more delicate facial features.

B. Educational Status

Alfred Malcolm, a retired naval officer, is a graduate of the naval academy. He rose to the rank of lieutenant commander while in the service, and since retirement has served as vice president of a manufacturing concern. Helen Malcolm did not attend college, having attended a small, southern school for girls during her high school years. She met her future husband at a house-party attended by many of the midshipmen from the academy.

Alicia is currently enrolled in a small women's college in the midwest. She is considering the possibility of pursuing a graduate degree in fashion design. She has submitted her transcript and portfolio and is anxiously awaiting word of their appraisal. Melba is attending a modeling school in New York City while working part-time as a professional model. She attended a midwestern junior college for women and received an associate's degree. Christina, the "intellectual" of the family, as she is referred to by her sisters, is currently in her senior year at the College Preparatory High School.

C. Economic Status

The Malcolms live in a large, older house in a quiet, respectable, but nondescript neighborhood. None of the neighbors are wealthy; however, most are old families who have lived there for some time. The neighborhood could perhaps best be described as "stable." The Malcolms are relative newcomers, having lived there for 10 years. Prior to Mr. Malcolm's retirement, the family lived somewhat more modestly in Baltimore. They moved to their present location because of the position Alfred Malcolm was offered upon his departure from the U. S. Navy.

Wanting to provide his family with comfortable, attractive, and spacious living quarters, Mr. Malcolm had gone alone to the city which would be their new home and gone house-hunting with a predetermined image in mind. He found just what he wanted, bought the house, and returned to his family in two short days.

The house is large, with three floors and 12 rooms in all. Each daughter has her own room. There is a study for their father's exclusive use and a sun room which is shared by all four women for sewing, card playing, and other feminine activities. Alicia, an accomplished pianist, is primarily responsible for the baby grand piano which commands one end of the long living room.

There are three cars in the garage. Mr. Malcolm drives an expensive foreign car. Alicia has a sports model of the same make, and Melba, who did not take her car to New York because of parking problems, has left behind a small economy car which Christina may use now that she is old enough to become licensed.

The family lives well, but wisely. There are no true extravagances, although Mr. Malcolm's income supplemented by his military pension, would certainly allow his family to live more lavishly. The only free-spending observable is in the quality of clothing worn by the Malcolm women. All are very clothes-conscious except for Christina, who perhaps just hasn't reached the age at which her interest in these matters will be piqued. The closets of her sisters and mother are packed with clothing of the latest styles and finest materials and tailoring. Mr. Malcolm dresses very conservatively and without much concern for the quality of his clothing. Mrs. Malcolm attributes his disinterest to the years and years of "sameness in uniform."

There are two servants who "help" with the maintenance of the home: Verna, the housemaid, who comes every day, and Hilda, the laundry woman, who washes and irons twice a week.

The elder Malcolms belong to several social clubs and civic groups which cater to individuals of their interests and income level.

D. Social Status and Adjustment

The mother, Helen Malcolm, is very socially oriented. Having come from a leading family in a small, southern town, she is very accustomed to being socially active and has tried to instill her interests into all three of her daughters. She has been very successful with the two older girls. Christina's lack of any affinity for the social graces, however, has caused her mother considerable concern.

The parents attend many social functions at the Country Club, the Fine Arts Center, the symphony, and the Civic Theatre. They also entertain frequently in their home. When guests are present for cocktails and dinner, the daughters are expected to attend, appropriately attired. When Alicia and Melba are away from home, Christina, although she is expected to appear, seldom does. On one occasion she did show up in time for dinner, but her appearance left a great deal to be desired from her mother's perspective.

Christina was attired in faded denims and a "disreputable-looking shirt of some sort." Mrs. Malcolm called her daughter aside and suggested that she "make a hasty change." Christina refused and the atmosphere at the dinner table was drastically affected by her blatant refusal to conform. Since that incident, Christina has avoided similar confrontations by simply failing to appear at any time during the evening. Because her parents are so socially active, she spends very little time with them and frankly admits preferring things this way.

The social lives of the older girls are very active and very similar. Alicia and Melba have always been exceedingly popular and sought-after by their age-mates. Both girls date regularly, but neither has gone with any young man on a steady basis. Mrs. Malcolm has begun to pressure Alicia about "settling down," but her admonitions have gone unheeded. Alicia is very career-oriented and Melba may follow the same pattern. The mother refuses to take either girl's ambitions seriously and expects both to marry soon and "begin raising a family."

Mr. Malcolm, who seems to picture himself as a "hail fellow well met," enjoys the social flurry of his household. In social settings he is somewhat of a "ladies' man," always catering to and seeking the attention of the most attractive women in the group. Mrs. Malcolm does not seem to resent this, even though she is frequently ignored by her husband. Being so attractive herself, she is seldom without the attention of other men.

E. Interests and Recreation

Basically, the interests of the Malcolm family are social. Their participation in country club activities is limited to dinner and dance attendance. No one engages in any athletic activities. Mrs. Malcolm plays bridge at the club at least once a week. Alicia and Melba have been a part of the young crowd at club functions, but Chris has never revealed an interest in any of the club offerings.

Musical interests are reflected in several ways. As previously mentioned, Alicia is a pianist. Melba studied the violin and although reasonably talented, eventually lost interest and stopped. Christina was encouraged to take up her sister's neglected violin, but it became evident that she did not share Melba's talent. Her interest waned also and she was no longer forced into practice sessions which were uncomfortable for everyone.

Alicia and Melba have always been interested in clothing, and as a result of parental encouragement of their respective talents in the form of art lessons and unlimited wardrobes, are pursuing fashion careers.

F. Ideology

The Malcolms are politically very conservative. Mr. Malcolm's military bearing makes him appear to be very rigid and commanding in his beliefs. Conformity, dependability, and responsibility would seem to be the watch-words of the Malcolm parents. They have certain aspirations for their children and expect each to follow parental prescriptions. They resent any infringement upon or any challenge to their way of life. They view from a prejudicial perspective anyone who "doesn't think or behave respectably."

The Malcolms are politically minded and speak out vociferously pro and con, depending upon whether or not their political party is in power. The "taxation and welfare mess" is an anathema to Mr. Malcolm, who is "damn sick and tired of supporting loafers and profligates." Mrs. Malcolm unerringly holds to her husband's views.

She believes that each of her daughters have particular talents which should be encouraged and allowed to develop. She's not quite sure where Christina's abilities lie, except for academic potential, which she tends to denigrate because "girls aren't supposed to be intellectual." In her southern heritage is embedded the belief that a girl is "smart" when she knows how to cook exquisite dishes, dress beautifully, entertain graciously, and raise a lovely family. She has plans for sending Christina to a small southern finishing school rather than to a regular college. There, she is convinced, her daughter's latent social proclivities will be brought to the surface.

Mr. Malcolm leaves the rearing of his family entirely up to his wife. Disinterested in feminine activities and points of view, he contents himself with providing for his family financially and seeing to it that they have every material advantage. Beyond this, he sees no other responsibility in their behalf.

Interpretive Questions

1. Describe the Malcolm family as seen through the eyes of the two older daughters. How does Christina's perspective differ from theirs?
2. What sort of female role example is Mrs. Malcolm setting? How well does Christina fit this pattern?
3. Speculate about Christina's feelings toward her father, and toward men in general. What might her opinion of marriage be, based upon her observation of her parents?
4. Do you see any evidence of sibling rivalry in the family? How do you think Christina views herself, as compared with her sisters?
5. Mrs. Malcolm seems unimpressed by Christina's academic achievements. What effect might this have upon her future school work?
6. How do you interpret Christina's lack of conformity in clothing and social behavior and interests?
7. How do you think Christina's ideology might differ from that of her parents and sisters?
8. Evaluate Mrs. Malcolm's future plans for Christina. How successful do you feel they will be?
9. In what ways are the Malcolms "good" parents? In what ways are they failing to meet Christina's needs?

10. If you could make one suggestion to the Malcolms at this point, what would it be? How do you think they might react to your suggestion?

III. THE CASE HISTORY

A. Health and Physical Characteristics

Christina Malcolm was a small, premature baby. The birth was accomplished by caesarian section and the mother remained in the hospital for a two-week recuperative period. Weighing only five lb. at birth, the infant was placed in an incubator for precautionary reasons. Christina, in spite of her slow start, soon began to flourish. The baby was bottle-fed and once the appropriate formula was devised, began gaining weight because of her hearty appetite. After mother and child left the hospital, Christina was turned over to a live-in nurse who remained with the family for over a year.

The developmental progress of the youngest child in the Malcolm family is best described by the notations in a *Baby Book* which were recorded by the nurse. Teething, crawling, walking, and talking all took place at significant intervals and were duly noted. Mrs. Malcolm, who remained semi-indisposed for several years, gives the impression that Christina's babyhood and its landmarks were afforded only casual consideration by the other members of her family. All three of the children spent much of their time in the company of baby sitters because of their parents' social preoccupations.

Christina proceeded through childhood with few physical difficulties. The minor bouts with measles, chicken pox, etc., caused only temporary discomfort. She had tonsils and adenoids removed at the age of 10. Since that time she has had strep throat and subsequent ear infections on three separate occasions. Penicillin shots have been administered and have successfully cleared up these infections.

During preadolescence, Christina developed a tendency to gain weight which has caused her some concern, but caused her mother much more. Many one-sided battles took place at mealtimes when her mother chastised Christina for dietary indiscretions. This constant nagging caused a reaction in Christina which simply compounds the problem. Instead of earnestly trying to keep her weight down, she deliberately eats unwisely, knowing this causes her mother considerable anguish. She admittedly "tunes out" whenever her mother's harangues begin.

Menarche occurred at the age of 13. Christina had been prepared for this event by the appearance of a book entitled *THIS IS YOUR FEMALE BODY*, which was placed in her room by Mrs. Malcolm. All three daughters had been provided with this same volume. Christina glanced through the book with considerable ennui, if not derision. Most of her friends had already passed this milestone and had shared their knowledge of such matters with their slower-developing friends. One episode which was particularly informative was a slumber party held the same week that their health class had seen a movie in cartoon form which explained the menstrual cycle and was sponsored by a sanitary napkin manufacturer. Each girl was provided with a sample of the company's product. This caused considerable hilarity among the members of the youthful audience. Perhaps it should be added that the health classes in Christina's school were not coeducational. Once Christina began having her periods, she experienced a certain amount of physical discomfort on a monthly basis. She would usually miss at least one day of school because of cramps. Her mother insisted on a thorough physical examination, since neither she nor the older girls had had this problem. The family physician assured Mrs. Malcolm and her daughter that dysmenorrhea was common at Christina's age and was "nothing to worry about." Helen Malcolm was convinced that Christina's problem was "all in her mind," and decided to pay no further attention to the problem.

Christina began exhibiting a predictable pattern. Several days prior to the onset of her period she became very moody and more antagonistic than ever. Deciding that the most effective way to contend with her mercurial daughter would be to ignore her, Mrs. Malcolm did so, for the most part. The psychological gap between her and her daughter continued to widen.

B. Educational History

Christina was often referred to by her less academically inclined sisters as "the whiz kid." By the first grade, having already completed one year of nursery school and two sessions of kindergarten, Christina's unusually high intellectual potential was unmistakable. According to the results of the Stanford-Binet Intelligence Scale Christina had an I.Q. of 145! Pleased, but not overjoyed by this report, the parents filed it away in the *Baby Book*. The older sisters, who had been tested at the same stage in their educational experience, achieved average scores.

Progressing through the elementary grades with enthusiasm and a perfect academic record, Christina was allowed to skip grade six. She was, as a result of this action, plummeted into junior high school well ahead of her age-mates. According to Mrs. Malcolm, this social upheaval caused her daughter no difficulty at all. Christina, however, views the circumstances from a different perspective as indicated in the following account:

> It was like entering a new world. I had to go all the way across town, alone, on a bus full of screaming, shoving morons. I would try to sit in front, near the bus driver, as though he cared for one minute what happened to me. I'd sit there, gritting my teeth 'til we pulled up in front of the school and then I'd jump out of the bus ahead of everyone else, and hope I wouldn't get mashed in the rush. I hated everybody. The school work wasn't too hard, but I buried myself in my books so I wouldn't notice how lonely I was.

According to school accounts, Christina never complained about the social isolation. This notation, made by the junior high school counselor, is part of Christina's file:

Christina Malcolm, age 11, seventh grade, Home Room 207, cumulative average: 4.00. Physically immature, but no signs of insecurity. Makes positive comments about school experience. Has not participated in extra-curricular activities. Will suggest that Home Room teacher encourage more active participation in class and school activities.

C. Emotional Development and Adjustment

According to Mrs. Malcolm, her youngest daughter was "always well-behaved, somewhat quiet, and for the most part, pleasant to have around."

Neither parent recalls any incident where physical punishment was ever necessary. The other daughters apparently had their share of "spankings," but Christina needed only to be admonished for whatever behavior was deemed objectionable and it never occurred again.

In school, as all reports have indicated, Christina exhibited similar behavior in the classroom. Her emotional development would seem to have reflected neither "ups nor downs" until the onset of puberty when menstrual cramps drastically affected her moods.

D. Psychosexual Development and Adjustment

As we have seen in the accounts of the subject's physical development, sexual factors have had some negative effects in Christina's life. There is some disagreement regarding the possible psychosomatic causes of dysmenorrhea. Some authorities, professional as well as self-appointed, attribute menstrual cramps to a woman's psychological make-up. Having been assured by the family physician that Christina's discomfort did not arise out of any physical problem, Mrs. Malcolm became less sympathetic about her daughter's difficulties. This lack of sympathy or understanding did not contribute to a nurturing mother-daughter relationship. Another vicious circle may have become established: the less empathy on the part of the mother, the more insecurity and/or resentment experienced by the daughter, causing greater psychosomatic reaction to the menstrual period.

Overtly, at least, Christina had no other difficulties in accepting an appropriate sex-role. While her appearance was less "dainty" or feminine than that of her older sisters, she none the less exhibited primarily feminine characteristics. Although she wore the typical casual garb of a teenager around the home, her school clothing was always "in good taste." She had taken a home economics course in junior high school and developed an interest in cooking. She was not interested in sewing, or clothing design. She spent considerable time and energy in the kitchen, preparing elaborate evening meals for herself and her sisters. She has not, according to the mother, ever been interested in cooking for the entire family. When Mr. and Mrs. Malcolm were home for dinner, Christina avoided the kitchen.

E. Social Development and Adjustment

Until Christina was separated from her age-mates at the beginning of junior high school, her social adjustment was normal. She related well to the other children in her immediate environment. Her friends were numerous and divided equally between boys and girls. She was invited to many parties, which she attended with the usual enthusiasm. Urged by her mother to invite groups into her own home, Christina never complied with this wish. Once a year Mrs. Malcolm would arrange and manage an elaborate party on her daughter's birthday. She would labor over lists of names before the final guest list emerged. The event would be catered and professional entertainment was always provided. On her 12th birthday, one that Christina remembers vividly, an instructor from a local dance studio was brought in to teach the youngsters "the latest thing in dance techniques." Although Mrs. Malcolm reports that "the boys and girls had a fabulous time," Christina's memory is one of "horror."

Once Christina was no longer in school with her former peers, her social contacts with friends were limited and, over a period of time, extinguished. Things seemed to go from bad to worse as this personal account indicates:

> I found myself moving about in a vacuum which I carried along with me, separating me from everybody else. Most of the time I could get through the entire day without saying word one to anybody. I never volunteered to recite in class. When called upon to do so, I didn't even recognize my own voice when it responded.

In the ninth grade, Christina made some attempt to crack the shell which surrounded her. Attracted to a teacher, a young woman who conducted "fascinating" English classes, Christina tried approaching her with questions and comments after class. She tried asking for extra work just as an excuse to talk with her teacher. Christina relates this interlude as follows:

> I tried so hard, too hard, to get her to notice me. She was so young, so pretty, so smart, and such a terrific teacher—she was my idol. Day after day I'd hang in there after class, just dying to talk with her. Sometimes I would succeed, but I could tell she thought I was a little pest.

During the third year of high school, at the age of 16, Christina's shell began to crack, leaving her exposed and defenseless. A young man in her advanced-placement history class found her shy and defensive behavior challenging. Knowing her to be a very capable student, he began asking her to look over his work after class. Christina obliged cautiously and became more communicative. Eventually they would meet briefly before and after class. The inevitable finally occurred; Christina was asked to go out on her first date. According to her mother, events proceeded in this manner:

Christina came home from school in a sort of 'tizzy.' Instead of going directly upstairs to her room, as usual, she literally bounced into the sunroom, rudely interrupting me and my guests at our card game. She asked to speak to me privately and I told her whatever it was, it would have to wait as I was obviously occupied. She flew out of the room in a most disrespectful way. I was embarrassed and had to apologize to my guests, for Christina had not even had the courtesy to speak to them.

That night Mrs. Malcolm met her husband downtown for dinner, so Chris had no further opportunity to approach her parents until 11:30 P.M. when they returned from their social engagement. At that time, in spite of her parents' impatience, Christina told them about her friend, Charles Kramer, and how he had invited her to a movie Saturday night. The bubble burst when she was informed that the young man "was not of our religion and it would not be wise to see him socially."

Christina found her parents' pronouncement incomprehensible, especially since religion had never been an important influence in the lives of her family. All three children had been christened, and annually the family would attend en masse Easter and Christmas Eve services, but that was their total participation in church activities. The fact that Christina's new friend was Jewish had "nothing to do with anything" as far as she was concerned.

Christina tried, unsuccessfully, for two days and nights to "get through" to her parents. Feelings of frustration began building up until she "thought she would burst." The night before she knew she must tell Charles whether or not they had a date, she recalls experiencing the feeling that she was "losing control." She was alone in the house, as her parents were out for the evening and both sisters were away at school. She found herself roaming from room to room, aimlessly, as though "trying to find an escape from unbearable loneliness and helplessness." The thought of trying to phone Charles Kramer occurred to her but was rejected because "it would have been mortifying to tell him I couldn't go out."

Chris found herself in her parents' bathroom staring at her image in the mirror. She relates her experience as follows:

> There I was, staring at that frantic face and wondering whose it was. Suddenly I realized that I was that pathetic girl with tears running down her fat, red cheeks and I hated her. I reached in the medicine cabinet and took out three bottles of pills. I began swallowing these as fast as I could. All I could think of was the desire to get out of my disgusting life.

Although Christina's dosage was lethal, a combination of narcotics (codeine) and sedatives (barbiturates), she was discovered by her parents in time to get her to the hospital for treatment.

F. Interests and Recreation

Prior to Christina's suicide attempt, she had revealed few specific interests. Cooking, a self-generated but seldom recognized interest, was the only activity outside of school work which occupied her thoughts and time. During her recuperative period, Christina has displayed some artistic interests and a modicum of talent. She has been "playing around" with oil paints and has produced some interesting results. Her pictures are of abstract designs which she paints with a pallet knife rather than a brush. Her paintings have been described as "aggressive and expressive" by her art teacher. Christina has been reading a great deal about art and has often expressed a desire to go to Europe especially to visit the Jeu de Paume and the Louvre in Paris as well as museums in other cities in Europe and Great Britain.

G. Ideology

Christina Malcolm's self-concept is in a state of flux. Her narrow escape from a tragic death has had a profound effect upon this young, intelligent, and highly sensitive girl. She views life from a dramatically different perspective and desires no longer "to escape," but looks forward with obvious enthusiasm to what lies ahead. Having spent a year at a private therapeutic convalescent center, where she could reassess, explore, and contemplate the past, present and future, she has returned to her home a much healthier and more independent young lady.

Interpretive Questions

1. What attitudes toward Christina are indicated by the fact that her *Baby Book* was kept by the nurse?
2. How typical of adolescent behavior is Christina's battle with her mother over her weight? What does she gain, and what does she lose, by this behavior?
3. Describe Christina's attitudes toward sex. How effective were her mother's, and her school's, efforts in this area?
4. Discuss possible psychological reasons for Christina's attacks of dysmenorrhea. Evaluate her mother's attitude toward this problem.
5. How perceptive was her junior high school counselor? What additional remarks would you add to her report?
6. Christina has been described as "sensitive." What evidence can you cite to support this statement?
7. Why did Christina apparently make no attempt to form new social relationships in junior high and high school?
8. Most adolescents experience a "crush" on an older person. What effect did Christina's crush have upon her development? How wisely did the teacher handle this situation?

9. Evaluate the way in which the Malcolms reacted to Christina's first date.
10. Advance possible reasons for Christina's suicide attempt. Did she really want to succeed? Defend your answer.
11. What lasting psychological effects might an attempted suicide have upon an adolescent?
12. Christina seems to be making an excellent recovery. How might the situation be different if her parents had been poor?
13. How does her brush with death seem to have altered Christina's outlook on life?
14. Do you think that this experience will change the behavior of her parents in any way? Defend your answer.
15. What key steps led up to the suicide attempt? Could it have been avoided by adult intervention at any point? How?

IV. CURRENT STATUS; DIAGNOSIS AND PROGNOSIS; RECOMMENDATIONS

Christina is currently enrolled in the senior year at her former high school. She studied a little during her recuperative period, but felt no urge, nor was she encouraged to, attempt to complete her secondary education in that setting.

She is attacking her studies with her usual vigor and will graduate cum laude this coming spring. In addition to her academic work, she is taking art classes at school and private lessons at the local art academy. She was asked to help with scenery painting for the school dramatic productions, and this has stimulated an interest in stage design.

Christina mixes socially with her classmates and, while she does not date regularly, she goes out with young men frequently and seems content with her social life. She has reported to her therapist and to the school counselor that she no longer feels "lonely or helpless."

Christina continues to attend therapy sessions once a week. Her parents also confer with the psychiatrist on a monthly basis. Mr. and Mrs. Malcolm, though reluctant at first, have finally accepted some responsibility for their daughter's emotional problems. Mr. Malcolm was profoundly affected by his daughter's attempted suicide. He has since become very attentive to Christina's needs and, on the whole, has exhibited much more concern than Mrs. Malcolm, who seemed more embarrassed than disturbed by her daughter's behavior.

Christina is being encouraged to be self-accepting and less dependent upon her mother's approval. She realizes that for a long time, perhaps all of her life, she had been trying to emulate her sisters who were lucky enough to personify all of Mrs. Malcolm's expectations. Cognizant of the fact that she is a unique individual of worth and dignity in her own right, Christina is now determined to "become the individual I am capable of becoming and with whom I can live comfortably."

Mrs. Malcolm has given up, under duress, her plans to send Christina to a "finishing school." Plans are being made for Christina to join her sister Melba in New York. Melba was very helpful during Christina's convalescence, visiting frequently and writing long letters on a regular basis. She has suggested that Christina share her apartment, at least for a year. Christina plans to enroll in several academic courses as well as take more art lessons.

Getting Christina Malcolm out of her repressive home, away from her mother's criticism and the psychological atmosphere which mirrors only negative images for her, should help immeasurably. Allowed to find herself in a different and accepting environment while still in the company of a sympathetic, accepting family member should help this young woman develop the self-direction and self-confidence she will need to operate effectively as an adult.

As her confidence increases, she will become more and more inclined to exude enthusiasm for life. On one of her last encounters with her local therapist, Christina was planning on an extensive trip to Europe the following summer and looking forward to a short course at Le Cordon Bleu, the famous cooking school.

Assuming there are no drastic setbacks, Christina Malcolm should soon be able to establish a life-style satisfying enough to allow her to escape from the stigma of past failures. Chris has every potential for becoming self-actualizing and making significant worthwhile contributions as an individual.

Interpretive Questions

1. How might this prognosis be different if Christina had not had a great deal of professional help?
2. What new abilities and interests has Christina discovered as a result of this experience? Do you think they might ever have emerged under normal circumstances?
3. In what ways has her suicide attempt proved beneficial to Christina?
4. Evaluate the current behavior of Mr. and Mrs. Malcolm.
5. What do you think of Christina's future plans? How successful do you predict she will be?
6. Do you agree that it is imperative for Christina to leave home? Defend your answer.
7. What might be the reaction of her peers to Christina's attempted suicide? Was it wise for her to return to the same school?
8. Do you agree or disagree with the author's prognosis for the future? Would you like to add any recommendations of your own?
9. What areas of development does Christina still need to concentrate on?
10. Do you think that she will ever marry? What sort of wife and mother might she be, based upon her own experiences?

10

Alienation from Society

The disenchantment of young people with the society created by their elders is certainly not a new concept. The same kinds of accusations being made by adolescents and young adults today have been voiced for centuries. What may, however, make this period in history different from those which have preceded it is the fact that large numbers of young people are acting upon their convictions, instead of merely talking about them.

Criticism concerning life in America today seems to center around what many people consider to be an artificial sense of values, generated in great measure by the depression of the 30s. People who are middle-aged today were children during that period. They remember what it was like to have parents who could not find employment of any kind, and who therefore were unable to provide food and clothing, let alone toys and luxuries, for their families. They recall having to drop out of school to help the family finances, having to work full-time while going to school, and having to do without a great many things in order to survive. Most of these people, now parents themselves, vowed that their children would never have to endure similar circumstances.

However, in their zeal to insulate their children from want of any kind, parents went to the opposite extreme in many cases. As a reaction to the poverty of their earlier years, these parents began to equate success and happiness with material possessions. Assuming that their children would feel the same way, parents concentrated upon providing them with every possible material object that money could buy. Naturally, the pursuit of financial rewards sufficient to underwrite such a program left very little time to be spent in personal attention to the children. Unfortunately, the adolescent beneficiaries now disdain the values of the previous generation, unable to understand them because material deprivation has never been a part of their lives. In addition, the parents are condemned because their children received too little attention and love.

Overly materialistic values are only a part of the adolescent's complaint against today's society. The rapid pace of living, international conflict, dishonesty in public and private life, unfair treatment of minority groups, pollution, and lack of personal gratification in work are a few of the multitude of additional charges hurled by dissatisfied young people across the country. Feeling they have been failed by the government, the educational system, their parents, and the world in general, many of these young people have become completely alienated from our current society.

Adolescents and young adults cope with this alienation in various ways. While some still seek change by working within the system, others find their needs met by membership in one or more of the counterculture groups which have recently emerged. Spawned by the "beats" of a previous period, and given impetus by the more recent "hippies," these groups offer a haven for the disenchanted of every age and persuasion, and especially for the adolescent looking for an emotional home. Depending upon the particular orientation of the group, members can demonstrate their alienation from the mainstream of American society by flagrant disregard of accepted values in every facet of life from cleanliness to sexual behavior. They can participate in radical political activity, return to nature in the form of communal living, travel around the country in search of meaningful experiences, retire from life by perpetual drug use, seek the true meaning of life through a variety of religious cults, or seek out any one of the dozens of other methods of aligning themselves with kindred souls.

While only a small minority of such groups express their alienation by behavior which is actually criminal, and therefore punishable by society, the impact of these groups upon the people of our society has not yet been evaluated, and perhaps can never be accurately measured. One part of this impact has to do with the feelings, and in many instances, suffering, of parents who must watch their son or daughter disappear into the twilight land of a counterculture group. Another part of this impact concerns the reactions of those who, having joined such a group, find that instead of throwing off the constraints of a plastic society, they are merely conforming to nonconformity. Despite these obvious negative considerations, and the honest attempts of

numerous groups of all kinds to improve our present society, youthful alienation continues to be a problem of serious magnitude and implications.

A Case Study of Harrison Whitcomb III

The Whitcombs appear to be a happy family despite the problem they
are having with Harry. The marriage is a successful one in spite of the
differences in the ages and backgrounds of the parents. They seem to have
gracefully achieved racial integration. Perhaps from Harry's perspective, they
have been too successful in this respect.

I. IDENTIFICATION OF SUBJECT AND SOURCES OF INFORMATION

Name: Harrison Whitcomb III
Address: Unknown
Race: Black
Sex: Male
Age: 18
School or Occupation: None
Sources of Information:
  1.   Personal observation
  2.   Interviews with parents
  3.   Interview with sisters
  4.   Interviews with relatives
  5.   Interviews with teachers
  6.   Interviews with peers
  7.   School records
  8.   Interview with police

II. THE FAMILY HISTORY

The Whitcomb family consists of the father, Harrison Jr., the mother,
Emily, and two daughters, Janet, age 11, and Barbara, age 14. Until three
months ago the family also included a son, Harrison III (Harry), age 18.

A. Health and Physical Characteristics

Harrison Whitcomb, Jr., is a tall, imposing-looking man 58 years old,
whose gray hair is in striking contrast to his dark skin. He is a general practi-
tioner, and looks exactly like one would expect a family doctor to look. Dr.
Whitcomb is slightly overweight, which he attributes to the fact that he gave

up smoking two years ago, after suffering what his own doctor diagnosed as a mild heart attack brought on by overwork and hypertension. This heart attack, and his subsequent hospitalization, frightened Mrs. Whitcomb, who insisted that her husband cut down on his practice. However, Dr. Whitcomb spends two days a week at a free clinic in a ghetto neighborhood, and the number of patients he treats there has increased so greatly that he is presently working just as hard as he ever did. His own physician constantly advises him to slow down, and fears future, and possibly more severe, attacks of a similar nature. To the casual observer, however, this man appears to be in perfect health and possessed of boundless energy. Outside of occasional migraine headaches and sinus problems in the winter, Dr. Whitcomb has no other health problems at present.

Emily Whitcomb is a beautiful woman in her early 40s, and thus almost 15 years younger than her husband. She is tall and stately in appearance, being only slightly shorter than her husband's height of 6 ft. Her complexion is much lighter than Dr. Whitcomb's, and is set off to perfection by her long, black hair, which she usually wears gathered together at the back of her neck. Mrs. Whitcomb had polio as a child, and as a result one leg is shorter and thinner than the other. She therefore must wear special shoes, and walks with a pronounced limp.

Both of the girls have inherited their mother's light complexion, while Harry is dark like his father. All three children tend to be tall and thin. Mrs. Whitcomb, in addition to the living children, had one miscarriage, caused when she was knocked down by a group of black teenagers who were attempting to snatch her purse. Since this incident took place in the black neighborhood where the Whitcombs formerly lived, they have moved into a white neighborhood and lived there without difficulty for the past eight years.

All of the children have contracted the usual childhood illnesses. In addition, they have all had their tonsils removed. Barbara fell from her bicycle and fractured her wrist several years ago. Harry was involved in an automobile accident which will be described later. Other than this, the children seem to have been quite free from accident or illness, probably due to the careful supervision of their health by both parents.

The maternal grandparents are both deceased. Mrs. Whitcomb's father deserted the family when his two children were both quite small. Word was received some years later that he had been shot and killed by the police during the attempted robbery of a liquor store. Mrs. Whitcomb's mother worked as a cleaning woman, laundress, and other similar jobs to support her daughters. Both girls worked their way through high school with part-time jobs to supplement the family income, and took secretarial courses so that they would be able to support their mother. Shortly before Emily, the younger daughter, graduated from high school, her mother began to feel ill. An examination revealed the existence of advanced cancer, and Mrs. Roberts died six months later.

Both parental grandparents are hale and hearty, although over 80. When Dr. Whitcomb's father, who was one of the first black physicians in the city, retired some years ago, the grandparents traveled about the country for a number of years, seeing things they had always wanted to see and visiting all four of their children. Five years ago, however, Mrs. Whitcomb's sight began to fail, and they decided to enter a home in this city. Mrs. Whitcomb is now completely blind, and Dr. Whitcomb is becoming somewhat deaf.

B. Educational Status

Dr. Whitcomb has, of course, completed medical school. Emily Whitcomb is only a high-school graduate, because she had to go to work immediately in order to support herself after her mother's death. However, she keeps abreast of current events, reads widely, and has attended numerous short-term evening courses offered by a local college. Dr. Whitcomb often suggests that she should attempt to earn a college degree, but Mrs. Whitcomb only laughs and says that she is "too old." However, several of her friends have begun to attend a nearby two-year college, and Emily has secured a copy of the bulletin and registration forms.

Mrs. Whitcomb's parents both dropped out of school at the age of 16, and were married at 17. Dr. Whitcomb's mother is a college graduate, a rather unusual accomplishment, in addition to the father's medical school training. The Whitcomb family obviously places a high premium upon education, especially for black people. Dr. Whitcomb is quite adamant on this topic, because he feels that he has never been discriminated against as an adult by whites simply because he had more education than most blacks receive. Mrs. Whitcomb feels that education is the key to upward mobility for blacks, citing her own case, plus her marriage, as an example. Both parents feel strongly that education is as important for their daughters as it is for their son, and had planned on sending all three children to college. There had been some discussion about a black college for Harry, but, like everything else connected with Harry, the subject has been dropped. At any rate, the Whitcombs are well able financially to send all three children to college.

C. Economic Status

The Whitcombs would obviously be classified as an upper-class black family. They live in a large, colonial-style house in one of the best sections of the city. There are only two other black families in the neighborhood. One of these men is a judge and the other a prominent college professor and administrator. Dr. Whitcomb drives a Cadillac, which he trades in for a new one every two years. Mrs. Whitcomb has a slightly older Mercedes for her use. Harry was given an expensive foreign sports car for his birthday, which he completely demolished two days later. All of the family members dress very well, and Mrs. Whitcomb owns two fur coats. Every summer the entire family spends a month in Florida, but other shorter vacation trips are ruled out by Dr. Whitcomb's busy professional schedule.

All of the children have been given private lessons of various kinds over the years. For example, Harry showed early musical ability and took piano lessons until he entered high school, when he suddenly lost interest in the piano and in any kind of music other than what he called "soul music." Barbara and Janet have also taken piano lessons, plus ballet, art, riding, and swimming lessons at various times, starting and stopping as their interests changed.

Dr. Whitcomb did not marry until he was 35. Thus his family was spared the problem of living in reduced circumstances until he had reached his full earning capacity. Dr. Whitcomb had a well-established practice by the time he hired Emily Roberts as his receptionist-secretary, fell in love with her, and married her six months later. In addition to the income which he has earned over the years, Dr. Whitcomb received a moderate inheritance at the death of his grandfather, and a much larger amount was given to him when his parents decided to sell their house and enter a home.

All of the family has therefore lived very comfortably. Dr. Whitcomb was used to a certain amount of luxury, but Mrs. Whitcomb confesses that her present life "sometimes seems like a wonderful dream." She admits to some surprise that Dr. Whitcomb's parents did not object to his choice of a wife from a background so different from his own. According to the doctor, however, they simply said that he "was old enough to make up his own mind." The marriage seems to have worked very well despite the initial disparity in socioeconomic status.

As might be expected, Emily Whitcomb has a slight tendency to spoil the children by catering to their every whim. Dr. Whitcomb, however, usually prevents her from going overboard, except in the case of Harry, who obviously was his father's favorite. Until rather recently the children have tended to exploit the situation to their own advantage. Since Harry's departure the girls have developed more "social awareness" and have cut down on their requests for material possessions.

D. Social Status and Adjustment

The Whitcombs do not have a very extensive social life, primarily because the doctor does not have the time. Family friends are both black and white, coming primarily from the neighborhood and from among Dr. Whitcomb's professional colleagues. Emily's sister and her husband and Dr. Whitcomb's parents are guests for the major holidays. Other relatives live too far away to be frequent visitors.

The family does not maintain membership in any church. Dr. Whitcomb belongs only to medical groups. Mrs. Whitcomb has an informal group of women her age with whom she sometimes plays bridge, attends a movie, or goes shopping. Since the other members of this group are all white, Emily once said jokingly that she probably "passes for white" when out with her friends. This remark infuriated Harry, who felt that his mother should take more pride in being black, and associate more with black friends and less with white ones.

The Whitcombs appear to be well liked and respected in the neighborhood. Friends of both races speak highly of them. A few friends have expressed surprise that the Whitcombs choose to live in a social environment containing people of both races who are their socioeconomic equals, rather than limiting themselves to a black society in which they might well be the leaders. One possible explanation is that the Whitcombs feel secure in their own position, and therefore race or the admiration of less fortunate people is immaterial to them. This is one of the basic issues upon which Harry and his parents often disagreed, for Harry felt that his parents were "turning their backs on their own race" by living in a predominantly white neighborhood and mixing socially with both races.

In point of fact, however, the Whitcombs have very little social life at all. They occasionally attend a neighborhood cocktail or garden party, have another couple or two in for dinner, or attend a play or concert. Otherwise, life centers around the doctor's schedule and the activities of the children. Dr. Whitcomb has little free time, and prefers to spend that quietly at home. Perhaps because of his recent heart attack, Mrs. Whitcomb encourages him to do this, and has stopped suggesting that he ought to get more exercise and recreation. If she feels somewhat constricted by this routine, it is certainly not apparent.

E. Interests and Recreation

Dr. Whitcomb's interests center primarily around the field of medicine, his work, and his wife and children. He spends most of his spare time in reading medical journals and reports in an attempt to keep up with the latest research. He watches a few favorite television programs and is an enthusiastic pro-football fan. However, he does not participate in any sports himself, although he admits that his life is probably far too sedentary to be a good example for his patients. He tried to take up golf a few years ago, and even joined a local country club, but gave up his membership when he found that he simply could not devote enough time to practice to develop any skill.

Emily Whitcomb reads a great deal. She enjoys mystery stories, current fiction, and women's magazines. She has also read a variety of nonfiction books in connection with the university evening courses she has taken, and enjoys discussion on almost any topic. She is also interested in growing flowers, especially roses, and has what is commonly known as a "green thumb," since everything that she plants seems to thrive under her care. The Whitcombs have a part-time yardman, and he and Mrs. Whitcomb have succeeded in making their yard one of the most attractive in the neighborhood. Emily has planned and supervised most of the landscaping herself. Her recreational activities, other than those already mentioned, consist of the infrequent afternoons with her friends and social events with her husband.

Dr. Whitcomb claims that his work at the free clinic is his recreation. Mrs. Whitcomb counters that her work around the house serves as recreation for her. Although the doctor has repeatedly suggested that she get full-time help, Emily refuses to have anyone but a cleaning woman who comes three times a week to do the washing, ironing, and cleaning. She prefers to do the cooking, marketing, and similar jobs herself.

Unlike the wives of many wealthy men, Emily Whitcomb has never become interested in "charity work." At first the children fully occupied her time, and once they were all in school she became interested in her classes and garden. Although several groups, both black and white, have asked Emily to join them, she has thus far refused to become involved in any of their projects, preferring to simply send them a donation.

Like most children, Harry, Barbara, and Janet have passed through many phases in their interests. All three have usually done very well in school, and have been encouraged to spend a large portion of their time in study. Whenever one of the children would express an interest in any particular area, the Whitcombs would do everything possible to encourage the child. This partially explains the numerous lessons each has been given. However, no one area has so far held either of the girls' attention for an extended period of time. At present, Barbara seems to be interested primarily in boys, clothes, popular music, and school activities. Janet, being somewhat younger, is just discovering these areas. Neither one has ever been particularly good at sports, so that their participation has been quite limited. Janet likes to ride her bicycle, attend Girl Scout meetings, and watch television.

F. Ideology

The Whitcombs appear to be a relatively happy family, despite the problem they are having with Harry. They are rather unique in a number of ways. For example, the marriage is a successful one despite the differences in the ages and backgrounds of the parents. In addition, they handle their wealth well, even though it is a relatively new situation for Mrs. Whitcomb. Finally, they seem to have achieved an ideal state of integration, or lack of discrimination. Perhaps from Harry's point of view, they have been too successful in many ways.

The basic family philosophy seems to be that democracy can work, and that they are proof of this. The parents feel that education and hard work are the keys to success for black people, and that too many blacks simply do not want to put forth the necessary effort. This idea, in particular, is reinforced by many of the stories Dr. Whitcomb tells about the people he treats at the free clinic. Everyone in the family, except Harry, seems content with the status and position of the family, their friends, and their style of life. They are comfortable with friends of all races and religions, believe in God although they do not attend church, and seem to think of themselves as just people, rather than as black people or wealthy black people.

Interpretive Questions

1. From what little you know about Harry, how important do you think his dark skin color, like his father's, might be to him? Why?
2. What aspects of Dr. and Mrs. Whitcomb's philosophy of life might be traced to the events surrounding her miscarriage?
3. Speculate as to the possible ways in which Emily Whitcomb's life before her marriage has influenced her current behavior and thinking.
4. How accurate, in your opinion, is the Whitcomb's thinking about the value of education, especially for blacks?
5. The Whitcombs have been described as an "upper-class black family." Would you agree with this description? In what ways are they like an upper-class white family? In what ways are they different?
6. Discuss possible explanations for Dr. Whitcomb's late marriage, and his choice of Emily for his wife.
7. Evaluate the author's explanation for the Whitcombs' friendships with people of both races. Are there any other possible explanations which could be advanced?
8. Harry feels that his parents have no pride in being black, and are "turning their backs on their own race." Would you agree or disagree with Harry, and why?
9. The children have been described as somewhat spoiled. What evidence has been presented to support this contention? Would you agree with this description?
10. In what ways does the ideology of the Whitcombs differ from that of a poor black family in the ghetto? Would you agree that they have been perhaps too successful? In what ways might this statement apply?

III. THE CASE HISTORY

Harrison Whitcomb III is 5 ft. 11 in. tall and weighs 190 lb. Three months ago, after a family quarrel, he packed his things and left home. So far he has failed to communicate with his parents in any way.

A. Health and Physical Characteristics

Harry Whitcomb was a rather large baby, weighing almost 9 lb. at birth. Despite the fact that Emily Whitcomb had an easy and uneventful pregnancy with Harry, the delivery was somewhat difficult because of the baby's size. Dr. Whitcomb insisted that Emily have regular checkups throughout her pregnancy, and after the delivery was more exhausted than the mother. Emily recalls that the Whitcomb grandparents also kept a careful eye on the proceedings, and were overjoyed to learn that the first grandchild was a son, who was promptly named Harrison III in order to carry on the family name.

Harry was a healthy, happy baby who grew rapidly and learned to walk and talk at the appropriate ages. His development appears to have been normal in every way. There were no feeding problems with Harry, his mother reports, because his appetite has always been excellent. In comparison with his sisters, Harry was an extremely active child who began to assert his independence at an early age and required almost constant supervision in order to thwart some of his plans. His most daring adventure occurred at the age of three, when he was discovered trying to manipulate the controls on a car parked in front of the house. Fearing that he might be successful in future attempts, Dr. Whitcomb subsequently engaged a woman whose sole responsibility was to supervise Harry's activities.

During the first 10 years of Harry's life the Whitcombs lived in an all-black, middle-class neighborhood close to Dr. Whitcomb's office, where he was in practice with his father. There were no nursery schools in the area, so Harry had no pre-school experience until he started to kindergarten. Therefore most of his early years were spent in the company of adults, for he was rarely allowed to go out and play in the neighborhood. Emily was afraid of the traffic and Dr. Whitcomb feared that he would lead the other children into all sorts of mischief which would anger their parents.

Harry has always been large and strong for his age, inheriting the stature and bone structure of both parents. He resembles his father quite strongly in terms of facial features and personality characteristics, a fact which delights the grandparents and has certainly pleased the doctor. After beginning his formal education, Harry soon contracted most of the normal childhood diseases. He had his tonsils removed at the age of six, and miraculously suffered no broken bones until his recent automobile accident.

Harry is described by his friends as a big, handsome boy with a pleasant smile and a "way with the girls." While not considered to be one of the leaders in his graduating class, Harry was known and liked by most of his peers, according to all reports. Most of them state that Harry could have been a leader, but that during his last two years of high school he seemed to withdraw inside himself and refused to participate in school activities.

B. Educational History

Harry entered kindergarten at the age of six, attending the grade school in his neighborhood. All of his fellow students were black, as were most of the teachers. The principal, however, was white. Surprisingly enough, despite his limited experiences in social interaction, Harry adjusted to kindergarten quickly and easily. Since Barbara's arrival two years earlier, Emily had tried to devote more time to her son, and had begun to teach him how to read and write. Thus Harry did well during his early school years and brought home relatively good grades. His only major problem centered around poor grades in conduct, for the teachers found Harry a difficult child to control. Accustomed to having his own way, Harry was quite indifferent to school rules and regulations, and not above picking fights with other children on the playground. As he grew older, Harry made more and more frequent trips to the principal's office, and the Whitcombs were mortified to be called to school to discuss Harry's behavior. One day, after a particular incident in which Harry was repeatedly rude to his teacher, the principal paddled Harry. Indignant at this treatment, Harry left school and came home, expecting sympathy from his parents and angry phone calls to the school. Much to his surprise, his parents supported the actions of the principal. After that, Harry's behavior, while not perfect, improved markedly. However, Harry never forgot the incident or forgave the principal for his actions.

Harry attended this same neighborhood school through the fourth grade. The above incident occurred in March of Harry's last year there. During the following summer Mrs. Whitcomb suffered her miscarriage and the family moved to a new home in a different neighborhood. Harry's grades at his old school were above average. Many of his teachers are still there and remember Harry as a bright boy who did not take well to discipline.

The school in which Harry was enrolled for the fifth grade was quite different from the old one. There were no black teachers, and only four other black students besides the Whitcomb children. While Harry had had some contact with his parents' white friends, he had never been exposed to white children of his own age, and his parents were quite anxious about the situation. Harry again surprised everyone by adjusting easily to these new circumstances. He found himself somewhat behind the other students and had to work very hard to catch up during that first year. His behavior problems seemed to disappear, and he became quite involved in the school sports program which his previous school could not afford.

Looking back upon this period in his life, Harry analyzed his behavior in the following way:

> For the first time in my life, I began to realize that white people were in charge of the world. That white principal got me to start thinking about it, and then the next year we moved and I had to go to a white school. Man, were things different there! All the equipment and supplies money could buy—that school had everything and my old school had practically nothing. I decided that I could do anything just as well as the white kids could, and I was going to prove it to them and make my parents proud of me. That was the start of my 'Uncle Tom' period—trying to prove I could compete successfully with whites.

Harry spent two years at this school, and then moved to a junior high for the next two years. The junior high had a few more black students, but Harry continued to hang around with his white friends from grade school. In retrospect, Harry admitted that he probably enjoyed being the only black in his crowd. "That was the era of the 'token nigger,' and I guess I was it," is the way Harry put it. Harry maintained above-average grades in an academic track, and participated in football and basketball, making the varsity team in both sports. His junior high teachers remember him as "that talented black boy we had a few years ago." His counselor recalls that Harry planned "to be a doctor like his father and grandfather."

After junior high Harry went on to a large suburban high school. He continued with an academic program and stated the same vocational interests to his new counselor. He made the freshman football and basketball teams and all signs indicated smooth progress.

At the beginning of his sophomore year, Harry's high school was ordered to integrate, and a number of black students were bussed in from other areas. Despite community and student protests, integration took place. Harry suddenly found himself in the middle of an emotionally loaded situation. Some of his former friends began to avoid him because he was black, and the new black students cut him because of his white friends. The entire year was a state of turmoil for Harry, who seemed unable to identify with either group. He was involved in several fights on the basketball floor with members of both races, and the coach finally benched him for the remainder of the season. The crowning blow came when Harry asked a white girl to the big school dance, and was told that her parents would not let her go out with him.

Harry's parents were extremely distressed at this turn of events, and discussed the possibility of sending Harry to a private school for the next two years. They finally decided against this plan, on the grounds that running away from the problem would not solve it.

While the racial situation in the high school stabilized over the next two years, Harry's thinking and behavior underwent a radical change. He dropped out of the athletic program, stating that sports were the only areas where whites would accept blacks, and he wasn't going to "play Whitey's games for Whitey's school." He stopped associating with all of his former white friends, and hung around exclusively with blacks. He joined several organizations in the city which his parents disapproved of, since they were primarily composed of radical blacks. All of these activities gave Harry a new status in the eyes of the black students, and by the spring of his junior year they had accepted him as one of them. Harry began to date a number of black girls, taking them to movies and dances in the black sections of town. His grades fell off badly, and when asked about his plans by the counselor, Harry replied that he no longer wanted to go to medical school, or even to college. The counselor assessed the situation in the following report:

> Harry Whitcomb confronted an "identity crisis" of a most serious nature when this school became integrated. He started life as a black child, and then became "white" in terms of his values and aspirations after his years in a

predominantly white-oriented educational system. The influx of a number of lower-class black students brought Harry face to face with racial conflict and identity, subjects both he and his parents have not confronted squarely. For perhaps the first time in his life, Harry was subjected to prejudice, and from both races. Forced to choose sides, Harry chose to be black, and has rejected everything connected with the white world, including friends, activities, and vocational and academic aspirations.

Harry's communication with his parents has been severely limited for the past two years, since he believes that they cannot possibly understand how he feels. They have repeatedly expressed alarm over his falling grades and lack of interest in school activities. Harry graduated last spring, well toward the bottom of his class, and refused to apply to any college, even the outstanding black schools eventually suggested by his parents.

C. Emotional Development and Adjustment

Emily Whitcomb remembers Harry as a happy baby and small child who enjoyed the company of adults and being the center of attention. He did not seem to be unduly concerned about the subsequent arrival of two sisters, since his status was in no way threatened. Harry was never given to temper tantrums, fits of anger, or moodiness, probably because most of his desires were fulfilled. Harry learned at an early age that he was his father's pride and joy, and has always tried to copy his father's qualities.

As a small child Harry was probably not given enough discipline, due to the fact that his father was rarely home while Harry was awake and he was overindulged by his mother and his nurse. Thus behavior problems could almost be predicted when Harry entered school, for this sudden enforcement of rules was bound to conflict with Harry's independent nature and previous spoiling. Perhaps if spankings had been administered earlier, many of the problems could have been avoided.

Harry's parents felt that he took the drastic changes in his life with a great deal of internal stability. Both parents and grandparents have literally showered Harry with affection, and therefore feel that he should be an extremely secure young man. His present attitudes and behavior are vastly different from anything they have learned to expect from Harry, and it is probably very difficult for them to understand his feelings. As a child Harry confided almost everything to his mother, but as he has grown older he has kept more and more to himself, until now his parents feel that he is almost a stranger to them.

Until the fourth grade, Harry's emotional development appeared to be relatively normal. The incident with the white principal was traumatic on two counts: Harry was struck, and by a white man, and his parents failed to sympathize with and support him. For the first time Harry was exposed to the concept that whites have more power than blacks, and that even his parents might be helpless in this situation.

Shortly after this incident, the same basic idea was reinforced by Harry's change to a white school. Harry's response to this situation was to become as much like a white child as he could, which happened to fit in perfectly with his parents' expectations for him. Then Harry's emotional adjustment was again upset by the integration of his school. Harry has come full circle and is back to being black again, and militantly so.

While Harry seems outwardly calm, he has learned to mask his emotions so that people will not know that he is upset. Perhaps this is a result of his repeated punishment for fighting, which is certainly an overt expression of emotion, or perhaps it is a defense which he has adopted against the outside world.

D. Psychosexual Development and Adjustment

From the beginning Harry was made much of because he was a boy. Until quite recently he has always identified easily with his father because of the similarities in appearance, personality, and, of course, name. Perhaps one of Harry's present problems is that he can no longer identify with the doctor, because of their vast differences in philosophy on the subject of race.

Brought up with two sisters, Harry has always been aware of the anatomical differences between the sexes. Dr. Whitcomb was in charge of Harry's sex education, and saw to it that he was provided with appropriate information and answers to his questions. Thus Harry was probably better informed on the subject than most boys of his age, and consequently was the one his friends turned to when they wanted answers. According to Dr. Whitcomb, Harry would always come to him when there was anything he or his friends wanted to know. Neither parent can recall that Harry was ever found participating in exploratory sexual activities with his sisters or friends.

Harry seems to have been a child with a healthy attitude toward sex, fostered by adequate information and a father with whom he could readily identify. He passed through the normal childhood stages of having little girlfriends whom he would marry when he grew up, then avoiding girls at all costs for a period of time, and finally rediscovering them during adolescence. The only problem was that Harry rediscovered girls during his turbulent sophomore year in high school, and the girls he knew at that time happened to be white. For his first date, Harry asked a white girl to a school dance, and was refused because he was black. From that point on, Harry became immersed in the black world and dated only black girls. It is difficult to know whether or not Harry's parents should have attempted to prepare him for this eventuality, if indeed they ever thought that it might happen. However, neither of them ever discussed the problem of whom he should date with Harry. Perhaps Harry felt that he would be refused, and deliberately precipitated this incident so that his decision would be made easier for him.

At any rate, Harry now claims to have had intercourse with several black girls, and claims that they all say he is "great." He also says that he would never have anything to do with a white girl, even though several of them have offered, according to Harry. All of this may be true, or it may simply be Harry's means of gaining additional status among his friends.

E. Social Development and Adjustment

Harry's early social experiences were limited primarily to adults, and, of course, his sisters. Since he possesses many natural leadership qualities, Harry learned to get along with other children rather easily when he started to school. His peers admired Harry for his superior size and motor skills, as well as his daring and independent behavior. Even his frequent punishments earned him a measure of respect among his more timid peers. As a child, most of Harry's conflicts with his schoolmates arose from situations in which Harry was prevented from assuming a position of leadership. His easy solution to this problem was to pound his rival into submission.

Going from a position as one of the leaders of his black fourth-grade class to the only black in a white fifth-grade class must have created a great deal of insecurity within Harry, yet he seemed to adjust to the situation without signs of stress that were visible to his parents. According to his own statement, he felt that he had to "prove himself" to his new peers. Apparently he was able to do so successfully, for according to Mrs. Whitcomb, Harry soon had friends of both sexes, just as he had had in his old school.

In junior high and high school Harry continued to be known and liked by most of his peers, and relatively successful as a leader in school athletics. In looking back upon those years now, however, Harry reports that he always felt as though he were just being tolerated, rather than really accepted, by the other students. "They were nice to me because they felt they should be, rather than because they wanted to be," Harry claims. "I never really was one of the group, or had any really close friends. I always had to keep my guard up and watch what I said and did so I wouldn't seem 'colored'—I couldn't ever be myself," he adds.

According to Harry, all of this has now changed. "I finally feel as though I belong. I can be myself with the brothers and sisters, and be accepted for just being me—Harry—not the token black in the class or Dr. Whitcomb's son. It feels great!"

For his final two years in high school, Harry devoted most of his time and effort to socialization with his black friends. He dated heavily on the weekends and spent most of his free time hanging around with "the brothers" in various sections of town. His parents became more and concerned about the situation, and tried to talk with Harry about it. Every discussion ended in a violent argument, with Harry either storming out of the house or locking himself in his room.

His parents were concerned about Harry's falling grades, his sudden change of vocational plans, his new friends of questionable reputation and background, and his emphasis upon his blackness. For his part, Harry accused his parents of selling out to the white world, pretending to themselves that they were really white inside, turning their backs on their own race, and having no pride in being black. He told his father that he was "trying to help the poor niggers out" by working at the free clinic, and that if the doctor were really concerned about the brothers and sisters, he would give up his private practice and work at the clinic full-time. Harry informed his mother that she probably enjoyed "passing for white" when out with her white friends, and that she should "drop" them. He argued that she should certainly understand what it was like to be poor and black, and that if she had been white, she probably never would have gotten polio. Therefore she should persuade the doctor to sell the house and go back and live "among their own kind," and give some of their money to organizations set up to help poor black families. Harry laughed at the idea that education would help improve the life of blacks, because they still could not get jobs even if they had proper education.

In short, Harry claimed that the only way blacks were ever going to get ahead was by banding together against whites. While not yet advocating violence, Harry felt that the Black Panthers "just might have the right idea." His grandparents tried talking to Harry, and were branded as "the original Uncle Toms who got this family mixed up in the first place." They quickly washed their hands of Harry, saying they "just can't understand what has gotten into the boy."

The rift between Harry and his parents grew wider and wider during his last year in high school. Harry began discussing radical black philosophy with his sisters, and was forbidden to talk with them on the subject. He insulted white friends who had come to dinner with his parents, and answered the telephone in Black dialect. He even tried to pick fights with his sisters' white girlfriends and neighbors' children.

In a final attempt to reach Harry, his parents allowed him to invite all his friends to the house for a big party on his 18th birthday. Harry's present from the family was an expensive new foreign sports car. Unfortunately, the party turned out to be a disaster. Harry's friends brought liquor and pot, got into fights and broke some of the furniture, and created so much noise that the neighbors called the police. After they had cautioned the group and left, Dr. Whitcomb, livid with anger and embarrassment, ordered everyone out of the house. Several of the boys made insulting remarks to the doctor, and he smacked one of them in the mouth. At this, Harry and three other boys jumped in the new car and sped off. Several hours later, the police called the Whitcombs to report that Harry had wrecked the car and was in a local hospital.

Fortunately, none of the boys was seriously injured. Harry had sustained a broken leg and some fractured ribs, and the others had similar injuries. Since no other car was involved, the police did not press charges against Harry, but his license was suspended. Harry spent several weeks in the hospital, and eight more with his leg in a cast. He showed no remorse at what had happened, saying that his father "could afford 10 cars like that one and never miss the money." In fact, his greatest concern was that "those honky cops" took away his driver's license.

After Harry had recovered from the accident, his father demanded that he get a job and pay for the car. Harry replied that his father had plenty of money and since he would not spend it for the brothers and sisters, Harry was going to waste as much of it as he could. When asked if he had wrecked the car deliberately, Harry refused to reply. As far as Dr. Whitcomb was concerned, that was the last straw, and he ordered Harry out of the house, telling him to go and live with his friends, and let them support him. Harry promptly went to his room, packed his things, and, despite his mother's pleading, left the house. His parents have heard nothing from him for the last three months.

While both of them try hard to conceal it, Harry's behavior has broken his parents' hearts. They have often discussed alternative courses of action that they should have taken, or things said and done that they wish back. The doctor is especially upset with himself for ordering Harry to get out. Perhaps, however, an open break of this sort was inevitable, and Harry really needs to be out on his own, living according to the principles which he feels are right for black people.

F. Interests and Recreation

As a child, Harry liked active sports and games, bicycle riding, and collecting toy cars and trucks. While he was never terribly fond of reading, he liked to look at the colored illustrations and diagrams in Dr. Whitcomb's medical books. The family interpreted this as a sign that Harry was going to be a doctor, but it is more likely that he simply was attracted by the colors. As he grew older, Harry developed an interest in music and took piano lessons for seven years. During his sophomore year in high school, Harry suddenly decided that playing the piano merely reinforced the concept that "all blacks have rhythm," and gave it up. At the same time he also dropped out of sports and all of his other school activities. At present he has no time for sports or music, even if he wanted to participate in these activities.

Currently, Harry's interests and recreation all center around the group with which he is living. Approximately 12 black men and women of Harry's age have rented an old house in the inner city and have set up a communal living arrangement. There are several married couples, and a few children, but most group members are single. They are all actively working to improve conditions for blacks living in the ghetto. Some of their projects include a day-care center for working mothers, helping blacks register to vote and campaigning for black politicians, contacting drug addicts and convincing them to seek help, and other similar activities. When money gets low, some of the members will take temporary jobs, and from time to time they are given money by various black groups. The situation is quite different from the luxury Harry is used to, yet he claims that he has never been happier.

In the little free time that Harry has at his disposal, he reads black literature. Several weeks ago he was arrested in a demonstration in a white-owned grocery store in the ghetto. Blacks felt that prices in the store were too high and carried out a protest demonstration to call public attention to the problem. When they refused to leave the store, they were arrested. During this whole process Harry came in contact with some extremely radical blacks who are now supplying Harry with literature advocating their point of view. So far, Harry still seems committed to relatively peaceful means of change, but the radical element is keeping in touch with him. Because of his father, Harry would be quite a "catch" for them.

G. Ideology

Harry Whitcomb is a young man who comes from a family that has given him every possible material advantage. Although he is black, Harry has really encountered very little discrimination in his contacts with white people. In fact, until quite recently Harry appeared to be perfectly content to live in a predominantly white world, both at school and at home. The combination of events previously described apparently served to make Harry suddenly conscious of his black heritage and to arouse some slumbering resentments against whites from his earlier years. Harry was, in effect, forced to choose between the races, and probably made the only real choice available to him. Having chosen to be black, Harry has rebelled against society in general and against his parents' philosophy in particular. He has decided to be militantly black and is angry about a number of things: the position of most black people in our society, the way that his parents have chosen to behave in order to get along in this society, the fact that society has probably forced them to behave in this way, their obvious success under these conditions, and the idea that he went along with this concept for so many years. Harry probably feels quite guilty about his own previous behavior and affluence, for this makes him a traitor to his people in his own mind. At the same time, he probably feels some guilt about rejecting the values of his parents and turning his back upon everything they stand for. Harry left home in order to do what he thought should be done to change society. Perhaps, in time, he can also reconcile the two conflicting philosophies which exist within himself, and come to terms with his parents, and with society.

Interpretive Questions

1. What factors made it easy for Harry to identify with his father as a child? In what ways might this identification now be creating conflict within Harry?
2. Advance some possible reasons for Harry's behavioral problems at school. Why was physical punishment so effective? Might there have been a better way to handle the problem?
3. Evaluate Harry's remarks about his feelings toward the white school. Do

you think that is the way he really felt at the time? If not, what might his real feelings have been?

4. Describe the kinds of thoughts and feelings that Harry might have had during the integration of his high school. Why did he fight with members of both races?
5. What was Harry's reaction to being refused a date by the white girl? Do you think that he deliberately set this up as a test situation?
6. What purposes were served, in Harry's mind, by dropping out of athletics and other school activities and by giving up the piano?
7. Harry is described by his counselor as undergoing an "identity crisis" during his high school years. Would you agree or disagree, and why?
8. Have Harry's parents failed to confront the issue of race? Cite evidence to support your answer.
9. Why has Harry learned to mask his emotions? Do most adolescents tend toward this kind of behavior? If so, why?
10. From what you know of Harry, do you believe that he has had intercourse with several black girls? What purposes do his sexually oriented statements serve in his own mind, and in the eyes of his friends?
11. What aspects of Harry's recent behavior might be defined as attempts to punish his parents? What might he be trying to punish them for?
12. How thoroughly is Harry alienated from society? In your opinion, will his alienation increase or decrease as time passes?
13. Describe the feelings which Harry's parents must be experiencing right now. What effects might Harry's behavior be having upon his two younger sisters?
14. How mature is Harry at the present time? Defend your answer.
15. Do you think that Harry really is happier in his present situation than he has ever been before? Do you agree that he is being completely accepted for himself for the first time in his life? Defend your answer.
16. Did Harry make the only real choice available to him when he chose the black world? Cite evidence to support your answer.

IV. CURRENT STATUS; DIAGNOSIS AND PROGNOSIS; RECOMMENDATIONS

Like so many of today's adolescents, Harrison Whitcomb III has rejected the values of his parents and of society as a whole. He has decided that blacks can best improve conditions for themselves by banding together, militantly if necessary, against whites. Harry no longer believes that equality can be achieved by emphasizing education and forced integration, but places his faith in black pride and black power. In order to put his principles into action, Harry has refused to continue with his formal education, thus breaking the tradition established by his father and grandfather, and has gone to live in the ghetto with a group of young blacks with similar ideas. In effect, he has turned his back upon everything his parents stand for and is striking out on his own.

While Harry's intentions are undoubtedly good, it will be difficult for him to adjust to a life-style so completely different from his former one. Although he says now that he is completely happy, after the newness and enthusiasm wear off, Harry may find that he is not so happy after all. The kind of work he proposes to undertake requires a great deal of patience and restraint, neither of which is characteristic of Harry. In addition, his own socioeconomic background will not contribute substantially to his understanding of life in the ghetto.

Harry may well stick to his present activities for a year or two. At that point, unless he sees considerable progress being made, Harry will either join a radical black group and possibly become involved in illegal activities, or he will give up the fight and reconcile with his parents. In the latter event, Harry probably will attend college and medical school, and become a doctor according to his family's wishes. In either case, Harry is likely to experience some kind of guilt for the rest of his life—guilt which is really not of his own making. There seems to be no logical way in which he can fulfill all of the expectations which have been imposed upon him by his race, his family, and his own social conscience.

Interpretive Questions

1. What kinds of values has Harry decided to reject? Which ones are typical of many adolescents, and which are unique to Harry?
2. How powerful are the forces of black pride and black power in changing society, in your opinion? Are they more effective than anything which has been tried previously?
3. Was Harry's open break with his parents inevitable, as the author of this case study seems to think? Defend your answer.
4. Which of the two probable courses of future action described by the author do you think Harry will take, and why? Can you suggest any other possible alternatives?
5. Do you agree that, whatever he does, Harry will probably suffer from guilt feelings for the rest of his life? Is there any way in which he could get rid of this guilt?
6. Describe Harry's life as you see it 10 years from now. Will any of his problems solve themselves with the passage of time?
7. Which, if any, of Harry's problems could have been prevented if they had been spotted early enough? How could they have been avoided?
8. Is there anything that could be done right now to help Harry, and by whom?
9. If you were a friend of the Whitcombs, what advice would you give to them?
10. If you were a friend of Harry's, what advice would you give to him?

11

Vocational Choice

One of the most complex series of decisions facing adolescents today concerns the area of vocational choice and training. A few generations ago, this phase of life was fairly simple for most teenagers. Boys were expected to follow in the vocational footsteps of their fathers and grandfathers, while girls could look forward to adult lives as wives and mothers. It was only when a boy preferred to pursue an occupation different from that of his father, or a girl failed to find a husband, that problems arose.

The next general trend in occupational thinking, closely tied to the advent of prolonged schooling described in Chapter 7, was that the son should occupy a higher rung on the vocational ladder than that occupied by his father. Since social status, friendships, residence, and a host of other factors are strongly influenced by occupation, this was an easy way of achieving upward mobility for the son. The daughter, however, was still compelled to find herself a husband. But assisted by additional schooling and the labor shortages created by two world wars, women soon began to assert their vocational independence, and were accepted, with some reservations which still exist today, into the world of work.

Occupational preparation, meanwhile, was gradually becoming more and more complex. As a result of advances in science and technology, the need for unskilled labor practically disappeared. People without high school diplomas could not find jobs. Whole new vocational areas requiring certain specific kinds of training suddenly appeared. The need for more education and training continued to grow. Then, quite suddenly, the United States found itself with a large proportion of overtrained, overeducated people in the work force—people who could not find jobs despite extensive preparation.

At present, we seem to be experiencing a revival of interest in vocations which do not require extensive technical or educational backgrounds. Young people appear to be rebelling against long years of schooling in preparation for a specific vocation. There is a resurgence of interest in jobs involving manual labor and almost-forgotten skills and crafts, in the hope that such occupations will bring with them a return to a simpler, more leisurely way of life, in direct contrast to the typical harried life-style of today. For many adolescents, the choice of an occupation will be a direct reflection of the kind of life they hope to lead as adults, and perhaps in some cases, a form of protest about conditions in this country as they view them.

Another factor influencing vocational choice today is the relatively new concept that one need not prepare for a specific job and plan to spend all of his working life in that same job. This new vocational approach is due, in part, to the fact that advances in technology make some jobs obsolete rather rapidly, and the people in those positions must then acquire new skills in order to remain employed. Perhaps through observation of this type of change, people have begun to think differently about their careers, and to anticipate several different occupations during their working lives. One large group of such people is the number of wives and mothers who return to school to pursue a second career after their children are grown.

One final trend in vocational preparation today is the fact that women are now being encouraged to prepare for careers in areas which have traditionally been open only to men. New civil rights legislation and the women's liberation movement have combined to encourage adolescent females to broaden their vocational outlooks and consider a wider range of occupational choices. While this new freedom is inappropriate in the eyes of some parents, it certainly will have a great impact on the lives of many teenage girls.

Until a new philosophy regarding prolonged schooling and extensive vocational training is developed, however, adolescents will still face several major problems in deciding upon an occupation. The basic problem is, of course, to match the skills and interests of the individual with the appropriate job. High school counselors can be very useful in helping adolescents along these lines, despite the increasing complexities of the world of work. A second problem to be overcome is the fact that most young people today are expected to begin aiming toward a specific career in junior high school, or at the very latest, at the beginning of their freshman year in high school. Very few teenagers are prepared to make these decisions at this age, despite relatively recent efforts to spend more time in studying various occupations in the elementary grades. However, because of the tracking system used in most schools, some sort of general vocational decision must be made at these levels, and should a student change his plans at a later date, he will encounter numerous difficulties in switching from one track to another. It therefore seems obvious that adolescents need either to be better prepared to make vocational choices, or allowed more freedom to change vocational plans as they move through the grades.

The choice of a vocation is one of the most important decisions facing an adolescent, and the young person who has always known what he wants to be, and therefore can proceed in a straight line toward his goal, is the exception rather than the rule. Most adolescents will change their vocational plans several times before they finally make up their minds. Some will seem unable to select any career at all, and just drift along from day to day, while others will choose occupations for which they have no aptitude. Some will have careers picked out for them by their parents, and others will deliberately select occupations which incur parental disapproval. Counselors, teachers, and parents who attempt to help adolescents make vocational decisions face a difficult and challenging task.

A Case Study of Betty Lou Dixon

Betty Lou, while not a victim of an inferiority complex in the classic sense, is rather sensitive about her family background and socioeconomic status. At the university she is being exposed to people from homes where they were given every possible material advantage and she has begun to be keenly aware of her own lack of cultural exposure, sophistication and general polish. In spite of this, Betty Lou is a young woman obsessed with the idea of making something of herself through education. Anything which does not make a direct contribution toward this achievement is unimportant to her right now.

I. IDENTIFICATION OF SUBJECT AND SOURCES OF INFORMATION

Name: Betty Lou Dixon
Address: 132 Central Avenue, Apt. 14
Race: Caucasian
Sex: Female
Age: 19
School or Occupation: State University, freshman and waitress

Sources of Information:
1. Interviews with subject
2. Interviews with parents
3. Interviews with siblings
4. Interview with high school counselor
5. High school records and test scores
6. Interviews with high school and college teachers
7. Interview with college advisor
8. Interviews with subject's peers
9. Personal observation

II. THE FAMILY HISTORY

Betty Lou is one of the eight living children of Billy Joe and Matilda Dixon. Two other children died in infancy, and a third was hit by a car and killed.

A. Health and Physical Characteristics

The Dixon family consists of the father, Billy Joe Dixon, age 44, the mother, Mattie Dixon, age 42, and the three children who still live at home, Luke, age 20, Matt, age 17, and Jess, age 14. Roy, age 26, Willie, age 25, Jenny Mae, age 23, and Laurie Ann, age 22, have all married and established homes of their own. The subject of this case study, Betty Lou, age 19, presently lives with Jenny Mae rather than with her parents.

Mr. Dixon is a short, thin man with a grizzled appearance which makes him look much older than his actual age. His health is rather poor, but he refuses to see a doctor, preferring to dose himself with home remedies and patent medicines. As a result he has missed quite a few days of work in the past five years, and only his long union membership has kept him from being fired. He usually has a racking cough, which may be due to almost constant cigarette smoking, plus a variety of other ailments ranging from chronic indigestion to chest pains. He also suffers from frequent toothaches, and usually gets relief only by having the tooth pulled, which at that point is so decayed that it cannot be saved. He already has false teeth for the upper jaw, and since there are only six teeth left in the bottom jaw, he will soon have to replace these as well. Meanwhile, eating has become rather difficult, which may account for his chronic indigestion.

Mr. Dixon distrusts doctors because they failed to save the lives of his two children who died in infancy. In all fairness, however, neither baby was taken to a doctor until they were so seriously ill that they were beyond medical help. One had a congenital heart defect and the other contracted pneumonia. Billy Joe is also bitter about the son who was struck by a car, although he was dead on arrival at the hospital and probably was killed instantly. It never occurs to him that part of the blame for these three deaths might rest upon his own shoulders, so he refuses to see a doctor himself or to let any family members over whom he still has control consult one.

Billy Joe Dixon walks with a peculiar gait because both of his legs are rather bowed. Since he has not spent much time on horseback, this is probably due to a case of rickets in childhood. He has also lost three fingers from his left hand as a result of an accident at work. Mr. Dixon's most outstanding facial characteristics are a pair of watery pale-blue eyes and a very prominent, beak-like nose, a feature which most of his children have inherited.

Matilda Dixon is also short and thin, with a pale, washed-out look and mild brown eyes which seem to bear mute witness to a great deal of patient suffering. Her habitual expression of total resignation to whatever may happen next, coupled with her completely gray hair, makes her look almost 20 years older than her actual age. If Mrs. Dixon has any physical complaints, she never mentions them. However, she frequently massages the fingers of both hands as though troubled by arthritis, and her feet tend to swell when she is on them for long periods of time.

Compared to her husband, Mattie Dixon appears to be a rather colorless, self-effacing person. At present, there is nothing remarkable about her physical appearance, although both she and her husband say that she was once a very pretty girl. Mrs. Dixon got a complete set of false teeth several years ago, but they are poorly fitted and cause her some discomfort. For this reason she usually wears them only when absolutely necessary, and therefore her conversation is sometimes difficult to understand.

Roy, the oldest son, is a career Army man. At present, he is living on a base out west with his wife, who is Japanese, and their two small sons. Judging from his pictures, he resembles his father very much. However, since his parents disapprove of his marriage, Roy and his family have never come to visit the Dixons. The second son, Willie, does not look like either parent, for he is a tall, husky man with piercing blue eyes. Willie is the family "success" and the apple of his father's eye, because he is a construction worker and apparently makes a very good salary. He married the sister of one of his fellow workers, and now lives in a small house of his own in this city. Willie also has two children, and his wife is expecting a third.

The next child, Jenny Mae, looks very much like her mother, except that she is somewhat taller. She is married and has one daughter, but is separated from her husband. She lives in another city and Betty Lou is presently staying with her. Laurie Ann, the fourth child, is also married and has one son. She looks like a female version of her father, and has exactly the same nose. She and the baby are living with her husband's parents, while her husband serves a prison sentence for armed robbery.

Luke, age 20, has just come home from the Army. He is short, thin, and wiry like his father and is already beginning to develop the same sort of disposition. Although he was trained to be a mechanic in the service, he has not made any attempt to find a job, but prefers to sleep most of the day and spend the night with his old buddies. When pressed about his future plans, he gets angry and claims that he needs a rest after everything that he has been through. However, Luke was never in combat and spent his entire military service in the United States. He was promoted twice and then demoted for disciplinary reasons, and his mother is afraid that he is already involved in criminal activities with his friends. She has no idea that Luke is obviously using drugs of some sort.

The two remaining boys are Matt, 17, and Jess, 14. Both resemble their father in appearance, being shorter and thinner than most boys their age, and both have the Dixon nose. Matt apparently has very bad eyesight, but does not wear glasses. He dropped out of school last year, having only completed the eighth grade because he failed so many times, and now works in a supermarket. Jess is now in the seventh grade, having also failed several times, and has already been taken to Juvenile Court twice, along with other members of the gang to which he belongs. Mr. and Mrs. Dixon have been warned that the next offense will result in his being sent to the Juvenile Detention Home, and this could happen at any time, for Jess and his gang are now actively involved in shoplifting.

The Dixon children appear to have had more than their share of illnesses and injuries. This may have been due to poor nutrition, the fact that there were so many of them living together in five rooms, or poor care and attention from the parents. Mrs. Dixon said that she could not begin to remember the illnesses and accidents that each child had, but remarked that "one of 'em most always seemed to have somethin' wrong." In case of sickness, home remedies were applied or the illness was simply allowed to run its course. In case of accident, the child was taken to the neighborhood clinic for attention. Fortunately, none of the family has been injured since Mr. Dixon issued his edict against doctors. Visits to the local dental clinic were also made only on an emergency basis for the Dixon children, hence most of them have problems with their teeth. Roy and Luke were taken care of in the service, and Willie and Betty Lou have taken it upon themselves to visit the dentist regularly. The others, like their parents, simply wait until a tooth is beyond repair and then have it pulled.

B. Educational Status

Mr. and Mrs. Dixon are both from the same small mountain community in a southern state. Their parents and grandparents were farmers who barely scratched out a living from the land. Formal education was not an important part of life in this area, nor were the laws about compulsory attendance very strictly enforced. Although there was a community school in the area, the education of both Dixons was quite sketchy. If the children were needed to help with the work at home, they simply stopped going to school. Billy Joe dropped out at the age of 14, having completed approximately the sixth grade. Mattie finished the eighth grade, and at the age of 15 married Billy Joe, who was then 17. While this seems like remarkably little education, only one of the four grandparents could read and write.

Education is of absolutely no importance in the Dixon family. Every one of the children, with the exception of Betty Lou, has dropped out of high school as soon as possible. They have been brought up with the idea that it is important to get a job and start making money as soon as possible. The Dixons feel that education is especially useless for a girl, since she is not going to work but simply get married and have children. Thus there was a constant battle in the Dixon household for the two years during which Betty Lou completed high school, despite the fact that she was practically a straight "A" student and graduated third in a class of 600. To avoid further arguments with her parents over this issue, Betty Lou moved in with her sister when she started college. Although Mr. and Mrs. Dixon do not approve, she plans to become a doctor.

Both Roy and Willie were average students, but were forced to quit school in order to help support the family. Roy subsequently completed high school courses in the Army, and Willie finished in night school after he was married. The other children have all been exceptionally poor students, failing at least one grade along the way. Their lack of success has probably been due primarily to lack of interest, effort, and parental encouragement rather than to lack of ability, but Betty Lou is obviously the most intelligent of the Dixon children.

C. Economic Status

Shortly after the Dixons were married, Billy Joe's cousin moved to a northern city and got a job in a factory. The letters which he wrote to the folks back home were so glowing that Billy Joe became more and more dissatisfied with life on his parents' farm, where he and Mattie were living, and decided to pack up and move to the same city. He and Mattie hitchhiked all the way to the city, carrying their belongings in two cardboard suitcases. The cousin was able to get Billy Joe a job in the same factory where he was employed, and the Dixons moved into a three-room apartment which at that time seemed to them to be the height of luxury.

However, their satisfaction with the city was relatively short-lived, for the Dixon babies began to arrive with alarming regularity, and within a few years they found that Billy Joe's salary was not always sufficient to cover their expenses. They were forced to move to a larger apartment in a poorer section of town. Billy Joe began to drift from one job to another in the hope of making more money, but his lack of education and training kept him tied to factory work. He finally landed a job in an automobile assembly plant, where he has worked for the past 15 years. He has never been promoted.

Meanwhile, the neighborhood in which the Dixons live has changed drastically. Most of the buildings, including their own, are badly in need of paint and repair. The owners are unwilling to do much in the way of mainte-nance, and so the families who could afford to do so have moved away. The remaining people comprise some of the worst elements in the city, and crime and drugs are rampant in the area. While the population seems equally composed of blacks and whites, Mr. and Mrs. Dixon blame present condi-tions on "all them niggers livin' here." The Dixons are equally prejudiced against members of other racial and religious minority groups. They wish the government would "do something" about these groups, but they have never voted or made any attempt to change things themselves.

With so many of the children grown up, the economic picture is some-what brighter for Billy Joe and Mattie, and the two oldest boys have begun to send money home every month. The Dixons sometimes talk about moving to another apartment, but seem unable to overcome inertia and take any positive action. They have very little money saved up, and recently Billy Joe has begun to drink more and more heavily, so it seems unlikely that they will ever move unless the building is condemned and they are forced out.

The Dixons have no car, so Billy Joe rides the bus to work. Their apart-ment consists of five tiny rooms plus a bath. The furniture is old and worn, clearly showing the use of a number of children. Mrs. Dixon tries to keep things clean, but is defeated by city dirt and the carelessness of her husband and sons. She usually spends a great deal of time watching the family's prize possession, a large color television set, which is being paid for on an install-ment plan. She does the washing at a local laundromat, and cooks over an ancient gas stove. The plumbing is equally old and uncertain, and the hot water frequently runs out. The Dixons cope with this by not washing very often. Every winter they hope that the old furnace in the building will last for another year. Mr. Dixon has been heard to say that they probably made a mistake in coming to the city, but they just have to make the best of it. He also claims that if his wife had not had so many children, they would be a lot better off. Even with the extra money from Roy and Willie, the Dixons just barely make ends meet, and there have been times when there was not enough food and the family lived on one meal a day.

D. Social Status and Adjustment

The Dixons appear to be a lower-class white family. While they once had friends in the neighborhood, all of those families have moved away. Since the Dixons have no car, it is almost impossible for them to visit Willie or Billy Joe's cousin, and in fact, they are never invited to do so. Willie reports that Mr. and Mrs. Dixon were invited for one Thanksgiving dinner at his house, and after that his wife absolutely refused to have them again because of their appearance and manners. Willie occasionally drops in by himself to see his parents, and Laurie Ann sometimes brings the baby for a visit. The other grown children, including Betty Lou, do not communicate at all with their parents.

In effect, Mrs. Dixon has very little contact with anyone except the other members of the family. Luke, Matt, and Jess all have their own friends with whom they spend most of their time. All of the boys seem to be followers rather than leaders in their respective groups, and Luke and Matt may well be headed for prison because of their criminal activities. Laurie Ann's husband is already in jail. However, in the Dixon's neighborhood this would not be a social handicap if the Dixons wanted to have friends, but they prefer to stay by themselves. Over the years, Billy Joe has made friends with some of the men at work, mostly men with the same kind of background as his own. Almost every day after work a group of these men stop at a bar near the plant to have several beers and talk. Billy Joe is always a part of the group, and he often does not come home until several hours later. Usually he is drunk by the time he arrives, and this appears to be the extent of his social life. Billy Joe is certainly not a leader among his friends at the plant, many of whom just tolerate him rather than really like him. Some of the men refer to him as "that funny old hillbilly," a description that would probably provoke a fight if Billy Joe ever heard it. Mr. Dixon used to have one friend in the neighborhood, a man who came from a small southern town much like the Dixon's. Since this man lived alone, he would spend many evenings with Billy Joe and Mattie, drinking beer which he brought and talking about old times. Unfortunately, he died about two years ago.

While the younger children appear to be content with the status quo, Roy, Willie, and Jenny Mae have made attempts to improve their social positions. Roy is a sergeant in the Army, and Willie has built his own home in a middle-class neighborhood. Jenny Mae has worked as a waitress since she and her husband separated, and plans to go to secretarial school as soon as her daughter is old enough to take care of herself. Betty Lou, in hoping to become a doctor, is the most ambitious of the children.

E. Interests and Recreation

Mattie Dixon's interests center around her home and family. She has no hobbies, so her only recreation consists of watching television and listening to the conversation of her husband and sons. The occasional visits of Willie and Laurie Ann are the highpoints of her life. Billy Joe's interests center around his physical ailments, which he describes in great detail, his work and the men there, watching sporting events on television, and drinking beer.

The family does not attend church or belong to any clubs. Neither parent seems particularly interested in the activities of the three boys still at home, unless one of them is involved in some sort of trouble or stays out all night. The school principal has repeatedly asked them to come for a conference about Jess, but has gotten no response. Mrs. Dixon's philosophy is that if Jess is a problem at school, it is up to the school to deal with him. The parents used to be quite strict with the children, and administered physical punishment regularly, but with Matt and Jess they seem to have given up. Consequently, the boys simply go their own ways and lead their own lives, joining their parents only to eat and sleep. Each boy seems to have his own money. Matt works for his, but where Luke and Jess get theirs remains unknown and unquestioned by their parents.

F. Ideology

One might almost say that Billy Joe and Mattie Dixon have given up on life. They came to the city from a rural, poverty-stricken area expecting to find that conditions were much better than the ones they had left. Instead, because of poor education and a large family, they were forced to lead almost the same kind of life they would have had back home. They must feel as though there is little hope of things ever improving for them, despite the fact that most of their children are grown up, because they have absolutely nothing to look forward to except a lonely old age with very little money. The Dixons are very proud, and would never accept charity or welfare. When asked what he planned to do at retirement, Billy Joe replied, "Ain't thought about it—won't live that long!"

Like many poor people, the Dixons started out by working hard. As circumstances continued to conspire against them, they gradually lost their drive and became content with whatever momentary pleasures life offered. They emphasized making money to their children, not realizing that it is very difficult in today's world to make money without having at least a high school education. Fortunately, some of the children learned this for themselves and obtained their diploma, but in so doing, they cut themselves off socially from their parents. Some of the other children appear to have opted for illegal means of making money. The Dixons' acceptance of this is typical of their current attitude, as though everything were in the hands of fate and they had absolutely no control over their own lives or the lives of their children. Although both parents have a strong religious background, they seem to have lost their faith in God as well. Life has become a matter of merely existing from day to day.

Interpretive Questions

1. What kinds of problems almost always arise when there are a large number of children in a family? Which problems are especially typical of poor families?
2. How might the factors mentioned in answering the above question influence the personality of the child as he grows into adolescence? Which of these problems are most acute as far as a teenager is concerned?
3. Contrast the personalities of Billy Joe and Mattie Dixon. What are the strengths and weaknesses of each? How successful is each of them as a parent?
4. Compare the personalities of Roy and Willie with those of Luke and Jess.

What might account for the differences? Do you agree with the author that the Dixons have simply given up on the last two boys?

5. How might the Dixons have reacted to the news that Laurie Ann's husband was a criminal? How do you think they would feel if one of their own sons were arrested?

6. Discuss Mr. and Mrs. Dixon's attitudes about education. Are these attitudes typical of people at this socioeconomic level? If so, is it possible to change their attitudes, and what would be the best way to do this?

7. Describe life in the Dixon household as seen through the eyes of Betty Lou. Compare her impressions with those of Jess.

8. Describe Billy Joe's social contacts. How satisfying do you think they are? What explanations can you offer for his drinking?

9. Why have some of the children attempted to improve their social status, while the others have not? Is this dichotomy due in any way to the attitudes or behavior of the parents, or is it simply a matter of individual differences? Defend your answer.

10. Discuss the Dixons' attitude toward the requests from the principal for a conference concerning Jess. How typical of lower-class parents is it?

11. What factors operating in the lives of Luke and Jess might well be pushing them into criminal activities? How much of the blame rests with the parents?

12. Would you agree with the author that the Dixons have "given up on life"? Why, or why not?

III. THE CASE HISTORY

A. Health and Physical Characteristics

Like all of the other Dixon children, Betty Lou was born at home with the help of a doctor from the neighborhood clinic when actual labor began. She was a relatively small baby, weighing a little over 5 lb. at birth. Since Betty Lou was the sixth child, Mattie Dixon has trouble in remembering details about the baby's early years. However, she seems to have exhibited early signs of intelligence, because Mrs. Dixon recalls that she was "always gettin' into things and takin' 'em apart." Betty Lou seems to have learned to walk and talk at an early age, or at least much earlier than her siblings did, according to her mother. Questioned about the age of toilet training, Mrs. Dixon could not recall the exact time, but admitted that she did not spend a great deal of effort on this project and Betty Lou "pretty much trained herself."

For two years Betty Lou was the youngest child in the family, but it is difficult to believe that she was ever spoiled in any way. Being the smallest, she usually got the least of whatever was being passed out among the children. However, her siblings were more generous about sharing their sicknesses, for whenever any of the Dixon children caught something, it usually spread to every one of the others. Mattie Dixon's memory is also hazy on this point, but it is probable that at one time or another Betty Lou had almost all of the usual childhood illnesses.

Although her childhood was a period of financial crisis for the Dixons, and the children were often hungry, Betty Lou does not seem to have had any serious health problems. In elementary school her eyesight was found to be impaired, and glasses were secured for her through a charitable organization. This caused quite a battle at home, for Mr. Dixon refused to let her accept the glasses. Finally a compromise was worked out whereby Betty Lou would only wear them at school. As Betty Lou got older and more glasses were required, the family was able to pay for them and the crisis was resolved. The only other major health problems involving Betty Lou which her mother can recall were a broken arm around the age of six when she fell off the fire escape, and a gash in her cheek when she was hit by a rock thrown by another child. The scar from this episode, while not disfiguring, is still visible today.

Betty Lou is somewhat shorter and thinner than average, being 5 ft. 2 in. tall and weighing 105 lb. She has pleasant, but not beautiful, features, brown eyes, and medium brown hair which she wears hanging straight down to her shoulders unless she is working. She is a rather shy and withdrawn person around those she does not know well. Among friends she is much more relaxed and outgoing. She still wears glasses and sometimes talks about getting contact lenses when she can afford them. Since she is on a very limited budget, her clothes reflect durability and easy care rather than style or attractiveness. She feels slightly self-conscious about the way she dresses, as compared with her peers, but laughs it off by saying, "Anything is better than the hand-me-downs I always had to wear as a kid." This is one of the few references that Betty Lou ever makes to her childhood.

In a large family, one of the older children usually looks after one of the younger ones, and in the Dixon family Jenny Mae, four years older than Betty Lou, became her mentor. Jenny Mae taught Betty Lou to dress herself, wash, and eat. According to her sister, Betty Lou "caught on real fast" to these skills. Once Jenny Mae was in school, Betty Lou still had plenty of other brothers and sisters at home to play with, and despite the fact that she was the youngest, until Matt's arrival, she seems to have been the one who organized their activities and gave the orders. When Jenny Mae got home from school, she and Betty Lou would go off by themselves and Jenny Mae would report everything that had happened during the day. Betty Lou was so fascinated by the books her sister would bring home that she would pour over them for hours. She and Jenny Mae would play "school," with Jenny Mae acting as "teacher" and repeating some of the lessons she had learned. In this way Betty Lou taught herself to read and write before she entered school. Once she could read, Jenny Mae began to bring her books from the school library, and Betty Lou spent most of her time reading. Both Mr. and Mrs. Dixon dismissed this activity as "foolishness," but since it kept her quiet and out of their way, they did not interfere. Betty Lou, of course, looked forward to school with a great deal of enthusiasm and was very excited when she was old enough to enter the first grade, since the local school had no kindergarten. Her teachers, expecting another indifferent student from the Dixon family, were pleasantly surprised by Betty Lou's attitude and ability.

B. Educational History

From the very beginning Betty Lou was an exceptional student, and the pride and joy of a school which did not have many students of her ability. Despite the lack of encouragement from her parents, the poor examples set by her older siblings, and the lack of books, magazines, and other educational stimuli in the home, Betty Lou's whole life became centered around going to school. Due to her head start in reading and writing, she moved rapidly to the head of her first grade class and maintained that position throughout elementary school. By the third grade she was reading at the fifth-grade level, and her teachers found it necessary to provide her with special materials in order to challenge her abilities. Since Betty Lou's school had no provisions for talented students, this was the only way in which the teachers could attempt to meet her special needs.

Betty Lou continued to be an avid reader, and spent most of her free time in the school library, where the atmosphere was much more peaceful than it was at home. By the time she reached the upper grades, she had already gone through the rather limited resources that the library had to offer. At about the same time, her parents decided that she was spending too much time with books and not enough time helping with the younger children and the housework, and so her reading was temporarily suspended. Neither of her parents felt that it was healthy for her to spend so much time "with her nose stuck in a book," especially when there was work to be done. The discovery of her defective eyesight gave the Dixons further support for this belief.

In elementary school, Betty Lou's favorite subjects were reading, social studies, art, and music. There was little in the way of a physical education program, but Betty Lou appeared to possess average motor skills. Being small and quick on her feet, she was especially good at games involving running and dodging. She did not display any particular talents in the areas of art and music. Math was her least-liked subject, although she did well in it.

Her first big educational transition was the move from the neighborhood elementary school to a much larger junior high school. Her parents were convinced that she would now get over her "foolishness about 'book lear-nin' " and settle down into the pattern established by the other children. However, Betty Lou's enthusiasm for school was undiminished. She began to read again, frequently in bed by the light of a flashlight, despite being forbidden to do so and sometimes punished by her parents. Although the competition for grades was somewhat harder, by the end of the seventh grade Betty Lou was again one of the top students in her school. A group intelligence test given that year placed her I.Q. at around 145. She continued to do well for the next two years, and her name became a fixture on the school honor roll.

Billy Joe and Mattie Dixon were not at all impressed by the academic achievements of their daughter. Mr. Dixon felt that she was wasting her time by studying so much, when she could be helping her mother out around the house. Mrs. Dixon did not think that it was a good idea for a girl to be so smart. Neither parent offered Betty Lou any support or ever praised her accomplishments. Her brothers and sisters often teased her and tried to interrupt her study schedule. It was almost as though the family was embarrassed by her success.

The whole situation came to a head in the eighth grade, when students had to begin to make tentative vocational choices and select the courses they wished to take. The Dixons thought that Betty Lou should take the easiest courses possible, since she would be dropping out soon anyway. Betty Lou announced that she planned to enter the academic track which prepared students for college. Her parents literally could not believe their ears. No Dixon had ever completed high school, let alone given thought to going to college. They flatly refused to even consider the idea, and suggested that she enroll in secretarial courses where she would learn something which would help her get a job. The school counselor offered to talk with the Dixons, but Billy Joe and Mattie refused to go and see him, their reasoning being that nobody else was going to tell them what their daughter should do. In desperation, Betty Lou agreed to take the secretarial course, and then signed up for the college preparatory course without telling her parents. Since they never asked to see her report cards, she simply had Jenny Mae sign them, and thus kept peace in the family.

The next crisis occurred when Betty Lou was 16 and old enough to drop out of school. Her parents insisted that she quit and go to work to help support the family. Numerous arguments on this subject took place, with Betty Lou insisting that she was going to finish high school, even if it meant running away from home. At this point her high school counselor visited the Dixons, and was able to work out a compromise with them. Betty Lou was allowed to finish high school if she could work part-time to help with family expenses. The counselor was able to get her a job in the school office during her free periods, plus an after-school job in a local store. The salaries from these two jobs somewhat mollified her parents, who remained convinced, however, that Betty Lou was wasting good years of her life in school.

Despite the fact that she now had very little time in which to study, Betty Lou was able to maintain excellent grades during her junior and senior years, and she eventually graduated with an almost straight "A" average. Unknown to her parents, she took college entrance examinations and earned very high scores in every area except math. Her teachers remember her as an excellent student with a great deal of enthusiasm for learning and an inquiring mind. Some of them expressed concern over the fact that she appeared to have very few friends in the school and never participated in any extracurricular activities. Her high school counselor, Mrs. Miller, got to know Betty Lou quite well. Here are some of Mrs. Miller's comments about the subject:

Betty Lou Dixon is the sixth Dixon child to attend Washington High School. There are two younger children in the family also. Judging from appearances, the family is quite poor. Betty Lou is a short, thin girl who wears glasses and is rather shy and reserved. However, her academic record in elementary and junior high school is outstanding. Last year's counselor reports that there was some question as to which track she should pursue in high school. Her parents were invited to come in for a conference but never appeared. According to the student, they were opposed to her enrollment in the college preparatory program. However, the difficulty seems to have been resolved, for she has been placed in academic classes. On the basis of grades and previous test scores, this is clearly where she belongs. . .

Betty Lou Dixon appears to have made an excellent adjustment to high school work. She has been on the honor roll both semesters. There are no disciplinary problems. She still seems quite shy, although she is more relaxed since we have gotten to know each other. Since she appears to have few friends, I suggested that she might like to join one of the school clubs. She replied that she had to ride the school bus and could not stay after school. She will continue in the college preparatory track next year . . .

Betty Lou Dixon came in to see me today in a very distressed state. It seems that she will soon reach the age of 16, and her parents expect her to quit school and go to work. She also confessed that she has lied to her parents regarding the kinds of courses she has been taking for the past two years. I agreed to discuss the problem with her parents and try to work out some kind of compromise. In my opinion, Betty Lou should complete high school if at all possible . . .

Last evening I had a conference with Mr. and Mrs. Dixon at their home. At first the parents were quite hostile, and seemed to regard my interest in Betty Lou's future as interference in the private affairs of their family. Neither parent seems the least bit impressed with the fact that their daughter has an excellent mind and could rise considerably above her present station in life. They regard education as useless, especially for a girl. However, when the dollars and cents value of a high school diploma was pointed out to them, they altered their position slightly. In the end, they agreed to let Betty Lou finish, providing that she will work part-time. While this will place an added burden on the girl, I am sure that she can cope successfully with the situation . . .

After receiving Betty Lou Dixon's excellent test scores on the college entrance examinations, I called the student in for a conference regarding her future educational plans. She reported that her parents would undoubtedly be opposed to college enrollment, an opinion which I share after meeting the Dixons. However, she confided that she had made up her mind to enroll at State University and stay with a married sister who lives in that city. Since she will be 18 by that time, her parents will probably make no attempt to stop her, but neither will they support her in any way. She has asked for my help in securing a scholarship, and hopes to work part-time as she has for the past two years. She plans to take a liberal arts program and eventually enroll in medical school. Although Betty Lou seems to have chosen one of the most difficult and demanding academic courses possible, especially for a woman, I believe that her chances of success are good. It is a shame that her parents are so disinterested.

Through the efforts of Mrs. Miller, Betty Lou was able to secure a complete tuition scholarship to State University. She worked the summer after graduation from high school, and that fall simply announced that she was going to live with Jenny Mae. When her parents objected, she waited until they were both out of the apartment, and then packed her few belongings and left. She had saved enough money from her salary to buy a bus ticket to Central City, where Jenny Mae met her. At present she has completed two quarters at the University and maintained a perfect 4.0 average. She works during the evenings and on weekends as a waitress in a local restaurant, and uses this money for room and board, books, and other expenses. So far, she is just managing to make ends meet, but she has almost no free time.

Her college advisor describes Betty Lou as "one of the most dedicated students I've ever seen." He feels sure that she has the academic ability to succeed in college and medical school, but expresses concern in two areas: her health, and the subtle discrimination a woman is likely to encounter in medical school. He has suggested that she might give some thought to taking a lighter academic load and completing school in five or six years rather than four, and has also suggested that she could make it easier on herself by becoming a nurse rather than a doctor. "After all, she would still be in medicine," he says.

As a freshman Betty Lou is in relatively large classes and therefore some of her teachers do not know which student she is. Those who do know her, regard her as an excellent student who always attends class and is well prepared. A few remarked that she was exceptionally quiet and never volunteered unless called upon directly.

C. Emotional Development and Adjustment

As a member of a large family, Betty Lou may well have suffered from a certain amount of emotional deprivation. Mr. and Mrs. Dixon do not seem to have been overly concerned about the welfare of their children beyond the basic elements of food, clothing, and shelter. Jenny Mae appears to have taken over the role of "mother" to Betty Lou, which explains the close attachment between the two sisters today. Mrs. Dixon cannot recall any particular expressions of emotion on Betty Lou's part, beyond crying when she was hurt or angry. She responded to teasing from her brothers and sisters by retreating to her books. Neither parent remembers any occasion on which the child was extremely happy.

Betty Lou recalls her childhood almost without emotion. She can remember being afraid of her big brothers and some of the older children and teachers at school, feeling angry when she had fights with her siblings, and very unhappy when her parents were fighting or her father would hit her mother or one of the children. Her happiest moments were connected with school activities—being praised by a teacher, getting good grades, or being selected for some special task. It seems accurate to say that there have been only two really emotional events in her life thus far, the decisions to finish high school and go on to college. Other than these, her life has been almost devoid of emotional response, either positive or negative.

Upon meeting Betty Lou for the first time, one is immediately struck by a feeling of reserve, as though she were waiting to know you better before passing judgment. Once you have broken through this barrier, she becomes a very warm and friendly person, quite mature for her age, and not given to extreme swings of mood like most adolescents. She does not have crushes on movie stars or other teenage idols, and says that she has never been in love. When teased about these things, Betty Lou replies, "I just don't have time for that sort of nonsense. Besides, who would fall madly in love with me?" In terms of emotional development, she seems to be a combination of small child and mature adult.

D. Psychosexual Development and Adjustment

Betty Lou was exposed to most of the "facts of life" at an early age. The children born into the family after her own arrival gave her a good idea of where babies came from, and since they were also delivered at home rather than in a hospital, she gradually became informed about the process of birth. Living with seven brothers and sisters in a small apartment provided very little privacy, and so she also was soon aware of the anatomical differences between the sexes. Any additional information which she desired was easily supplied by one of the older children.

According to Jenny Mae, the male siblings were quite interested in the topic of sex, and would frequently hold discussions to which the girls were not invited. However, as the oldest girl, she was sometimes asked questions by the boys, and received several invitations to participate in sexual experiments with them and their friends. She can also recall one occasion in which Billy Joe's best friend made advances toward her. To the best of Jenny Mae's knowledge, nothing like this ever happened to Betty Lou, or at least she never mentioned it.

The Dixon apartment contained three bedrooms. The parents occupied one, the boys shared the second, plus the couch in the living room, and the girls had the third room. Since the walls were quite thin, the parents' sexual activities could be heard clearly. Betty Lou's earliest sexually oriented memory is of being awakened by strange noises from her parents' bedroom, and being afraid that something horrible was happening to one of her parents. Fortunately she awakened Jenny Mae, who was able to explain the situation and calm her down. Betty Lou remembers that she hated those sounds, which almost always woke her up, and the way the boys would laugh and joke about it the next day. She says she could never go back to sleep until her parents were quiet.

Betty Lou has never had a boyfriend or been out on a date. She has had a few offers, but has always refused because she either had to work or study. Because of her brothers, however, she has spent a great deal of time around males and seems to get along well with them. She claims that she really is not interested in dating, even if she had the time, and that she plans to remain single and devote her life to her career. She does not want to have children, and therefore see no point in getting married. When questioned about her attitudes, she replied:

> I know it must seem funny that I don't want to get married and have children, especially when Mom and Pop think that's all women are good for. Maybe I'm just going to the opposite extreme to spite them. But I had plenty of time to see what it was like to be married with a big gang of kids, and poor besides, mostly because of having so many kids. It wasn't a good thing for us, or for Mom and Dad either. I want something more out of life than they have, and I don't think I can get it and be married too. Maybe I can—I'll just have to wait and see. But right now, getting through school is the most important thing in my life. Maybe if I met someone and fell in love with him, all this would change. I don't know. I sometimes wonder if I'm capable of loving anyone.

Betty Lou is going through a normal adolescent period of self-doubt and questioning of the goals she has set for herself. She knows that she has had almost no experience on a romantic or sexual level with men, and is honest enough to admit that such experiences might eventually change some of her attitudes. At this point, she seems determined that nothing will prevent her from becoming a doctor, and she is willing to give up almost anything else in order to achieve that goal.

E. Social Development and Adjustment

Betty Lou might be described as quite different from the average adolescent in that she displays few signs of emotion, no interest in the opposite sex, despite the fact that her sexual orientation and physical development is apparently normal, and cares very little about social contacts with other people. While she was living at home, she was constantly surrounded by other family members, and as a small child she displayed many qualities of leadership. However, as she grew older and became more and more immersed in school, work, and her plans for the future, she seemed gradually to withdraw from social contacts. Part of this was due to an increasing lack of time, and part to a voluntary wish to be alone. It may be that privacy is important to someone like Betty Lou, who has never had very much of it, or it may simply be that all of her energies are so concentrated on her own plans that she cannot afford to waste any on other people. At any rate, she does not seem to need many social contacts the way most girls her age do.

This is not to imply that Betty Lou is at a complete loss in a social situation. While her family background and lack of polish makes her uncomfortable in a formal situation like a tea, she is quite relaxed and charming with people she knows well, and her depth and breadth of knowledge enable her to carry on fascinating conversations. People who meet her for the first time consider her shy and reserved, terms used by both high school and college teachers to describe Betty Lou's personality. Fellow students in her classes react in much the same way, and several of them added comments about her obvious intelligence. Some of the students appear to be "turned off" by this. For example, one girl reported that Betty Lou does not seem to want to talk about anything but what goes on in class. A young man said that he had thought about asking her out for coffee, but decided against it because she is so smart and his grades are rather poor. These responses are typical of the ways in which their peers tend to react toward bright young women.

Betty Lou, while not a victim of an "inferiority complex" in the classic sense, is rather sensitive about her family background and socioeconomic status. In elementary school, and perhaps to a lesser extent in high school, everyone she knew came from the same kind of background. At the university she is being exposed to people from homes where they were given every possible material advantage, and she has begun to be keenly aware of her own lack of cultural exposure, sophistication, and general polish. Perhaps her firm belief in education as the means by which she can better herself has been partially shaken, for she realizes just how far she has to go to reach a level that others achieved at birth. It may well be that new experiences and perceptions like these have combined to make her even more inclined to withdraw from people, especially those who appear to possess the sophistication she lacks.

F. Interests and Recreation

During childhood Betty Lou developed a fondness for reading, which continues to be her chief interest and only form of recreation. Other interests include Jenny Mae and her young daughter, and, of course, her academic work at the university. The remaining family members are of little importance to Betty Lou. She regards her job as a waitress as a necessary evil, and does not enjoy the work at all. However, she is quite good at it, has built up a clientele of people who always sit at her tables, and usually earns generous tips. The owner of the restaurant considers her the best waitress he has, and her fellow employees think highly of her. Surprisingly enough, Betty Lou is almost like a different person at work. She is friendly, outgoing, jokes and laughs with strangers, and seems completely at ease. Either she is playing the part of a waitress simply because such behavior is expected of her, or the situation presents no threat and she can afford to be herself.

Outside of a few hours a week spent in watching television, working around the apartment, or playing with her niece, Betty Lou has no recreation. When asked about such activities, she replied, "I thrive on work. The kind of schedule that she follows cannot be considered good for her mental and emotional health.

G. Ideology

Betty Lou Dixon is one of eight children from a lower-class white family. Possessed of superior intelligence, she wishes to rise above the station in life occupied by her parents, and firmly believes that education will enable her to do this. Despite a lack of support from any other family member except Jenny Mae, Betty Lou has managed to complete high school and begin college, maintain excellent grades, and work to support herself at the same time. She has set an extremely difficult goal for herself in deciding to enter the field of medicine, for this requires additional years of schooling and is still considered primarily a male field. Although she obviously does not think so, this goal may well be an unrealistic one and she might be wise to lower her sights somewhat. Her desire to enter medicine appears to be based on a cold appraisal of how best to exploit her intellectual gifts, rather than upon a strong emotional desire to help others or heal the sick

In terms of personal values, Betty Lou does not have any strong religious faith. She believes in education and hard work as the keys to success, and has adopted a set of beliefs worked out by herself and quite different from those of her parents. Some of her other siblings have also adopted middle-class values, but not to the extent that Betty Lou has.

Marriage, children, and personal or emotional relationships of any sort with other people apparently are unimportant to her. This may simply be a reaction to the imposed relationships of a large family, or it may well be that Betty Lou, at this point in her life, does not feel a need for emotional ties with others. Perhaps she will feel this need as she grows older, depending upon the amount of fulfillment she is able to find in other areas.

Betty Lou is a young woman obsessed with the idea of making something of herself through education. All of her time, effort, and energy is directed toward the eventual achievement of the goals she has set for herself. Anything which does not make a direct contribution toward this achievement is unimportant to her right now.

Interpretive Questions

1. What inferences can be drawn from the fact that Betty Lou is reluctant to discuss her childhood? In view of what you know about her, is this reluctance understandable, or does it seem strange?

2. Describe the attitudes of Mr. and Mrs. Dixon toward their children. How do they seem to have felt about Betty Lou in particular?

3. What part did Jenny Mae play in Betty Lou's childhood? How instrumental was she in determining the course of Betty Lou's future? Is this common in large families?

4. Describe the ways in which Betty Lou's elementary school teachers might have reacted to her. How well did they meet the challenge of her ability? What efforts did she make on her own?

5. Attempt to explain the parents' negative attitudes about Betty Lou's success in school from their point of view.

6. What are the outstanding points in Mrs. Miller's anecdotal records of Betty Lou's high school years? How successfully were the crises met, in your opinion? Could Mrs. Miller have done anything further to help Betty Lou? Was she correct in encouraging and helping Betty Lou to pursue a course of action which was contrary to the wishes of her parents? Why or why not?

7. Do you believe that Betty Lou was right in making plans for college and leaving home to pursue them, since she knew that her parents would never agree? Defend your answer. Would you feel the same way if her plans had been of a different, less wholesome nature?

8. Describe Betty Lou as seen through the eyes of her recent teachers. Evaluate the suggestions made by her college advisor. Would you agree or disagree with his comments, and why?

9. The author of this study suggests that Betty Lou may have been "emotionally deprived" as a child. What evidence is presented to support or refute this theory? Judging from her behavior as an adolescent, would you agree or disagree?

10. In terms of emotional development and adjustment, in what ways is she "a combination of small child and mature adult"? Could this description be applied to her in any other areas? Explain why.

11. Evaluate Betty Lou's sex education. Describe her current attitudes toward sex as you think they might be, based upon the information in this study.

12. How typical of her social class were her early experiences in the area of sex? Would you evaluate these as positive or negative in character? What kinds of effects might they have on children?

13. Discuss Betty Lou's remarks about marriage and children. In the light of her family background and previous experience, how reasonable do her attitudes seem to be to you? Do you think that these will change as she grows older?

14. Discuss possible reasons for Betty Lou's voluntary social isolation. Do you consider this an unhealthy situation?

15. Advance reasons for her drastically different behavior in her job as a waitress.

IV.   CURRENT STATUS; DIAGNOSIS AND PROGNOSIS; RECOMMENDATIONS

At this point in her life, Betty Lou Dixon seems to be relatively content. She has broken away, both physically and mentally, from her parents and their lower-class values which were so different from her own. She has gained freedom in the sense that she can now openly pursue goals which they disapproved of, but she still operates under a very strict set of self-imposed constraints. At 18, she accepted full responsibility for herself, although these responsibilities may not be "adult" ones in the usual sense of the word, since they do not include marriage and a family.

It is difficult to think of Betty Lou as being "happy," but who knows what happiness means to another person? From an outsider's perspective, this young woman has never been happy, and perhaps her ambition will never allow her to reach that state. She appears to be satisfied with her life as it is now, revolving primarily around school and work, and almost devoid of any but the most superficial relationships with other people.

Although she has set a difficult educational goal for herself, if her health holds up and she is able to maintain her scholarship, her chances of success are quite good. There is, however, some doubt as to whether or not medicine is really the field for her. This doubt does not stem from the fact that medicine is primarily a male field, but rather from her choice of a career based primarily upon its social status.

In childhood, following a very common pattern, Betty Lou used books to escape from a reality which she found unpleasant. Later on, her obsession with education took the place of reading, and still enables her to find rational excuses for avoiding social situations, which she now finds painful because of her background. In addition, Betty Lou is socially and emotionally imma- ture, and will never develop adult perspectives in these areas unless she allows herself to interact with other people. Since most human happiness comes from relationships with others, Betty Lou Dixon will never be a happy person, no matter how much success she achieves in other areas, until she allows people into her life.

Betty Lou needs to take the time to reassess her life. She should give careful consideration to her choice of medicine as a career, and think about other possible careers which would be equally challenging but require less education and be better suited to her personality and interests. Betty Lou should also think about taking a longer period of time to complete college, which would mean a lighter academic load and more free time. Pursuing her present schedule for the next six or eight years seems physically and mentally impossible for anyone. Even if she were able to do so, Betty Lou would one day discover that she had passed through adolescence and young adulthood without even knowing it. In fact, this may have already happened.

Interpretive Questions

1. Would you agree with the author that Betty Lou is content but not happy, and that she has never been happy? Why, or why not?
2. What are "adult" responsibilities? Must they include marriage and children today? Has Betty Lou accepted adult responsibilities?
3. Evaluate Betty Lou's choice of medicine as a career. How do you see her chances of achieving this goal?
4. Are there any other career choices which you think might be better for her? Explain your answer.
5. Would you agree that Betty Lou is using education as a means of escaping from social relationships? How important is it that she have more social contacts, from your point of view?
6. Evaluate the suggestion that Betty Lou attempt to lighten her schedule. What do you think her reaction to this idea might be?
7. Has adolescence already passed Betty Lou by, or is it perhaps yet to come? Defend your answer.
8. How might Betty Lou's life be quite different at this point if she were not gifted with superior intelligence?
9. Advance reasons for the fact that Betty Lou developed a set of values so different from those of her parents.
10. Assuming no change in the present circumstances, describe Betty Lou's life as you think it might be in 10 years.
11. Suppose something happened which prevented Betty Lou from becoming a doctor. How do you think she would react to the situation? What would this do to her total pattern of adjustment?
12. What common problems concerning vocational choice are illustrated by this case study? What aspects of Betty Lou's story are unusual in this respect?

12

Minority Group Problems and Pressures

The population of the United States has traditionally been composed of numerous minority groups. The earliest settlers in this country were members of religious minorities persecuted in their native lands, the first of many groups to seek freedom from oppression by settling in America. More recent immigrants came to our shores in search of economic and educational opportunities and a better life for themselves and their children. However, most minority-group members found that prejudice and discrimination were as much a part of life in the United States as the opportunities they had come here to find. For some, this was merely the continuation of a pattern they had been exposed to all their lives. For others, this was a totally new and unexpected experience.

Reactions to prejudice are, of course, as varied as the people who are exposed to it. Generally, however, some minorities tried to accept the status quo and succeed as best they could within these limits. Others attempted to fight back with prejudices of their own, or by any other means at their disposal. As might be expected, the young of each succeeding generation became more militant about existing conditions than their parents had been, and less accepting as they grew older and became parents themselves.

In recent years the problems of minority groups have been brought to the attention of the general public with increasing frequency, and more and more members of the majority have become involved in helping to solve these problems. Although mass guilt and further exploitation have been advanced by some as explanations for the current, almost universal, interest in better conditions and fairer treatment for minorities, perhaps it is the realization that unity cannot exist without some measure of equality that is the basic motivating factor. No matter what the reasons, however, public support for action favorable to minorities seems firmly marshaled. Almost every minority group which exists in the United States seems to have recognized this, and has begun to clamor for attention. Those who have been discriminated against because of race, sex, religion, or ethnic background are all calling for equal rights, and demanding solutions to problems which are of greater magnitude in the United States than in any other country in the world. However, the same sort of movement seems to be appearing in other countries which contain minority groups of any size.

Prior to the present day, the adolescent member of a minority group probably found the common problems of this age more difficult to cope with because of his race, religion, ethnic background, or sex. Almost all of the aspects of adolescence already covered in this book are slightly more complex for the minority group teenager than for his majority group peer. In addition, these problems may well be compounded by poverty and a pervasive sense of hopelessness. Today's adolescent must also concern himself with two critical decisions, one old, the other relatively new. The old situation revolves around whether to retain or reject the values of his parents and the subculture into which he was born—whether or not to allow himself to be assimilated into the culture of the majority. The new situation involves the fact that more and more minority group members are rejecting assimilation and demanding that equal validity be granted to their values, customs, and mores. The question then arises as to just how militant one should become in pressing these demands, and what forces one should bring to bear in working toward the achievement of these goals. Thus the adolescent member of a minority group must face, not one, but two identity crises.

Many of these young people need help from outside the family in coping with such problems, yet they are among the most difficult to reach. An intense sense of pride and independence, coupled with suspicion of anyone who appears to be trying to "help the less fortunate" makes minority group adolescents reject many of the offers of assistance that are extended to them. Perhaps the best source of help in this area comes from members of the same group who have their own experiences as points of reference. In addition to this, everyone working with adolescents should make an effort to understand minority group problems and pressures.

A Case Study of Juan Hernandez

Juan likes to tell stories about how he and his friends made life so miserable for one young teacher that she quit her job. Today, Juan still has no use for women except as sexual objects. While many of Juan's tales are rather far-fetched, there must be an element of truth to some of them because he has already made two trips to the clinic to be treated for venereal disease. With little education and no job skills, Juan and the other members of his gang appear to be headed for a life of crime.

I. IDENTIFICATION OF SUBJECT AND SOURCES OF INFORMATION

Name: Juan Hernandez
Address: 42 King Street, Apt. 1
Ethnic Background: Puerto Rican
Sex: Male
Age: 17
School or Occupation: none
Sources of Information:
  1. Personal observation
  2. Interviews with subject
  3. Interviews with father
  4. Interviews with siblings
  5. School records and test scores
  6. Police and court records
  7. Interviews with relatives
  8. Interviews with high school teachers and counselors
  9. Interviews with peers

II. THE FAMILY HISTORY

A. Health and Physical Characteristics

The Hernandez family consists of the father, Manuel Hernandez, age 37, and four children. Juan, age 17, is the son of Manuel and his first wife, Carmella, who died of leukemia when Juan was 6. The other three children are Teresa, age 10, Roberto, age 8, and Tomas, age 7. They are the children of Manuel and his second wife, Rosita, who died from complications following a miscarriage four years ago.

Manuel Hernandez is a short, slim man with black hair and a swarthy complexion. He has brown eyes, regular features, and is considered to be very handsome by the women of his acquaintance. He has no apparent health problems at this point, although he has not seen a doctor since he was in the army almost 20 years ago.

His first wife was a rather pretty woman, judging from the few pictures of her which exist. She was also short and slim, with long dark hair pulled back from her face in a severe style. According to Manuel, Carmella was a delicate, sickly child whose health seemed to improve after they were married and Juan arrived. Then she began to complain of various symptoms, and her illness, which ended in her death two years later, was diagnosed as leukemia. Rosita, the second wife, was a tall, buxom woman quite different in appearance from Carmella. Her health was robust, and she produced three large, healthy babies in four years. Then things somehow began to go wrong, and her next two pregnancies ended in miscarriages. After the second, the doctors suggested that she should not become pregnant again. However, she and Manuel did not heed their advice, and as a result Rosita had a third miscarriage. This one occurred at home and was accompanied by such severe internal hemorrhages that she apparently bled to death before medical help arrived.

The three youngest children all resemble their mother in appearance and bone structure, although they are not husky. Juan is short and thin like his mother, and quite handsome like his father. All of the children show their Puerto Rican parentage with brown eyes, black hair, and swarthy complexions.

Manuel is extremely vague about the early health problems of the children, as these were dealt with by his wives. He recalls that the four births were normal and without complications, and that Juan was the smallest baby, as might be expected. The youngest child, Tomas, has recently had the measles, and both he and Roberto had mumps about two years ago. The only other thing Manuel knows is that Roberto had a severe ear infection just after Rosita died, and his hearing in the left ear is somewhat impaired. All three seem to be in average health, but rather listless and apathetic due to an improper diet and insufficient sleep.

The family's three sets of grandparents are all still living and, since they reside in the same community, take an active interest in the lives of their grandchildren. However, their information in regard to health problems was also vague.

B. Educational Status

Manuel's parents came to this country from Puerto Rico 30 years ago, bringing their five small children with them. Manuel, the oldest, was about 10 years old at the time. Neither of his parents had any formal education at all. They could not read or write, and spoke only Spanish. They settled in the Puerto Rican section of a large eastern city, where Manuel's father found work as a day laborer, a job he still holds today. Since Mrs. Hernandez has had very little contact with the world outside this small community, she has mastered only a few words of English. However, Mr. Hernandez has learned to write his name, and can read and speak some English.

Both parents were determined to see that their children took advantage of the free schools in this country. However, education was a difficult process for the Hernandez children, and especially for the older ones like Manuel who were already so far behind. Since they spoke no English to begin with, all five of the children failed at least one grade along the way. Manuel was able to complete the eighth grade by the time he was 16, at which point his parents decided that he was a man and should stop going to school. The two youngest children were the only members of the family to successfully complete high school. No one has ever considered the possibility of going to college.

Carmella Hernandez came from a relatively similar family background. Her parents have been in the United States for almost 40 years, and she was born in this country. However, both parents learned to read, write, and speak English to some extent, and made an effort to speak English in front of their children. Thus school was somewhat easier for Carmella than it was for Manuel, and she completed the 10th grade. At this point she reached the legal age for dropping out, and since her parents believed that too much education was bad for a woman, her formal schooling ended.

Rosita Hernandez was the only child of relatively wealthy parents who were both born in the United States. Her father owns a small business and is a high school graduate. Her mother has less education, but both parents speak and understand very little Spanish. Rosita graduated from high school with secretarial training and helped her father in his business before marrying Manuel.

Juan has been exposed to two different educational philosophies, as have the other children. While Carmella was alive, little attention was paid to report cards or school progress. When Rosita became his stepmother, she followed his academic progress quite closely, enforced study periods, and impressed her own children with the importance of doing well in school. After her death, the children were left to their own devices and the various philosophies of grandparents and other relatives. Manuel is uninterested in the education of the children and never looks at their report cards. As a result, Teresa, who is self-motivated, is doing well, but the two boys are poor students and put forth little effort.

C. Economic Status

The Puerto Rican section of the city in which these families reside has a social structure all its own, based upon wealth, family background, education, and numerous other factors. By community standards, Rosita's parents are upper class. Both Manuel's and Carmella's parents are lower class, here as well as in the outside world. Manuel's father works as a laborer. When questioned as to what this meant, Manuel replied that his father picks up odd jobs cleaning out stores, warehouses, and occasional basements, garages, and attics in the suburbs. At an earlier age he dug ditches and did similar kinds of jobs, but now such work is too hard for him. Manuel's mother is a housewife and has never held a job.

Carmella's father works in a neighborhood produce store. He has had this kind of job all his life in various different stores. The one where he is now employed is owned by another son-in-law. Carmella's mother is also a housewife. Rosita's father owns a small food-import business which he inherited from his father. He is the third generation to operate the business, which was once thriving but is now beginning to lose money. His wife has never been anything but a housewife. Although they are probably middle class by American standards and could have afforded to move out of the area, they preferred to stay in the community where they are thought to be the wealthiest family. They own one of the few houses occupied by a single family. Most of the others have been broken up into apartments. Both Manuel's parents and Carmella's live in such apartments, which are quite small. The buildings themselves have fallen into disrepair, despite the efforts of the occupants, and the whole area is considered a slum section of the city.

Manuel and the four children occupy a four-room apartment on the second floor of what was once a grocery store. The store went out of business several years ago and the ground floor is now empty. The children sometimes play down there, although they have been warned not to because of the broken glass, rusty nails, and rats. Both rodents and bugs are a problem in the apartments upstairs. In the winter the heat is often insufficient to warm all three of the apartments, and the ovens are pressed into service. The supply of hot water is equally erratic, but on a year-round basis. The Hernandez apartment is furnished like most of the other apartments in this neighborhood. The kitchen contains an ancient gas stove, a refrigerator, and a chipped, rusty sink. The furniture consists of odds and ends contributed by the various parents, plus a few items purchased from the local Goodwill Store. All of the furniture and bedding is dirty and in the process of falling apart. The dishes are chipped and, like the knives and forks, are pieces from various different sets. There is a single bathroom located in the main hall of the second floor which serves the occupants of all three apartments—15 people in all. The bathroom plumbing leaks and there is usually water on the floor, which also attracts bugs. The entire hall has an extremely unpleasant odor. Manuel acts as the caretaker for the building, and in return lives there rent free. He does very little besides fire the furnace in the winter, but the owner does not seem to care as long as there is no trouble with the tenants.

When Manuel left school at the age of 16, he had absolutely no vocational training. He worked at odd jobs for two years, never lasting more than a couple of months at any one job. Part of the problem was his terrible temper. If anything happened that he did not like, he would argue with the boss and wind up quitting or being fired. Several times these episodes ended in fights, with Manuel getting the worst of it because of his size. After one particularly unpleasant incident, Manuel enlisted in the army in a fit of anger. He was in the service for a little over a year and then was discharged because of bad conduct. In the service his behavior was much the same as it had been before he enlisted—arguments with officers and fights with other men on the base. However, he did learn some skills as an automobile mechanic which enabled him to secure a job in a garage when he was discharged. He came back home, moved in with his parents again, and seemed to settle down. His mother and father felt that having a wife and children would help keep Manuel on an even keel, and they kept suggesting that he begin to court Carmella, whom he had known since childhood. Although he was already dating a number of other girls, Manuel also began to date Carmella in order to please his parents and soon discovered that she had been in love with him for years. This made her quite receptive to all of Manuel's suggestions, including physical intimacy, and resulted in Carmella's becoming pregnant. Terrified by what their strict Catholic parents would do if they ever found out, the couple hastily announced that they wanted to get married. Both sets of parents agreed, and the wedding took place almost immediately. Fortunately Juan was several weeks late in arriving, and the grandparents apparently never discovered the truth.

Manuel and Carmella lived with Mr. and Mrs. Hernandez until after the baby was born. Then they wanted to get a place of their own and selected the apartment where Manuel still lives. At that time it was in somewhat better condition than it is now. For four years things seemed to go well for the young family, despite the fact that no more children arrived. Manuel was able to keep his job, and his income, although not large, was adequate for the needs of a small family. Then Carmella's health began to fail, and the bills began to pile up. Although both sets of parents did what little they could to help out financially, by the time of Carmella's death Manuel was deeply in debt.

All of the neighbors attended Carmella's funeral, because they felt sorry for Manuel and little Juan. One of the mourners was Rosita Perez, who knew the couple only slightly because she was five years older than they were. Everyone said that it was very kind of Rosita to come and very sad that she apparently was never going to find a husband. Manuel confesses that as he listened to the talk he suddenly discovered a solution to his financial problems, because if he married Rosita he could borrow enough money from her father to pay off his debts. Having decided upon this plan, he set out to capture Rosita and was so successful that they were married three months later. Mr. and Mrs. Perez were completely against the marriage on the grounds that Rosita was marrying beneath her social status, but Rosita was a very strong-willed woman who probably realized that Manuel was her last chance. At any rate, each of them felt that marriage was appropriate for rather practical reasons rather than because they were deeply in love.

As Manuel had expected, Rosita was able to persuade her father to loan them enough money to pay off their creditors. However, Manuel has never repaid his father-in-law. After their marriage Manuel and Rosita continued to live in the same apartment. When her parents begged them to move to a nicer place, Rosita replied that they would do so when Manuel made more money. Then the children began to arrive and expenses mounted. Manuel changed jobs several times in an attempt to make more money, but there never seemed to be quite enough. From time to time Rosita's parents would give her money, until Manuel found out and refused to let her accept any more "charity." As their financial situation grew worse and worse, Manuel began to behave in the old way. He started to pick fights with the other men at work and to slap Rosita and the children when they annoyed him at home. He was fired from several jobs and had difficulty in finding new ones because of his reputation as a troublemaker. At this point Rosita suffered her first miscarriage, and Mr. Perez stepped in and used his influence to secure a job for Manuel, who had been out of work for several weeks. Sobered by the loss of the baby, Manuel calmed down and held this job until Rosita's death.

When Rosita died, Manuel seemed to fall apart. For the first time in his life, he drank heavily. He simply stopped going to work and neglected the children completely. The grandparents and other relatives took turns in taking care of the children and bringing food into the apartment. Mr. and Mrs. Perez finally threatened to go to court and take the three younger children, but not Juan, away from Manuel. This seemed to frighten Manuel and he stopped drinking, found a job in a local gas station, and began to take care of the children after a fashion.

At present the family's standard of living is quite low. Each of the younger children has three changes of clothing and one pair of shoes. Meals are irregular and poorly balanced, often consisting of bread and beans, or hamburgers and potato chips. Fortunately each child gets a free lunch at school, since they rarely eat breakfast. The children are usually dirty, and Manuel makes no effort to see that they wash regularly. Teresa is in charge of the washing and ironing, and the two boys are supposed to keep the apartment clean. Manuel does the cooking and washes the dishes when everything is dirty. All of these duties are carried out in a rather haphazard way and often forgotten completely. Unfortunately the family is not poor enough to qualify for welfare. Social workers have made a few attempts to help out, but Manuel has refused their assistance.

D. Social Status and Adjustment

The financial status of the Hernandez family is typical of people living in this neighborhood, so there are almost no distinctions made on the basis of wealth. Family background is important, as well as how long the family has been in this country, what occupations the males follow, the connections made by marriage, and how closely the customs of the old country are followed. Regular attendance at Mass is an important part of the local social structure. Many of these items are currently in a state of flux, as the children are beginning to turn away from the patterns of their parents and create a new structure based on the one which exists outside this particular community.

Manuel probably falls somewhere in the middle of the old social pattern. The status he loses in occupation he regains through marriage connections. Most of the neighbors feel sorry for him and blame the death of both wives on "bad luck" or "the will of God." A few hint that perhaps he is being punished for something. In general, Manuel is not disliked, but not terribly respected either. He fancies himself as something of a "ladies' man" around the women of the neighborhood, which does not endear him to their husbands.

While the Hernandez children play with the other children in the neighborhood, Manuel has no close friends other than his relatives and never entertains. He and the younger children go to Mass and Sunday dinner at his parents' apartment, and that is the extent of the family's social life. For his part, Manuel does not seem to be overly concerned about what other people think, and such an attitude is unusual in this neighborhood.

E. Interests and Recreation

None of the family members appears to have any hobbies or special interests. There are no books, magazines, or newspapers in the house except those that the children find in trash cans and bring home. Teresa spends her time on household chores, school homework, and play. Roberto and Tomas spend most of their free time just roaming around the neighborhood. Manuel sometimes has to work the night shift at the gas station, and when this happens, the boys often stay up half the night watching the ancient family television set. When Manuel is home in the evening, he does not insist that they be in bed before 11 P.M. Manuel often goes out in the evening with women friends. According to gossip, he is visiting married women whose husbands work at night.

Family conversation is usually quite limited, and consists of the children screaming and fighting over something, or Manuel yelling at one or more of them in a mixture of Spanish and English. When Juan is home Manuel usually tries, without much success, to find out where he has been and what he has been doing. Juan rarely speaks at all, and simply ignores his father's questions. This irritates Manuel so much that he loses his temper and hits the boy. When this happens, Juan spends the night with friends.

Manuel also works on the weekends, so he really has very little free time. He used to be interested in cars, but has lost interest since it has become apparent that he will never own one. He questions Juan about his activities simply to exert parental authority and has frequently said that he really does not care what any of the children do, as long as they stay out of trouble and do not bother him. To Manuel, taking care of children is a woman's job.

F. Ideology

Manuel Hernandez seems to be a rather weak, immature man. Handicapped by a lack of education and probably a lack of ambition, he is stuck in a poorly paid job with no future from which he gets little satisfaction. When he was younger he was able to express his frustration in outbursts of temper and physical fights, but has apparently learned that such actions do more harm than good in the long run. He certainly has had more than his share of tragedy in the death of two wives, but instead of accepting the additional responsibilities thrust upon him, he simply ignores the children as much as possible, until it must seem to them that they have neither mother nor father.

All of the family members are Catholic, and attend church regularly. Yet Manuel does not appear to be deeply religious or to get much support from his faith. It looks as though he is simply going through the motions from force of habit. The church has taught the Hernandez children everything they know about their religion.

Manuel seems to have the idea that fate is against him, and nothing that he attempts is going to work out, so he simply makes no effort to control his own destiny and drifts from day to day. While they were alive, Carmella and Rosita apparently gave him some sense of direction which he cannot maintain by himself, even for the sake of the children. Like so many minority group members, he is unable to overcome the obstacles of poverty, traditional ways of thinking, and insufficient education. Unfortunately, Tomas and Roberto are already beginning to think and act like their father.

Interpretive Questions

1. What kinds of problems might Juan have because of the deaths of both his mother and stepmother?

2. Compare the family backgrounds of Manuel, Carmella, and Rosita. Which of them had experiences most like those of an average American? How were these experiences reflected in their attitudes and behavior?

3. What effect would being exposed to two different educational philosophies by two different mothers have upon a child? Which one would you expect Juan to choose, and why?

4. Describe his home, family, and relatives as you think Juan might.

5. How does Manuel seem to feel about his children, especially Juan? What sort of relationship exists between father and son? What developmental problems could result from such a relationship?

6. What sort of a person is Manuel? Cite key incidents which led you to your conclusions. How might he be different if either of his wives had lived?

7. How typical of minority group problems are the various situations reported in this study? Discuss some of the basic reasons for the problems encountered by the Hernandez family.

8. Is there any evidence to suggest that Juan may feel unloved and unwanted? If so, how has he handled these feelings? Can you suggest any other course of behavior open to him?

9. Why does Manuel's apparent lack of concern about what his neighbors think appear unusual to the author of this study?

10. Describe a typical day in the life of Teresa, Roberto, or Tomas. Speculate as to the future lives of these children when they are teenagers and adults.

11. What is Manuel's attitude toward women? Is this typical of his ethnic background, or a result of his own personality and experience?

12. Many poor people feel that fate is against them. In Manuel's case, how accurate is this belief? How much control does he really have over his own life, and the lives of his children?

III. THE CASE HISTORY

A. Health and Physical Characteristics

The early life of Juan Hernandez is difficult to reconstruct because little information is available. He was conceived before his parents were married, and fortunately was several weeks late in arriving. By giving out the story that Juan was premature, a fabrication supported by the small size of the baby, Manuel and Carmella were successful in hiding the truth from their parents. Juan has never been told these facts, and probably never will. Knowing the truth might help him to understand some of Manuel's feelings and attitudes toward him, or it might make him lose the little esteem for his father he has left.

Juan was born at home with the help of a midwife and several female relatives experienced in these matters. Although small, he was a healthy and perfectly formed baby. No one seems able to recall any unusual events in Juan's early childhood. He was breast-fed and obviously learned to walk and talk, feed and dress himself, and to master the other skills of this developmental period, but the exact ages cannot be recorded. Carmella's parents remember Juan as a lively little boy who had to be watched constantly because of his inquisitive nature. On one visit to their apartment he was allowed to go and play with the boy who lived upstairs. Within five minutes he had dismantled this little boy's toys so effectively that it took his father and grandfather an hour to repair the damage! At first Manuel and Carmella found their son's energy and fearlessness amusing and devoted much of their time to the supervision of his activities. Then Carmella's health began to fail and she simply could not keep up with Juan. When Manuel was home he was more concerned about his wife than about his son, and consequently Juan was left pretty much to his own devices. He can still recall two distinct periods in his early childhood, one when he was the center of parental attention, and one when he was almost ignored except to be told to be quiet or punished for some misdeed. Juan remembers being bewildered and frightened by the change in his parents. As Carmella grew sicker and the doctor held out little hope for her recovery, her parents tried to explain what was happening and prepare Juan for her death. Juan, however, did not believe them and refused to listen. He recalls that he prayed every night that his mother would get well, and believed that it would happen, for he had learned in church that God answers prayers. When Carmella died, the grandparents were again given the job of trying to explain what had happened to the six-year-old boy. Juan could not believe that God had actually taken his mother away from him. He remembers that he blamed his father for allowing such a thing to happen.

After the funeral Juan was sent to live with Carmella's parents for a few months. During this period his appetite dropped off, and he was frequently sick with colds, stomach aches, and various other complaints. His illnesses were most frequent when his father came to visit on the weekends. Three months later Manuel married Rosita, whom Juan had seen only four or five times, and took Juan home again.

At first Juan was determined to hate Rosita, for she had taken the place of his real mother. However, she was so kind and so affectionate with him that he began to like her in spite of himself. Gradually his appetite returned and his "illnesses" disappeared. At various times during the next few years Juan remembers having measles, mumps, a sprained wrist from a playground accident at school, and an infected foot from stepping barefooted on a piece of broken glass. As he grew older he suffered countless bumps and bruises, plus one black eye, as a result of fist fights with other boys at school. He has twice sustained minor cuts in knife fights involving the gang to which he belongs, but no really serious injuries have occurred to date. Juan has experimented with "soft" drugs of various kinds, but is not a habitual user.

At the age of 17 Juan Hernandez is approximately 5 ft 6 in. tall and weighs around 135 lb. He is shorter and thinner than most of his peers and finds this quite disturbing. He hopes to grow more in the next few years, but his irregular hours of sleep and dietary habits, plus his inherited bone structure and body build make this rather unlikely. Juan has extremely handsome features, with dark wavy hair, big brown eyes, and very white teeth. He is rather vain about his appearance and takes great pains with his clothes and personal grooming. All of these factors lead some people to suspect that Juan is effeminate, but in fact he is a very masculine young man.

B. Educational History

Juan grew up hearing a mixture of Spanish and English spoken by the people around him, and thus he learned to speak in the same way. When he entered school at the age of six, he was somewhat handicapped in terms of his English vocabulary. It was several years before his teachers could get him to respond completely in English. While some of his other classmates had the same problem, many did not. Some of Juan's earliest memories of school involve fights with children who made fun of the way he talked. This particular problem also carried over into the area of reading, which was Juan's most difficult subject in elementary school and continued to cause problems for him throughout his academic career. According to school test results, Juan reads at about the sixth-grade level.

Juan's school career began at the neighborhood grade school a few blocks from his home. This school served children from other areas besides the predominantly Puerto Rican section where Juan lived, and for the first time in his life he was exposed to black and white children from backgrounds which were quite different from his own in many ways. While all of the children came from approximately the same socioeconomic level, they talked and behaved in ways which were quite new to Juan. He claims that he learned very quickly that the teachers liked the white children best and the Puerto Rican children least, and that the situation was the same in all of the schools he attended. Juan's report may very well be true. At any rate, it was unfortunate that Juan started to school during the last year of Carmella's life, when things were so unsettled at home. Neither parent had attempted to prepare him for school and, in fact, they probably gave him a negative attitude through various remarks about their own school experiences. Juan did not want to go to school, he was very insecure in his relationship with his parents, and he was suddenly thrust into a new situation with new and strange children who laughed at him. All of these elements combined to make Juan hate school, and he was a discipline problem from the very beginning. As he gradually realized that many of the other children were doing a much better job of mastering basic skills than he was, his resentment and poor behavior increased. As an added bonus, he attracted a great deal of attention from his teachers to make up for what he was not getting at home. Juan learned very little during that first year, and as a result he had to repeat the first grade.

His second year started off in much the same way, but then Manuel married Rosita, whose ideas about education were quite different from any Juan had ever heard before. Rosita supervised the preparation of homework, helped Juan to understand material he was having trouble with, and forced him to practice his reading. While Juan was still something of a discipline problem, his grades began to improve, and at the end of the year he was promoted to the second grade. Meanwhile baby Teresa had been born, and Rosita could not supervise Juan as closely, so he gradually lost much of the ground that he had previously gained. Eventually Juan's elementary school life settled into a pattern which consisted of doing as little work as possible and just managing to make passing grades. The folder pertaining to his behavior grew thicker and thicker over the years, and his parents were summoned to the school on several occasions. Rosita apparently tried various methods of improving Juan's work and conduct, including punishment, and there would be improvement for a time, but nothing permanent. In explaining his behavior in those days, Juan claims that the other children made fun of him, and being small, he was constantly fighting them or getting into trouble to prove himself.

Juan next moved to a large junior-senior high school in the inner city.

He had to ride a school bus, which gave him further opportunities to misbehave and to observe the kinds of things done by the older, more experienced boys. Juan learned how to "cut" classes and skip school completely, the fine art of forging excuses from home and hall passes, the best times of day to sneak a quick cigarette in the rest room, and other similar skills. He continued to be uninterested in his classes and his grades hovered on the borderline between passing and failing. His counselor had several talks with the boy, usually when Juan was sent to him by a teacher for acting up in class, and found him sullen and uncooperative. The counselor attempted to set up an interview with Mr. and Mrs. Hernandez, but they never appeared. His teachers reported that Juan was seriously deficient in basic skills, especially reading, and this handicapped him in almost every course. Although this school had no remedial program, several of the teachers created an after-school tutorial class for weak students. Juan was invited to participate in this class, but refused to attend. At the beginning of the eighth grade Rosita died, and Juan's behavior was somewhat better for the first part of the year. Then he and some of his friends formed a gang, and almost immediately were involved in a fight with another gang in the school yard which resulted in a week's suspension for everyone involved. Juan claims that after this incident the teachers and counselor gave up on him and passed him along to get rid of him. He seems to take some pride in this statement.

By the time Juan entered high school, he had a reputation as a troublemaker and a very poor student. Several teachers had him transferred out of their classes because they could not cope with him. Juan likes to tell stories about how he and his friends made life so miserable for one young female teacher that she quit her job. According to school records, Juan failed almost every subject he took in high school, partly because of poor attendance and failure to make up missed tests. His high school counselor, a white woman, felt that she was unable to reach Juan in any way, and that he was insolent in every interview she had with him. An I.Q. test administered to all pupils in the 10th grade reported a score of 90 for Juan Hernandez. As soon as he reached the age of 16, Juan dropped out of school. "I'll bet they were really glad to get rid of me," Juan laughs.

Since leaving school Juan has worked at a number of odd jobs, never for more than a few months at a time. His lack of education and job skills has forced him to take low paying jobs in which there is a rapid turnover of personnel. Juan also has made some serious mistakes on jobs which have caused him to be fired. Whenever this happens, Juan blames it on the idea that the boss is prejudiced against Puerto Ricans. He cannot admit that such incidents are his own fault. After spending almost a year in jobs like stock clerk, gas station attendant, window washer, and parking lot attendant, Juan has become disgusted with working for a living. He feels that the entire world is against him because he is neither rich nor smart, and because he is a member of a minority group. This is his explanation for the fact that he cannot get a decent job. In order to make money for the things they want, but cannot achieve through the usual means, Juan and his gang have turned to stealing.

Although they will steal anything if the opportunity presents itself, their specialty is cars. At present Juan has an income of several hundred dollars a week from this source, most of which he immediately spends.

C. Emotional Development and Adjustment

Juan Hernandez is a good example of the person whose life has been shaped primarily by his environment. To begin with, he was born to parents who were members of a minority group in this country. Because of this, and several additional factors, the family was poor and living conditions were substandard. Yet Juan appeared to be a healthy, happy child for the first few years of his life. At this point, however, his mother became ill, and both parents seemed to withdraw their affection from the child, either out of concern for each other or a feeling that they were being punished for an earlier act. From this point on, Juan was forced to grow up with very little emotional contact or support from anyone. For a time Rosita, his stepmother, attempted to make contact with the boy, but the arrival of her own children soon cut down on the amount of time she could spend with him. Then she died, leaving him without a mother again. Meanwhile Manuel, after his early pride in his son, seemed to turn his back on the boy completely. Part of his behavior was due to the fact that, according to Manuel's cultural background, it was the woman's job to take care of the children. In the absence of a woman, Manuel apparently could not bring himself to assume these responsibilities. He may also have grown ashamed of himself, in view of his inability to support his family adequately, or ashamed of Juan when he discovered that the boy had no desire to "make something of himself." Further problems developed as Juan grew up and rejected the Catholic church and his own Puerto Rican heritage.

Juan's emotional difficulties probably began with his apparent rejection by both parents around the age of four or five. He was then forced to go to school, which brought about a physical separation as well. If Juan had turned out to be a good student, he might have been able to form some emotional ties with his teachers, or derive satisfaction from his academic accomplishments. As it turned out, however, his poor cultural background in the home and his poor command of English proved to be early handicaps which he was never able to overcome, through either lack of motivation or lack of intelligence. Added to this was the fact that the other children laughed at his speech and his slowness in the classroom. The only possible way in which Juan could achieve a measure of recognition or status for himself was to become a discipline problem, and this was the route he took. If an understanding teacher had reached Juan during his elementary school years, he might well be a very different person today, but nobody made the effort until he was in junior high school, and by then it was too late.

Juan quickly became an aggressive, unhappy little boy. His antisocial behavior was a cry for help which went unheeded by his parents and the school authorities except for regular punishment. Because he had no alternative, Juan continued with this pattern of behavior. Meanwhile he got farther and farther behind in academic skills, and his teachers simply moved him along through the grades to be rid of him. A lonely boy with nobody to relate to, Juan eventually fell in with a group of misfits like himself who were drawn to each other out of desperation. By the time Juan became a member of this gang, his bitterness concerning parental rejection, lack of academic success, almost constant punishment, and what he viewed as prejudice had crystal-lized into rejection of society as a whole. Neither Juan nor the other gang members see anything wrong in stealing or the other kinds of things they do. They simply feel that they are getting even with society.

At 17, Juan Hernandez is "turned off" about almost everything. He has no social contacts outside of the five other members of his gang, and several people whom he feels are his enemies and would harm him if they ever got the chance. Before becoming a member of the "Knights," he was a loner, both at school and in the neighborhood. Parents refused to let their children play with Juan because he hurt them or got them into trouble in some way. Despite his relatively small size, Juan's toughness and aggressiveness usually ensured his position as leader. Juan says that he hates his father because "he is a weak, stupid man who lets people step all over him." He claims that he feels nothing about either of his mothers. Juan's only human ties are the loose bonds with the other gang members which could be broken at any moment.

D. Psychosexual Development and Adjustment

As an only child until he was seven years old, Juan learned almost nothing about sex during his early years. He can remember being faintly curious about the whole process when Teresa was born, but as neither parent volunteered any information, he did not ask questions. Outside of some joking references by the grandparents, Juan cannot remember the topic of sex ever being mentioned in his presence. While he was in elementary school Juan gained bits and pieces of information from the other children. He also began to notice the mating activities of the numerous stray dogs and cats in the neighborhood. However, his most informative early experience with sex occurred when he accidentally discovered that a teenage couple met regu-larly in an abandoned building in the neighborhood to have intercourse. For weeks Juan hid himself behind a pile of refuse and watched them. He recalls this experience quite vividly because it was during these observations that he learned to masturbate. Juan thinks that he must have been eight or nine at the time.

Some of his childhood activities which caused parents to forbid their children to play with Juan involved sex. On one occasion a group of children, led by Juan, was discovered in the middle of their version of "Doctor and Patient." Another time Juan attempted to have intercourse with a little girl who became frightened and told her parents. When her enraged father came to see Manuel, he simply laughed the matter off and refused to punish Juan.

By the time he entered junior high school Juan knew everything there was to know about sex, according to his own report. However, he was somewhat behind his peers in reaching puberty, which distressed him a great deal. It also caused some of the other boys at school to tease him and call him "fairy." One very big black boy seemed to take special pleasure in tormenting Juan in this way. Unfortunately, this boy was enrolled in Juan's gym class, where he had a receptive audience for his remarks. One day Juan was punished by having to run laps after class and was late in getting back to the locker room. When he got there everyone else had gone except this boy, who tried to assault Juan sexually. Fortunately a teacher heard the struggle and came to Juan's aid. The other boy was subsequently expelled from school, but many of the students heard the story and continued to tease Juan. These sessions usually ended in fights, and the incident caused Juan to be terribly sensitive about his masculinity.

At present he still has relatively few secondary sex characteristics, and is sometimes propositioned by homosexuals on the street and in rest rooms. Juan reports that this makes him so angry that he wants "to kill those dirty queers." Fortunately, he has learned to simply walk away from the situation. Juan claims that he has had numerous sexual experiences with girls and women since junior high school. At present he dates a number of girls, all of whom he claims to be sleeping with. There are also three girls who hang around with the "Knights" and seem to be available to all of the members of the gang. Some parts of his story must be true, for Juan has already paid two visits to the local V.D. Clinic.

His attitude toward women is much the same as his father's. Juan says that he has never been in love, and probably will never marry. "Why should I, when I can get it free?" he asks. He feels that women are useful only as a means of satisfying sexual urges, and that is probably the only kind of relationship he has ever had with a woman since Rosita died.

E. Social Development and Adjustment

Juan started out as a very outgoing little boy in a world composed of doting parents and grandparents. He was the first child, and a boy, which made him a very special person. When the attention of his parents was withdrawn, Juan certainly did not understand what was happening and probably felt rejected, even though his grandparents tried to fill the gap. Aggressive by nature, he soon learned that such behavior in the school situation brought him some measure of the attention he needed but apparently was not going to win by academic success. Since misbehaving was Juan's only method of gaining the attention of teachers and peers, he continued to act in this way throughout his school career. Many children follow this pattern, feeling that negative attention is better than none at all, and gaining some measure of respect from their peers in the process.

All of the schools Juan has attended have been inner-city schools, with a racially mixed student body of predominantly lower-class social status. Although a majority of the students are black, there are always a number of white and Puerto Rican children in the schools. Juan had never been exposed to white or black children before entering the first grade, and was totally unprepared for this experience. Unfortunately, Juan's mixture of Spanish and English speech and his academic slowness seemed funny to his new classmates, and they laughed at him. This automatically precluded the possibility of making friends with any of them, as far as he was concerned, and so he tried to become one of the group of Puerto Rican students. As time passed these students, who were more strictly disciplined in the home than Juan was, also rejected him because of his behavior, and Juan became a "loner." For a few years he still had the social contacts of neighborhood children, but eventually even that was cut to a minimum and Juan was pretty much on his own. His half-sister and half-brothers were much too young to be of any interest to Juan, and because he had failed the first grade, he was a year older than his classmates. Older students found him too short and skinny to take part in their activities, and Juan was simply shut out on all sides.

Until he became a member of the "Knights," Juan really had no friends. He was never interested in sports, probably because of his small size, and so that area of social contact was closed to him. None of the school activities interested him, and he had no special talents to exploit. In fact, his primary ability seemed to be a knack for getting into trouble, and this was how he came to the attention of the "Knights." They discovered that he was stealing hubcaps from cars in their "territory" and lay in wait for him one night. When he came along, they all jumped him and beat him up. The next night, Juan was right back, armed with a knife, and ready to take on the whole gang again. Some of the boys knew of Juan's reputation at school and in the neighborhood, and after these incidents they decided to invite him to join the gang. Juan was suspicious of their invitation, since nobody had ever wanted him before, but finally decided to join. From this point of view it has worked out well, since he finally has some friends to whom he can relate. From the point of view of society, Juan has become a member of a dangerous street gang which fights other gangs, terrorizes innocent people, and engages in criminal activities.

All of the members of the "Knights" are Puerto Rican, and this probably influenced Juan's decision to join. All of the boys have faced the same kinds of problems while growing up. They come from poor families, many of them large, where the father makes very little money. Living conditions in the home are terrible, and the boys want to break away from their families and strike out on their own. Yet all of them have quit school because they were not learning anything, and now cannot find any decent kind of job. As they look around and see the kinds of lives that people outside the ghetto live, these boys want some of these pleasures for themselves. Since this all takes money, the "Knights" steal.

They are very ambivalent about their Puerto Rican ethnic background. All of them have been subjected to some prejudice because of it, either at school or in the outside world, and they are bitter about this. They frequently imagine insults which do not exist and have fought other gangs for racial reasons. Yet each of the boys has rejected the Catholic religion and the cultural patterns of their parents, and is determined to "make it" by the standards of the outside world, which to them means having money. Typical of the way in which the "Knights" are caught between two worlds, they speak to each other in a mixture of Spanish and English.

The way Juan lives is very upsetting to his relatives. His various sets of grandparents have tried to talk with the boy and explain what a terrible thing he is doing to the family, but Juan simply will not listen to them. They predict that God will punish him for turning his back on his religion and his background. Manuel does not seem to care and says only that Juan will end up in jail, where he belongs. Manuel may be right, since Juan already has a police record as a juvenile for petty theft and gang fights. So far he has escaped with a warning, but soon he will be old enough to be treated as an adult by the courts. Unfortunately Roberto and Tomas admire Juan and brag about his exploits to their friends. His former teachers and counselors agree with Manuel's prediction that Juan will eventually wind up in jail. They say that he was one of the boys who just could not be reached or helped by the schools.

F. Interests and Recreation

As a child Juan never had any clearly defined interests or hobbies. He displayed no talent in any of the special subjects given at school, like art, music, or physical education. All of his free time was devoted to play activities in the neighborhood, which in early childhood consisted of the usual street games and scavenger activities of the inner-city child. In later childhood Juan engaged in petty theft, shoplifting, rummaging in refuse for articles which could be sold, and various activities of a similar nature.

In high school Juan claims to have spent a great deal of his free time in sexual activities. He joined the "Knights" and became involved in "rolling" drunks, fights with other gangs, and stealing of a more organized nature. Since leaving school and trying unsuccessfully to hold a job, Juan has immersed himself completely in the activities of the "Knights" and spends most of his time in their company. For recreation the boys go to movies, hang around the streets, or sit and talk in their "headquarters," an empty apartment they have furnished with discarded bits and pieces of furniture. The boys say they date, which seems to mean that they take girls out to a movie or dance. All of them claim to lead active sex lives involving black and white girls, but never Puerto Rican girls. The "jobs" the boys work at are their various illegal activities.

Juan and the others always seem to have plenty of money. Juan has an extensive wardrobe of cheap, flashy clothes in the latest styles which he wears when he is "dressed up." Most of the time he wears the traditional blue jeans and jacket with "Knights" painted on the back. Like the other boys, Juan wears his hair rather long.

Each of the gang members seems to use his own home simply as a place to keep his clothes, eat, and sleep. Frequently one of the boys will go home with another, so that his parents may not see their son for a week at a time. If the parents get upset at this, the boy just disappears until they calm down. Most of the parents, like Manuel, have given up trying to keep track of their sons and let them come and go as they please. However, the parents have learned to dread a knock on the door, which may mean that the police have come. Should this happen, the parents would be unable to face their friends and neighbors.

G. Ideology

Juan Hernandez is a bitter, unhappy young man. He has little education and cannot get a decent job. He feels that he has been discriminated against because he is Puerto Rican. His home life has been poor, emotionally and economically, since he was four years old. Rejected by most of the world for 13 years, Juan has in turn rejected almost everything—his religion, his background, his family, and their values—and has created a new set of values for himself based upon what he sees as worldly success. His present life is based upon immediate gratification through the acquisition of money, in this case by illegal methods. Juan sees money as the key to happiness.

In his gang, Juan "belongs" for almost the first time in his life, and has friends who care about him. He is not likely to sever his relationship with the "Knights" and probably will eventually move on to bigger and bigger crimes until he is arrested and put in jail. Should this occur, Juan may turn into a hardened criminal, a pattern he might follow for the rest of his life.

Juan really does not believe in anything, including himself. His tough exterior conceals a frightened, lost young man. Having rejected the values of his family, he has found nothing to take their place. Religion, the work ethic, education, and social status are all meaningless to Juan, and so he lives from day to day in the hope that something will happen which will give meaning to his life. Meanwhile he relies on sex and whatever can be bought with money, plus the thrill of danger, to keep him going.

Interpretive Questions

1. What lasting effects on Juan's life seem to have been caused by Carmella's death?
2. Explain various possible reasons for Juan's sudden period of illness in childhood.
3. Evaluate the ways in which Juan's early teachers handled his learning problems. What sort of lasting effect did this problem have upon his life?
4. Discuss the reasons for Juan's behavior problems. How accurate, in your opinion, is the author's explanation of this situation?
5. What part, in your opinion, did Rosita play in Juan's life? How did he react to her death?
6. Discuss possible ways in which Juan's junior high and high school

teachers and counselors might have attempted to reach the boy. Do you agree that he was "beyond help" by this time? Defend your answer.

7. How typical of the average "dropout" are Juan's problems in finding and keeping jobs?

8. How much factual basis is there, in your opinion, for Juan's feeling that he has been discriminated against at school and at work? How much is this feeling due to a lack of ability to admit his own weaknesses and faults?

9. Evaluate the reasons that the author advances for the lack of rapport between Juan and his father. Are there any additional factors that should be mentioned?

10. In several sections Juan's childhood and present life have been described as "unhappy." Would you agree or disagree with that evaluation, and why?

11. How would you describe Juan's present state of emotional development and adjustment? Give reasons to support your answer.

12. What sort of moral code does Juan have? How has this evolved over the years?

13. What critical events in Juan's life have created his present attitudes toward sex?

14. How typical of inner-city teenagers do the lives and activities of the "Knights" appear to be?

15. Would Juan's life be very different today if he were not a member of this group? Cite reasons for your answer.

16. Would you agree or disagree with the idea that Juan's "tough exterior conceals a frightened, lost young man"? Support your answer.

IV. CURRENT STATUS; DIAGNOSIS AND PROGNOSIS; RECOMMENDATIONS

Life has rarely been kind to Juan Hernandez. Born into a poor Puerto Rican family living in a slum area, Juan had two strikes against him almost from birth. Everything that could possibly go wrong in this boy's life seems to have done so. His own mother died, and then his stepmother. His father ignored the child. Handicapped by his background, Juan was a poor student. Now he is unwanted on the job market. With almost every door closed to him, Juan has chosen a life of crime as his only means of gaining some satisfaction from life. It is probably only a matter of time before he is caught and this avenue also closed to him.

To add to his other problems, Juan is a social misfit as well. He has difficulty in relating to other people, especially women, and has finally been accepted by a group of boys as poorly adjusted as he is. Juan's preoccupation with sex leads one to suspect that his attitudes in this area are unhealthy as well. Juan may be fighting against the idea that he is a latent homosexual.

While apparently rejecting the values of his ethnic background, Juan probably still feels considerable guilt about his behavior. Perhaps he has chosen this particular life style because he knows that eventually he will be caught and punished. Meanwhile he is standing halfway between two cultures.

The prognosis for Juan Hernandez is not good. Unless he receives a great deal of intensive counseling at some point in the immediate future, which is not likely, he will probably spend the rest of his life in and out of prison, becoming more bitter and hardened with each experience. Juan's life will be completely wasted through no real fault of his own. Unfortunately, there is nobody in Juan's present life who can attempt to help him, or persuade him to seek the help of others.

Interpretive Questions

1. Would you agree or disagree with the idea that Juan is a victim of his environment and "had two strikes against him almost from birth"? Support your answer.
2. Discuss the possibility that Juan might be a latent homosexual.
3. Do you feel that Juan is "standing halfway between two cultures"? Does he really feel guilty about this and want to be punished?
4. Evaluate the author's prognosis for Juan's future. How do you see him 20 years from now?
5. How might Juan have been different today if:
   (a) Either of his mothers had lived?
   (b) He had been born into a poor white family?
   (c) His father had been a stronger type of person?
   (d) He had been a good student instead of a poor one?
6. How have some of the adjustments made by Juan, that society would call "bad," really been "good" from his point of view?
7. Which, if any, of the developmental problems of adolescence have been more difficult for Juan because of his ethnic background?
8. Discuss the statement that "Juan really does not believe in anything, including himself." Is this a phase typical of most adolescents, or does it go deeper than that in Juan's case?
9. What would happen to Juan if for some reason the "Knights" were suddenly dissolved? Would this be "good" or "bad" for Juan, from his point of view, and from your own?
10. What are the chances that Juan may eventually see the error of his ways and "straighten out" by himself? Does he have the intelligence and experience to help himself?
11. How typical is Juan of the adolescent who lives in the inner city? What needs to be done to help these young people?